TESI GREGORIANA

Serie Teologia

93

JAMES OLAITAN AJAYI

THE HIV/AIDS EPIDEMIC IN NIGERIA

Some Ethical Considerations

EDITRICE PONTIFICIA UNIVERSITÀ GREGORIANA
Roma 2003

Vidimus et approbamus ad normam Statutorum Universitatis

Romae, ex Pontificia Universitate Gregoriana
die 08 mensis novembris anni 2002

R.P. Prof. MARK ATTARD, O.Carm
R.P. Prof. AURELIANO PACCIOLLA, O.Carm

ISBN 88-7652-955-1
© Iura editionis et versionis reservantur
PRINTED IN ITALY

Finito di stampare
nel mese di Gennaio 2003

presso la tipografia
"Giovanni Olivieri" di E. Montefoschi
00187 Roma - Via dell'Archetto, 10,11,12

GREGORIAN UNIVERSITY PRESS
Piazza della Pilotta, 35 - 00187 Rome, Italy

This work is dedicated to:

Felix Ola Soga (1969 - 2001)

and

Karl E. Dowd Jr. (1934 - 2002)

ACKNOWLEDGMENTS

I would like to thank the Lord for the gift of life, and all the blessings he has shown me since the day of my birth to this present time.

I owe a debt of gratitude to my supervisor, Professor Mark Attard, O. Carm., for accepting to moderate this work. I am particularly grateful for his guidance, encouragement, constructive criticisms, and for his understanding. My profound thanks go to Prof. Pacciolla, O. Carm., the co-moderator of this work. I am also grateful to the dean of the faculty of Theology, Professor Sergio Bastianel, SJ., and all my Professors at the department for their guidance in my quest for truth and knowledge. I am equally grateful to Jim Keenan, SJ, Professor of Moral Theology, Weston Jesuit School of Theology, Cambridge, Mass., and Jon Fuller, SJ, MD., associate Professor of Medicine, Boston University School of Medicine, for their time, invaluable suggestions and assistance in getting the materials for this research.

This work could not have been possible without the love and support of Mother Chiara Stucchi, who stood by me through thick and thin. To her, I shall remain ever grateful. I also would like to acknowledge the loving care and support of all the Poor Clare Sisters of Cortona and Siena. My profound thanks also go to His Grace, Prof. Mons. G. Pittau, SJ, Rector emeritus and Secretary of Congregation for Catholic Education, and Prof. Franco Imoda, SJ, the present Rector, Sr. Adela Engelmann, and all the Franciscan Sisters in Salzkotten, Germany, Sr. Mary-Lou, for their care, support and encouragement.

I cannot forget the supportive company of all my numerous friends to whom I owe a great deal. Kieran O'Reilly, SMA, Superior General, Karl E. Dowd Jr. (RIP), Jerry Desmarais, Helen and Phil Forrest, Barbara Cosgrove, Helen and Roger Dumont, Helen Aubin, Linda and Fern Vachon and all the members of St. Joseph, Nashua, NH. I am especially grateful to Basil Matuluko, Sylvester Onasanya, Aunty Gbonju, Henry Yanju, Omololu Falobi, Anita and Augusto Prada, Federica and Andrea Di Pietro, Christian Pristipino, Rolando Castro,

Francesca, Fabrizio Giuli, Manuela De Lorenzo, Amelia Rossi, Ethelbert Ukpabi, Paschal Nweazeapu, Richard Omolade, Dr. Peter Odetoyinbo, Dr. Uma Balakrishnan, Chair, Department of Government and Politics, St. John's University, Queens, New York, Dr. Frank Le Veness, Dr. Bill Gangi, Dr. Massimiliano Tommassini, Director / Ass. Dean St. John's University Graduate Center Rome, and all my friends at St. John's University, for their love, understanding and various contributions to the completion of this work.

I would like to register my indebtedness to Rt. Rev. Albert Fasina, the ordinary of the Catholic Diocese of Ijebu-Ode, and all the clergy, religious and the laity of the Catholic Diocese of Ijebu-Ode, Nigeria, for their love and prayers.

I owe a debt of gratitude to my parents, uncles and aunts, my brothers and sisters, cousins, nephews and nieces. I am blessed to have them as my family. I love you all and I will always be there for you as you have always been for me.

Finally, I would like to thank all who have had anything to do with everything I have done… You know who you are! Peace.

GENERAL INTRODUCTION

1. Thesis statement

This dissertation is devoted to examining some of the ethical problems of human immunodeficiency virus (HIV), the causative agent of the acquired immunodeficiency syndrome (AIDS) in Nigeria, and how the Catholic Church should respond to these problems.

The thesis demonstrates that infection with HIV/AIDS is not just a cultural issue or a result of moral decadence; rather, the social and economic problems of the country are the contributing factors. Thus, these are the real issues that must be addressed and tackled once and for all.

In addition, and more importantly, this thesis contends that the Nigerian Church is not doing enough to address this human tragedy especially in the area of prevention. I believe that the Church must be in the forefront of working for the prevention of the disease. Everyone is morally obliged to work for the prevention of this deadly disease especially as there is as yet no known cure. The moral obligation to work for the prevention of the transmission of HIV/AIDS has been emphasized by notable moral theologians around the world.[1]

Yet in Nigeria, the local Church as a body has been silent in giving guidelines. The silence may not be unconnected to the fear that the leaders might be accused of undermining the Church's teaching. I think that this fear is unjustified. I argue that if we truly explore the moral traditions and teachings of the Church, it will be discovered that some of the preventive methods like the use of prophylactics and needle exchange programs, in some given situations, are not in conflict with the Church's teaching as some people fear. Therefore, this thesis seeks to challenge the local Church in particular, to look into the Church's rich traditions and give directions as to the ways and manners that an effec-

---

[1] Cf. M. VIDAL, *Diccionario de Etica Teologica*, 555. See also, J.F. KEENAN, ed., *Catholic Ethicists*. This book highlights various contributions of moralists' efforts to respond to HIV/AIDS prevention.

tive preventive approach policy could be formulated in the country. One of the traditional teachings that provide basis for my conviction is *Humanae Vitae* no. 15.

Furthermore, the reason that the Church must be actively involved is that to date this disease, that made its appearance about three decades ago, has proven to be the second most deadly and most puzzling disease experienced by the human race (second to the «Black Death»). Needless to say that the disease has some profound implications not just on individuals infected but also on the whole of society at large. As Pope John Paul II remarked:

> Compared with many infectious diseases faced by mankind in the course of history, HIV/AIDS has by far many more profound repercussions of a moral, social, economic, juridical and structural nature not only on individual families and on neighborhood communities, but also on Nations and the entire community of peoples.[2]

Although the disease is not limited to one geographical area of the world, it has proven to be a greater calamity for Africa in general than for any other part of the world. According to UNAIDS and the World Health Organization (WHO)[3] update report of 2000, out of the estimated 36 million persons living with HIV in the world, sub-Saharan Africa alone is said to have 25.3 million or about 70 per cent of the world total.[4]

The above data shows that the disease has reached an epidemic level in Africa in general and if not arrested might reach that level in Nigeria as well. Also, HIV/AIDS has proven to be a threat to the survival and economic growth of the continent. There are a number of reasons for this sad development. First, there was a general attitude of silence and denial about the existence of the disease in the continent at the early stage of its discovery. Second, social and economic factors have contributed significantly to the spread of the disease in the continent.

2. Aim and methodology

The theme of this thesis is to consider some of the ethical issues around HIV/AIDS. Thus this dissertation seeks first to examine some of the problems that have led to the increase in the number of HIV in-

---

[2] JOHN PAUL II, «The Church», 662-669.

[3] These are bodies responsible for monitoring and coordinating the HIV/AIDS activities in the world. They are based in Geneva, Switzerland.

[4] Cf. UNAIDS – WHO, *Statistical Report* (2000).

fections and to offer insights through which we can slow the tide of the infection in the country. I therefore argue that the economic and social barriers must be dismantled in order to have any positive result of containing the further spread of the disease.

This dissertation therefore aims to challenge the religious and political institutions in Nigeria about the way to respond to this human tragedy. It is my hope that on the social and political level this study can lead both the ecclesial and government leaders to develop processes and procedures that will ensure a higher degree of commitment at all levels of governance that will be translated into concrete and valuable plans of action.

To achieve its aim, this study first adopts an expository and analytic method in examining the facts and ethical issues that are confronted with regards to the problems of HIV/AIDS, especially as regards the prevention of the disease.

3. **Division of work**

The work is divided into four chapters. Each chapter begins with a brief introduction and is concluded by summing up the major findings of the issues raised.

The first chapter examines the nature and meaning of the disease and its manifestations. It also examines the issue of the origin, though that remains inconclusive. This chapter also devotes time to examining the modes of transmission of the disease.

The second chapter leads to the main body of the dissertation. It gives the description of the HIV/AIDS situation in Nigeria. The chapter is divided into four sections. The first section gives a general description and location of Nigeria. The second section gives an overview of the HIV/AIDS situation in the country. The third section examines the causes for the rapid spread of the epidemic in the country, ranging from social and moral to economic and political factors. The effects like increased poverty, loss of manpower or labor force and AIDS orphans are also the focal points of this chapter.

The third chapter contends that the present preventive measures are not sufficient. Therefore, it offers insights on what needs to be done, namely, the need for a moral vision based on the principles of responsibility, non-discrimination and confidentiality. The demands of justice and the gender power dynamics are also areas of focus in this section. Here, I try to point out how the Catholic Social teachings could be a useful instrument in responding to the problems that have led to the

spread of the virus. Finally, the chapter examines the responsible a-
gents for the preventive approach and proffers ways through which
preventive goals could be achieved.

The fourth and final chapter examines some specific moral issues
regarding the prevention of the disease. In the first place, it confronts
the Church's theology of human sexuality, where it is emphasized that
both the procreative and unitive aspects of sexuality in marriage must
be strengthened in the time of HIV/AIDS. It also examines extensively
the prophylactic debate and the needle exchange programs. The contention here is that while immoral sexual practices must be discouraged
and condemned, the duty to save lives is also a value that must be protected. In saying this, it is, important to note, that the duty to save life is
not in competition with the Church's teaching on sexual activity, if
anything, it fully respects it. Based on this conviction, the chapter tries
to look at how theological discourse can help in the prevention of the
disease in the country. It does this by specifically looking at some traditional Catholic principles to argue in favor of prophylactics and the
needle exchange programs for the prevention of HIV/AIDS in some
given situations.

4. Limitation of study

However, I must admit that this work has some limitations as well.
One of the reasons for this limitation is due to the fact that the multi-
faceted nature of the disease does not give room for an exhaustive
study of HIV/AIDS.

In addition, there have been difficulties in getting the needed materials especially with regards to Nigerian traditional teachings and customs which point to the fact that though cultural issues are part of the
problems yet they are not the central issues. The main difficulty is that
most of these traditional sayings are not in writing hence the problem
of documentation in some areas. It is however my hope that with this
study and the work of other native people, we can begin to have proper
literature on issues in Africa in general and the local Church in particular.

Finally, I do not attempt to lay claim to an exhaustive originality of
thoughts in this thesis. As the references and bibliography demonstrate,
I relied on some notable authors in the field of this research. Nonetheless, I tried to demonstrate my own contribution in this field by trying
to examine the local problems that the disease is generating and will
likely generate, and then confront them with the Catholic moral tradi-

tion. Furthermore, my contribution in this field is also in the area of trying to break the silence that many people, including the local Church leaders, associate with HIV/AIDS. I believe that remaining silent about the disease is dangerous, and sometimes immoral. This is where I think the living tradition of the Church challenges us to act responsibly in the face of suffering and death.

CHAPTER I

HIV/AIDS: An Overview

1. Introductory Remarks

A previously unknown disease suddenly appeared among mankind and before many people came to be aware of its severity, the disease had already begun to spread like a raging fire with its roots in almost every part of the globe. After a series of observations and examinations, the disease was given a name, the «Acquired Immunodeficiency Syndrome», commonly called AIDS, and the Human Immunodeficiency Virus (HIV) was regarded as the causative agent.[1] In this work, I shall be referring to this disease simply as HIV/AIDS.

This chapter seeks to explore and clarify this disease. To achieve this objective the chapter is divided into four sections. The first section looks at the nature, meaning of this disease and how it operates. The second section examines the manifestations of the disease from its asymptomatic stage to the full-blown AIDS. The third section looks at the modes of transmission, that is, the route through which the disease is transmitted from one person to another. The final section examines the issue of its origin, looking at the different hypotheses and theories.

2. HIV/AIDS : Meaning and Understanding.

It is not easy to define with precision HIV / AIDS. The difficulty lies in the fact that the symptoms of the clusters of diseases now associated with HIV/AIDS were first noticed and recorded in medical journals and newspapers under various forms of diseases like «Pneumocystis pneu-

---

[1] It must be noted that I deliberately used the phrase that HIV is regarded as the causative agent of AIDS since some people are disputing this claim. This issue will be looked into later on in this chapter.

monia»,[2] «Rare cancer»,[3] «Kaposi Sarcoma»,[4] in 1981. The conclusion on the above is that the «observations suggest the possibility of a cellular-immune dsyfunction related to a common exposure that predisposes individuals to opportunistic infections such as pneumocystosis and candidiasis».[5] As a result, the investigators came to the conclusion we are dealing with a new disease entity within the human community, which came to be known as the acquired immunodeficiency syndrome, AIDS.[6] Leibowitch reports that based on the grouping of symptoms, as reported by and observed in the patients, this grouping of signs of «something wrong», permit the outlining of a «syndrome», a group of symptoms.[7]

AIDS is the acronym for the «acquired immunodeficiency syndrome», which is the English language terminology.

It is called syndrome because «a syndrome is a range of manifestations and symptoms, which characterize an illness and which, in this case, include a serious weakening of the immune system».[8] This means that the disease is not just a single disease presentation.

It is called «acquired», because «it is not hereditary, but the product of an acquired virus».[9] «Acquired», as Hooper notes, «also indicates that this unknown causative agent is transmitted to human beings exogenously, from external sources in the course of their natural life span (rather than passed endogenously, in the germ line)».[10]

This is where the human immunodeficiency virus (HIV) dimension of the disease is very important. The majority of scientists maintain that the human immunodeficiency virus (HIV) is the causative agent of AIDS.[11] It must, however, be noted that the conclusion that HIV is the cause of AIDS is still being contested. One of the notable critics, Peter

---

[2] CENTERS FOR DISEASE CONTROL, «Pneumocystis Pneumonia», 250-252.

[3] L.K. ALTMAN, «Rare Cancer», 20.

[4] CENTERS FOR DISEASE CONTROL, «Kaposi's Sarcoma», 305-308; ID., «Follow-up on Kaposi's Sarcoma», 409-410; ID., «Diffuse, Undifferentiated Non-Hodgkins Lymphoma», 277-279.

[5] CENTERS FOR DISEASE CONTROL, «Pneumocystis Pneumonia», 251.

[6] M.S. GOTTLIEB – al., «Pneumocystis Carinii Pneumonia», 1425-31. H. MASUR – al., «An Outbreak», 1431-38. J. FULLER, «HIV/AIDS: An Overview», 2.

[7] J. LEIBOWITCH, A Strange Virus, 16-17.

[8] F.J.E. BASTERRA, Bioethics , 288.

[9] F.J.E. BASTERRA, Bioethics , 288.

[10] E. HOOPER, The River, 8.

[11] R. GALLO, Virus Hunting, 283; B.D. SCHOUB, AIDS and HIV in Perspective, 21-22; W. BLATTNER – R. GALLO – H. TEMIN, «HIV Causes AIDS», 514-517.

Duesberg[12] claimed that AIDS might be caused by some other unknown pathogen (a disease-causing agent).[13]

Viruses are «intracellular parasites».[14] There are many viruses. As
Leibowitch explains, a «virus can exhibit the long delays which separate contamination from the disease's appearance. ... Viruses can be
carried by apparently healthy individuals», whereas, «no toxins», he
says, «could be present in the blood for so long without that individual's being distressed».[15] This is to say that the presence of toxin mani-
fests itself in the individual host quickly, whereas, it takes a longer period for the manifestation of viruses to cause distress in human body.

«HIV infection», is clinically described as «a continuum of conditions associated with immune dysfunction».[16] «Immune deficiency»
indicates that the symptoms result from «a fault in the immune system,
the very mechanism that has evolved to combat disease».[17] Therefore
HIV has a striking effect on the immune system of the patient by de-
stroying the cells that naturally help fight diseases and germs in the
human body.

It is believed that the human immune system's response to infectious
agents is shared by two subgroups of white blood cells: CD4 (also
known as T4 or helper cells) and CD8 or suppressor cells.[18] The CD4
cells have protein known as CD4 receptors, which regulates the immune system's mechanism for recognizing and responding to foreign
agents, through which the CD4 cells orchestrate the immune response
to such an invasion, hence, its vital role in the immune function.

The mechanism of these two subgroups of white cells could simply
be understood or explained in the following way. The helper cells send
the immune system a stimulating, or «on» signal, whereas suppressors
counterbalance this with a suppressing, or «off» signal. What happens
then is that in a healthy person, the presence of infectious agents stimu-
lates the helper cells by sending a strong activating signal to the im-

---

12 Peter Duesberg is a molecular biologist and AIDS researcher. He championed
the theory that HIV is not the cause of AIDS. See P. DUESBERG, «HIV is Not the
Cause of AIDS», 514-517.

13 For a greater insight into this theory, see P. DUESBERG, *Inventing the AIDS Virus*.

14 J. LEIBOWITCH, *A Strange Virus*, 11.

15 J. LEIBOWITCH, *A Strange Virus*, 11.

16 J.L. FAHEY – D.S. FLEMMING, ed., *AIDS/HIV*, 2.

17 E. HOOPER, *The River*, 8.

18 See J. FULLER, «HIV/AIDS: An Overview», 8.

mune system, tipping the balance in favor of a vigorous immune response. When this happens, the invading organisms are neutralized; in
that case, the suppressor cells appropriately «turn down» the immune
system response to prevent over-activity that would result in autoim-
mune disease.[19]

The above helps to understand how HIV works in relation to immune deficiency. HIV is believed to be unable to reproduce on its own.
Thus in order to replicate, HIV targets specifically the CD4 cells
through the CD4 receptor that manufactures proteins for the virus.[20] In
other words, HIV replicates on the CD4 receptors, which causes a depletion and deficiency of the CD4 cells' population and a dominant
suppressor signal, consequently, the immune system becomes unre-
sponsive in spite the presence of infecting organisms.

The other cells that HIV targets are macrophages, which also have
the CD4 receptors.[21] The infection of the macrophage cells by HIV is
believed to account for HIV's transport into the central nervous system,
by acting as the «biological Trojan horse».[22]

The loss of the CD4 or helper cells and the macrophage cells affect
the immune function system.[23] Given the fact that the dysfunction of
the helper cell is not congenital as has been explained above, that is, is
acquired with HIV-related destruction, the collection of secondary diseases caused by HIV is referred to as the acquired Immunodeficiency
syndrome (AIDS).

Therefore AIDS can be described as a group of sign-symptoms,
which bears witness to a collapse of the human's immune system. It is
also important to note that the disease AIDS is seen to be the last stage
of the group of sign symptoms that destroy the immune system.

3. HIV/AIDS: Clinical Manifestations.

There are basically three stages in the overall HIV/AIDS manifestations namely, the Asymptomatic Stage, the Pre-AIDS stage and, the
full-blown AIDS stage.

---

[19] J. FULLER, «HIV/AIDS: An Overview», 8.

[20] Cf. J. FULLER, «HIV/AIDS: An Overview», 2-3.

[21] Cf. A. AMADORI – P. ZANOVELLO, *Immunologia Cellulare e Molecolare*, 545.

[22] J. FULLER, «HIV/AIDS: An Overview», 13, 21-22.

[23] J. FULLER, «HIV/AIDS: An Overview», 13. See also, A. AMADORI – P. ZANO-
VELLO, *Immunologia Cellulare e Molecolare*, 550-552.

3.1 *The Asymptomatic Stage*

This is the first stage of HIV/AIDS, which is the initial exposure to the infection to what would later develop into recognizable HIV/AIDS. At the time of the initial contact with the virus, the exposed person goes through a phase called the «window period»[24] – which is the interval between infection and development of antibodies. During this period, even if the person takes an antibody test, he or she will test HIV negative. However, the infected person is already capable of transmitting the virus to other persons.

The next development in this stage is the «sero conversion», which represents the appearance of HIV antibodies.[25] «Antibodies are custom-made proteins which the body creates to fight specific infectious agents».[26] At this stage, the infected person may experience «sero conversion illness», which occurs about two to four weeks after infection, and lasts for about one to two weeks.[27]   The illness may be characterized with fever, swelling of the lymph glands, a measles-like rash over the body, etc.[28] Though the person recovers fast, he or she henceforth becomes seropositive for HIV antibodies. The only proof or evidence is through the antibodies test.

The characteristic feature of this stage is that the infected person appears healthy and for that reason, this stage is called an «asymptomatic», or even «silent», «incubating» period. During this stage, the virus works slowly but progressively, with its target being the T-helper or CD4 lymphocytes, which regulate the immune system. In such a situation, the person is unaware of this risk and, if the person does not belong to the «high risk» group, the situation becomes even worse, because he or she continues to infect others if he or she engages in intimate, unprotected, sexual contact.

This incubating period normally takes between six to ten years, depending on the overall well being of the infected individual person and the level of his or her immune resistance capacity.

---

[24] J.L. FAHEY – D.S. FLEMMING, ed., *AIDS/HIV*, 3.

[25] J.L. FAHEY – D.S. FLEMMING, ed., *AIDS/HIV*, 3.

[26] J. FULLER, «HIV/AIDS: An Overview», 7.

[27] B.D. SCHOUB, *AIDS and HIV in Perspective*, 33-34; A. AMADORI – P. ZANOVELLO, *Immunologia Cellulare e Molecolare*, 553.

[28] B.D. SCHOUB, *AIDS and HIV in Perspective*, 33-34; A. AMADORI – P. ZANOVELLO, *Immunologia Cellulare e Molecolare*, 553.

3.2 *Pre-AIDS Stage.*

This is the period immediately after the incubating period. This becomes dangerous if the person is unaware and so does not begin with immediate treatment. The weakening of the immune system opens the person to various attacks and, since the immune system is unable to ward off these attacks, there begins manifestations of various illnesses and diseases. At this stage, the person begins to show manifestations of what is known as AIDS Related Complex, (ARC). At this stage, the infected person is susceptible to various biological attacks caused by viruses, bacteria or parasites.

The characteristic features or manifestations at this stage is that the infected person experiences illnesses like chronic diarrhea, which will result in severe weight loss, repeated fevers with high temperature, unexplained fatigue, the swelling of the lymph glands, especially in the head, neck, armpit, the groin areas etc.[29] Other features include some forms of cancer as well. These symptoms however are not limited to HIV/AIDS cases.[30]

3.3 *Full – Blown AIDS*

This is the final stage, the full manifestation of what is known as AIDS. At this stage, there is a combination and cumulation of infections called «opportunistic infections». These are infections that could normally happen to a person that may or may not cause disease when the immune system is fully functioning.[31] But because of the collapse or suppression of the immune system, these infections now result in diseases that, more often than not, are fatal.[32] They are thus called «opportunistic infections» because these usually benign organisms are taking advantage of the immune suppression.

---

[29] B.D. SCHOUB, *AIDS and HIV in Perspective,* 33-34; A. AMADORI – P. ZANOVELLO, *Immunologia Cellulare e Molecolare,* 553.

[30] J. LEIBOWITCH, *A Strange Virus,* 107-109. He calls these symptoms as «Non-Specific Symptoms», to show that they are not limited to AIDS cases alone.

[31] A. AMADORI – P. ZANOVELLO, *Immunologia Cellulare e Molecolare,* 553; J. FULLER, «HIV/AIDS: An Overview», 17; B.D. SCHOUB, *AIDS and HIV in Perspective,* 26.

[32] A. AMADORI – P. ZANOVELLO, *Immunologia Cellulare e Molecolare,* 553; J. FULLER, «HIV/AIDS: An Overview», 17; B.D. SCHOUB, *AIDS and HIV in Perspective,* 26.

The opportunistic infections are classified either into yeasts or fungal, protozoa, viruses and bacteria.[33] Examples of such opportunistic infections are:

Fungal: Candida albicans (infection of mouth or esophagus),[34] Cryptococcus neoformans (meningitis).[35] Protozoal: pneumocystis carinii (pneumonia),[36] Toxoplasma gondii (brain infection),[37] Cryptosporidium (diarrhea).[38]

The bacterial/mycobacterial opportunistic infections are: Mycobacterium tuberculosis,[39] Salmonella.[40] The viral opportunistic infections are: Cytomegalovirus (retinitis),[41] also included are herpes simplex, a skin eruption that causes, painful and severe ulcers around the mouth and lips, herpes varicella zoster, which causes eruptions known as shingles.[42] Also in the viral group is the Human Herpesvirus 8 (Kaposi's Sarcoma, KS), a malignant vascular neoplasm.[43]

The above manifestations notwithstanding, the task before the medical community is the ability to really differentiate AIDS cases from diseases that occur but are not due to AIDS. For instance, the symptoms in the Pre-AIDS stage and even the opportunistic infections are not necessarily limited to the presence of HIV/AIDS. A good example

---

[33] J. FULLER, «HIV/AIDS: An Overview», 17-21, also B.D. SCHOUB, *AIDS and HIV in Perspective,* 26.

[34] J. FULLER, «HIV/AIDS: An Overview», 17, 21; B.D. SCHOUB, *AIDS and HIV in Perspective,* 28; A. AMADORI – P. ZANOVELLO, *Immunologia Cellulare e Molecolare,* 554.

[35] J. FULLER, «HIV/AIDS: An Overview», 21; A. AMADORI – P. ZANOVELLO, *Immunologia Cellulare e Molecolare,* 554.

[36] R. GALLO, *Virus Hunting,* 237; J. FULLER, «HIV/AIDS: An Overview», 18, 21; B.D. SCHOUB, *AIDS and HIV in Perspective,* 29.

[37] J. FULLER, «HIV/AIDS: An Overview», 18, 21; B.D. SCHOUB, *AIDS and HIV in Perspective,* 29-30.

[38] J. FULLER, «HIV/AIDS: An Overview», 18, 21; B.D. SCHOUB, *AIDS and HIV in Perspective,* 29-30.

[39] B.D. SCHOUB, *AIDS and HIV in Perspective,* 26-28; J. FULLER, «HIV/AIDS: An Overview», 20-21.

[40] B.D. SCHOUB, *AIDS and HIV in Perspective,* 26-28; J. FULLER, «HIV/AIDS: An Overview», 20-21.

[41] J. FULLER, «HIV/AIDS: An Overview», 19, 21; B.D. SCHOUB, *AIDS and HIV in Perspective,* 26.

[42] J. FULLER, «HIV/AIDS: An Overview», 19, 21; B.D. SCHOUB, *AIDS and HIV in Perspective,* 26.

[43] J.L. FAHEY – D.S. FLEMMING, ed., *AIDS/HIV,* 191; A. AMADORI – P. ZANOVELLO, *Immunologia Cellulare e Molecolare,* 554; B.D. SCHOUB, *AIDS and HIV in Perspective,* 31; J. FULLER, «HIV/AIDS: An Overview», 21.

is Kaposi's Sarcoma, KS, which is said to be common among people in the Mediterranean region and even found among Africans, unrelated to AIDS.[44] This is the type that is described as «indolent» form. The other, much less frequent but much more severe, «aggressive» form is more or less due to AIDS. In the «aggressive» form, lesions are not limited to the skin but affect many organs (glands, lungs, intestines, heart, etc.).[45]

It becomes obvious that when there is a breakdown of the immune system as a result of HIV/AIDS, and regardless of the combinations of treatment, the end is usually fatal, leading to death. This is because the direct effect of AIDS normally involves various organs like the kidneys, the central nervous system, etc., depending on the organism responsible and which organs are infected.

From what has been seen, we now know that the general consensus is that HIV is the viral agent that is responsible for AIDS. Besides, we have come to know as well that not every illness that is characterized by the immune breakdown is a result of HIV/AIDS infection. This therefore calls for caution both in diagnosing and stigmatizing people who might exhibit traits of illnesses that resemble AIDS but which in reality are not caused by HIV/AIDS. This will definitely allow proper treatment to be followed.

4. Modes of Transmission

One undeniable fact about HIV/AIDS disease is it poses a great threat to the human race and will continue to do so as long as there is no effective treatment and vaccine. However, it is also a transmissible and infectious disease.

This section examines the different modes of transmission or the route from which this disease passes from an infected person to another non-infected person. This section becomes even more important when we consider the different assumptions and fears associated with the disease.

There is fear, doubt, panic and even trauma everywhere as some claim the disease could be air-borne, contacted casually through such activities like hugging, kissing, etc. But the real question is are these fears really justified? There seems to be consensus of opinion about the modes of transmission of this disease.

---

[44] Cf. B.D. SCHOUB, *AIDS and HIV in Perspective*, 31.

[45] J. LEIBOWITCH, *A Strange Virus*, 18; A. AMADORI – P. ZANOVELLO, *Immunologia Cellulare e Molecolare*, 554.

4.1 *Sexual Route*

First, the most common and frequent mode of transmission is of the intimate and private nature, intimate sexual contact or activity. The irony here is that intimate sexual relations that ought to be a very natural way of expressing love and generating new life have also become a channel of pain, agony and death. There is no dispute or divided opinion about the fact of HIV/AIDS being transmitted as a result of intimate sexual contact from one infected person to another. This disease differs, however, in different ways from other known sexually transmitted diseases (STDs), both in its nature and impact.

In addition, in the case of HIV/AIDS, all persons who are infected are potentially agents of infection and remain so probably for the rest of their lives.[46] It is equally important to know that intimate sexual contact could either be heterosexual, homosexual or even bisexual.

4.1.1 Homosexual Route

HIV/AIDS was initially considered to be the disease of homosexual men, that is, men having sex with men (MSM).[47] The reason for this is that the HIV/AIDS epidemic was initially recognized among white male homosexuals in the US, and later in other developed countries. Consequently, various nuances and descriptions surfaced. «The Gay Plague», «Gay menace», «Gay killer».[48] The very fact that the disease was initially recognized and seen among homosexual men also meant that it was called in those early times as «Gay Related Immune Deficiency Syndrome – GRIDS».[49]

I shall not go into a detailed analysis of homosexuality or homosexual practice in this work. Suffice it to say that the practice is more rampant in the developed countries than in Africa. This of course does not suggest that such practices do not occur in Africa. Perhaps its infrequency in this region might be connected with the societal perception

---

[46] This assertion is based on the fact that there is no effective cure or vaccination to contain the spread of the disease for now. This assertion is thus conditional given the fact that there is hope of finding an effective vaccine in the future.

[47] Cf. D.L. KIRP – R. BAYER, ed., *AIDS in the Industrialized Democracies*, 189; R. SHILTS, *And the Band Played On*, xxi.

[48] These are just some of the nuances one finds in the newspaper editorials at the beginning of the epidemic. See R. BRENNAN – D. DURACK, «Gay Compromise Syndrome», 1338-1339.

[49] R. SHILTS, *And the Band Played On,* 121.

of the practice as an aberration. Therefore, homosexuals or those who exhibit this tendency tend to hide their identity.

Regarding homosexuality and AIDS, it is claimed that «in the United Kingdom, around 90% of all reported AIDS cases occur in sexually active, male, homosexual or bisexual men».[50] By the same token, homosexual HIV/AIDS transmission is not limited to the developed countries alone. In places like Thailand, the Philippines, and much of South and Central America, the first AIDS cases reported were found in homosexual men.[51]

In fact, the figures between 1983 and 1994 show that over 40 percent of AIDS cases in Mexico and most of South America resulted from homosexual transmission, as is true for over half of the known cases in Indonesia.[52] In Africa, there is some difficulty in obtaining accurate statistics since homosexuality is less an issue.

How does homosexuality constitute a greater risk for HIV/AIDS transmission? Homosexual intercourse involves rectal or anal penetration. Rectal intercourse, that is penile-anal, is said to constitute a danger for HIV/AIDS transmission because «of the high frequency of trauma to the mucosal lining of the rectum» during such activity. As Schoub explains:

> The rectal mucous is a relatively delicate and friable epithelium composed of a lining of one cell thickness in contrast to the multi-cell layered and relatively robust vaginal epithelium which is far better equipped to withstand the injuries which may take place during intercourse. Furthermore, the rectal wall is richly supplied with lymphoid tissue, which can provide a ready access for the virus to susceptible lymphocytes. … Finally, the M-cells in the rectal mucous are energetic transporters of foreign material to the underlying lymphoid tissue and lymphocytes.[53]

Apart from these biological factors, another important factor was the alleged sexual promiscuity found among homosexuals, that is, the practice of having multiple sex male partners, especially in bathhouses.[54]

It is also important to note that homosexual practice could either be penile-anal, oral-anal or oral-penile sex, also known as fellatio. In these different categories, penile-anal, which involves rectal intercourse constitutes a major route for transmission. Some believe that oral-penile

---

50 B.D. SCHOUB, *AIDS and HIV in Perspective*, 96.
51 D. ALTMAN, «HIV, Homosexuality, and Vulnerability», 254.
52 D. ALTMAN, «HIV, Homosexuality, and Vulnerability», 254.
53 B.D. SCHOUB, *AIDS and HIV in Perspective*, 97.
54 Cf. G. CINA – E. LOCCI – C. ROCCHETTA – L. SANDRIN, ed., *Dizionario*, 19.

sex too can serve as a route of transmission because of the deposition of semen in the oral cavity, becoming even more dangerous if lesions or abrasions are present. However, transmission via the oral-anal contact has not been established.[55]

One final consideration is the need to know if homosexual activity per se is the source of HIV/AIDS. If a person is already infected then the consideration above is sufficient to explain the transmission route. It is however yet to be determined, and no explanation has been offered for sexual practices that might enhance the transmission of the HIV/AIDS virus from woman to woman, since women too are involved in homosexual practice, otherwise known as lesbianism.

4.1.2 Heterosexual Route

As just seen, attention was focused more on the homosexuals as the early manifestation of the disease was common among this group. Unfortunately, this disease has also been feasting and spreading unnoticed among those who have intimate heterosexual contact. The focus on the heterosexual transmission route especially in the developed countries started very late[56] and this awareness became heightened in 1986 at the Paris AIDS Conference.[57] This conference signaled the beginning of the awareness of the risk of heterosexual transmission of HIV/AIDS in the developed countries.

Whereas homosexual route has been of high prevalence in the US and most other developed countries, in Africa, especially the central, eastern and southern parts where the disease is quite prevalent, heterosexual contact remains the main route of HIV/AIDS transmission. In this region this disease was dubbed the «slim disease»,[58] because it makes people skinny. Slim disease is simply due to the loss of the capacity to absorb food that leads to a chronic, malabsorptive diarrhea.

Across the globe, heterosexual transmission has been on a steady increase. In Europe alone, heterosexual transmission of HIV is said to have «increased from 11.4 percent in 1990 to 16.5 percent in the first six months of 1995».[59] It is even believed that worldwide, over 70 percent of HIV infections today is as a result of heterosexual activity.[60]

---

[55] G. CINA – E. LOCCI – C. ROCCHETTA – L. SANDRIN, ed., *Dizionario,* 101.

[56] R. SHILTS, *And the Band Played On,* 510.

[57] J. BALLARD, «Australia: Participation and Innovation»,145.

[58] E. HOOPER, *The River,* 34, 36, 39; R. SHILTS, *And the Band Played On,* 510.

[59] B.G. WENIGER – S. BERKLEY, «The Evolving HIV/AIDS Pandemic», 58.

[60] A.A. EHRHARDT, «Sexual Behavior Among Homosexuals», 259.

In these cases of heterosexual transmission, it unfortunately appears that women are the most vulnerable. The vulnerability of women especially in Africa may be tied to social and biological factors. In Africa, for instance, it is almost a general assumption that women are often expected to be submissive to the demands of men even when the lifestyles of some of these men are deplorable. In this situation women are at greater risk of acquiring the disease.

There is also the biological dimension that predisposes women to acquiring the disease more than men. Biologically, Schoub explains:

> As in the case of rectal intercourse, trauma to the vagina significantly increases the chance of transmission. Traumatic disruption of the vaginal mucous is seen in rape… and also following the insertion of sex toys and other foreign objects into the vagina.
>
> In addition, the vagina is a receptacle for relatively large volume of infected semen, which remains in contact with a substantial area of susceptible vaginal and cervical epithelium for prolonged periods of time. Whereas, the exposure of a susceptible male to an infected female involves only a brief contact with an infected epithelial surface and the retention of a thin film of vaginal or cervical secretion onto susceptible epithelial surfaces of the penis and the urethra.[61]

Like in homosexual activity, heterosexual intimate practice could be penile-vaginal or oral, which in turn could be fellatio-oral-penile sex or cunnilingus-oral-vaginal sex. Any of this could constitute a route of transmission. But the important point is that one of the partners must have been infected already. In fellatio or cunnilingus, the risk is always there because the semen and the vaginal fluid are rich in lymphocytes including CD4 lymphocytes. Additionally, the genital mucous membranes are extensively supplied with langerhans cells. These cells are the major presenters of foreign antigen to the immune system. They are highly susceptible to HIV infection, as their surface is rich in CD4 receptor sites. They can therefore function as vehicles to transport HIV from peripheral mucous membranes centrally to the lymphoid tissue of the immune system.[62]

Heterosexual transmission route is commonly passed more from male to female. But there have been cases of female to male transmission, for example by female prostitutes to their male client.[63] However,

---

[61] B.D. SCHOUB, *AIDS and HIV in Perspective,* 100.
[62] B.D. SCHOUB, *AIDS and HIV in Perspective,* 93.
[63] R. SHILTS, *And the Band Played On,* 511.

it still could be argued that the prostitute was originally infected by one of her male clients.

4.1.3 Other Sexual Factors

Other factors could facilitate in the sexual transmission of HIV/AIDS either through homosexual or heterosexual practice. These factors are called «co-factors». They are biological factors like the presence of some sexually transmitted diseases (STDs). These diseases are due to a variety of microorganisms, which could be viruses, bacteria, fungi and parasites. STDs clinically manifest themselves in genital ulcers, genital discharges and genital warts. When STDs are present, they can facilitate the easy spread of HIV/AIDS.

In this situation, the female to male transmission is as great and likely to occur as from male to female. The high cases of the HIV/AIDS infection rate in Africa could probably be tied to these co-factors as well since many with STDs do not have access to quality health care compared to people in the developed countries. In some hospitals, there are hardly enough doctors and other health care personnel.

In addition, drugs are not readily available. And where you find quality hospitals and availability of drugs, many of those in need of treatment cannot afford this treatment as a result of poverty. These co-factors together with intimate heterosexual contact make transmission of HIV/AIDS easy in Africa. It is said that 94 percent of HIV/AIDS infection in sub-Saharan Africa is as a result of heterosexual contact.[64]

4.2 Intravenous Drug Users (IDU)

HIV/AIDS transmission in the developed countries as has been seen was prevalent mainly among homosexuals especially at the initial stage of the epidemic. The second major risk group has been recognized as intravenous drug users. Intravenous drug users are people who use hard drugs not normally prescribed by doctors and pharmacists, such as heroin, cocaine, etc. by injecting the drugs into their veins by needles and syringes. As Leibowitch reported, HIV/AIDS virus is very rampant among drug addicts of both sexes in the US. In «a small group of New York drug users» alone, «alarming figures of over 80 percent have been found».[65]

---

[64] P.O. WAY – K.A. STANECKI, *The Impact of HIV/AIDS*, 6.
[65] J. LEIBOWITCH, *A Strange Virus*, 154.

Apart from the US, it is said that in some European countries, the IDUs comprise the largest group of AIDS patients. For instance, in Italy and Spain, over 50 percent of AIDS patients are said to be intravenous drug users.[66] A late 1992 report puts the case of IDUs and AIDS in Spain and Italy at 64 percent and 65 percent respectively, which is considered to be the highest in Europe.[67]

In the case of those intravenous drug users who are addicted, the same syringe and needle is often shared among them. In this case, if one person is already infected, he or she passes the virus on to another person. Again Leibowitch offers the following explanation: «Although the syringes and needles may be rinsed, they may not be clean enough to neutralize the fluids of the preceding user». This method of sharing syringes and needles, he concludes is economical and convivial, but also hygienically unsafe and dangerous.[68]

One should not forget to note also that some of these intravenous drug users are also homosexuals and bisexuals, as well as heterosexual drug users. It is easier therefore for the already infected person whether homosexual or heterosexual, or both, to spread the disease easily to another person due to blood contact occasioned by the sharing of syringe.[69] In the case of the heterosexual drug user already infected, he or she through the practice of sharing syringes and needles serves as an agent of infection to his or her partner in heterosexual intimate contact.[70] The double routes could best explain the observation that the intravenous drug users who are HIV positive are quick in manifesting the symptoms of the last stages of the disease, and so die faster.[71]

4.3 Medical Intervention Route

HIV/AIDS could be and has been transmitted through medical activities like the following:

---

[66] B.D. SCHOUB, AIDS and HIV in Perspective, 112; G. CINA – E. LOCCI – C. ROCCHETTA – L. SANDRIN, Dizionario, 19.

[67] P.O. WAY – K.A. STANECKI, The Impact of HIV/AIDS, 6.

[68] J. LEIBOWITCH, A Strange Virus, 32.

[69] R. SHILTS, And the Band Played On, 83. See also M.F. GOLDSMITH, «HIV and Intravenous Drug Users», 102.

[70] R. SHILTS, And the Band Played On, 126.

[71] R. SHILTS, And the Band Played On, 97.

4.3.1 Blood Transfusion

Since the beginning of the epidemic, it has been generally recognized and known that the HIV/AIDS virus has been transmitted through blood transfusion. The virus is actually found in the blood, and «feeds» on the white cells, which are the blood cells responsible for immune response.

Blood transfusion is a common practice in the medical environment. There are those who opposed the practice of blood transfusion based on religious belief and practice, for example the Jehovah Witnesses.

Blood is needed in cases of major surgeries, the treatment of accident victims or those who are anaemic, etc. All people in these categories depend on blood for their survival. This common and accepted medical practice, which is meant to save life, has also become the source of infection for some people. What happens is that during blood transfusion, some people are given blood that is already contaminated and infected.

Since the beginning of the HIV/AIDS epidemic, there have been reported cases of infections as a result of blood transfusion. These incidences have been recorded in both the developed and developing countries.[72]

The first known case of HIV/AIDS blood transfusion is the case of a baby born at the University of California, San Francisco (UCSF). The case of what Shilts calls «Rh baby». This baby was born with a defect as «his body had antibodies to his own blood», so he needed a complete blood transfusion for survival. As it turned out, the transfused blood was already infected with the HIV/AIDS virus.[73] Another incidence of infection as a result of blood transfusion involved a Hispanic man, who «received massive blood transfusions for a coronary bypass operation» at Bellevue, New York in January 1981. He was said to not have belonged to the high-risk group, but by 1982, developed symptoms related to AIDS disease. [74]

There is also, in retrospect, a case of a young Frenchman, who in 1978 was on the National Service Obligations at Port-au-Prince, Haiti. While there, he was involved in a car accident and received blood during his treatment. He recovered from the accident, but by 1982, he

---

[72] Cf. R. SHILTS, *And the Band Played On,* 116.
[73] R. SHILTS, *And the Band Played On,* 45, 57, 206-208.
[74] R. SHILTS, *And the Band Played On,* 176.

showed symptoms of AIDS. Again, the striking thing being that he was not known for activities that put him in the risk group.[75]

While the earlier cases occurred in the US, similar cases have occurred elsewhere in the world, for instance in Australia. In 1984, it was announced that three babies died of AIDS – related diseases as a result of receiving HIV-contaminated blood donated by a homosexual person. That incident became a significant political event as an opposition leader accused the ruling party of being responsible for it. He was quoted to have said: «If it wasn't for the promotion of homosexuality as a norm by Labour, I am quite confident that the deaths of these three poor babies would not have occurred».[76]

While the cases above are recorded in the developed countries at the early stage of the epidemic, it is no longer a serious problem now as blood and blood products are continuously screened before any transfusion is done. We can only imagine what could have happened, and perhaps is still happening in the developing countries, like Africa, where many hospitals still lack screening kits.

4.3.2 Haemophiliac Transmission

Haemophiliac transmission represents another medical means by which HIV/AIDS has been and can be transmitted.[77] Haemophilia is a genetic anomaly. This defect involves a profound disorder of coagulation. However, injecting a blood product called «Factor VIII», lacking in haemophiliacs, can rectify this condition. This factor VIII helps the blood to clot, normally compensating for the inherited defect. This type of intervention, unfortunately, has also proved to be a means of HIV/AIDS transmission, as there have been cases where the coagulant fractions received proved to be HIV contaminated.[78]

4.3.3 Other Medical Means

There are some other medical routes like the use of unsterilized syringes and needles. This practice is not common in the developed countries especially at this age of HIV/AIDS. But it was not uncommon in Africa, though it is perhaps a bit reduced now as a result of the awareness of risks involved. It is likely that most of the syringes and needles

[75] J. LEIBOWITCH, A Strange Virus, 30.
[76] J. BALLARD, «Australia: Participation and Innovation»,134.
[77] Cf. M. VIDAL, Diccionario de Etica Teologica, 554.
[78] Cf. R. SHILTS, And the Band Played On, 115-116, 160-161.

used during the various vaccination programs in the late fifties through sixties, and even in the seventies, might not have been sterilized at all or not properly sterilized. This would then have been a feasible explanation for the high prevalence of HIV/AIDS in the region today.

In addition, there is also the accidental inoculation of infected blood through needle-stick injuries. According to Schoub, up to 1995, some 73 such professional cases of infection have been documented worldwide.[79] It is not unlikely that the figures could be more if thorough investigation is carried out. The cases of accident have led to serious debate about the safety of medical personnel.

4.4 *Vertical Transmission – Mother to Child*

Since the beginning of the epidemic, vertical transmission or transmission from an infected mother to her newborn child has been recognized as one of the modes of transmission[80] and has been a great issue of concern. Vertical transmission could either occur while the fetus is developing in the womb or at childbirth. It has also been noted that vertical transmission does occur in the course of breast-feeding.[81]

Apart from cases of blood transfusion, vertical transmission accounts for most cases of HIV/AIDS infections among children in the world and in Africa in particular, especially in the central and eastern regions of Africa.

It must be borne in mind however, that the likelihood of transmission could also depend very much on the stage of infection of the mother, that is, the amount of viral load in her body. If the viral load is high and the mother is pregnant around the last stage of the disease, the likelihood of vertical transmission would obviously be very high.

Here too, we can note various ethical issues and considerations, for example the issue of pregnancy for infected women. These considerations will be examined at the latter part of this work, when we discuss the issue of prevention.

4.5 *Casual Transmission*

There have been opinions and debates about the possibility of transmission taking place as a result of casual contacts. That is, whether

---

[79] B.D. SCHOUB, *AIDS and HIV in Perspective*, 113.

[80] M. VIDAL, *Diccionario de Etica Teologica*, 554.

[81] J. LEIBOWITCH, *A Strange Virus*, 33. See also B.D. SCHOUB, *AIDS and HIV in Perspective*, 118; G. CINA – E. LOCCI – C. ROCCHETTA – L. SANDRIN, *Dizionario*, 19.

exposure to the virus can occur through such activities like kissing, hugging, touching, insect-bites, sharing kitchen and bathrooms.

The general conclusion tends to be that casual transmission is not likely to occur.[82] Gallo, for instance, dispels as unfounded the notion of casual or insect-borne transmission of the virus. He says:

> The ability (of the virus) to be casually transmitted would change the very essence of the virus. The reason for its lethal effect is chiefly due to its uncanny knack for targeting the most critical cells of the immune system. That is, the CD4 molecule of the T4 helper lymphocytes and macrophages.[83]

The point is that many scientists believe that the HIV virus multiplies in a host cell, which is chiefly the T-lymphocytes, which is not likely to occur through casual contact.[84]

It is therefore important for people to know that there is no risk of acquiring the virus from living together, from being in the same workplace, from coughing or sneezing, from using public toilets, or from nonsexual physical contact. An awareness of these facts can, and should help to reduce, if not to eliminate, the discriminatory attitude towards the people living with HIV/AIDS.

The above notwithstanding, people have called for caution. For instance, in contacts involving «deep» or «French kissing» which entails the exchange of saliva, one cannot be too sure. There is a risk though if blood is present in the saliva, or abrasions or lesions in the mouth. In this case, it is not the casual act of kissing that is the problem, but rather these other factors mentioned above.

5. The Origin of HIV/AIDS

I did mention previously that AIDS was recognised to be a new phenomenon, or at least was not known before.

This section seeks to highlight some of the various discussions that have arisen on the origin of HIV/AIDS. Some preliminary observations are necessary.

---

[82] G.H. FRIEDLAN – al., «Lack of Transmission», 344-349; F.H. MESSERLI, «Transmission of AIDS», 379-380; M.A. SANDE, «Transmission of AIDS», 380-382; G.H. FRIEDLAN, «Risk of HTLV-II/LAV Transmission», 258; G.H. FRIEDLAN – R.S. KLEIN, «Transmission of the Human Immunodeficiency Virus», 1125-1135.

[83] R. GALLO, Virus Hunting, 232.

[84] J.E. KAPLAN – al., «Evidence», 468-471.

First, there are social, political and human implications tied to this disease, hence the various speculations and hypotheses. In addition to this is the fact that there have been some recent outbursts among scholars, that people are not being told the truth as to what causes AIDS and its origin. This fact makes the question of origin more challenging and worth reviewing and evaluating.

There are those who think the debate over the origin of HIV/AIDS is unnecessary as that does not solve or offer the solution of a cure. Furthermore, such debates compound the already tense and traumatic experiences of people living with HIV/AIDS and society at large. The origin of this disease, they argue, does not mitigate the urgent need for the management and control of the disease. Consequently, the concern should be how best we can manage it and prevent its further spread.

While the above is true and valid in some regard, it is equally valid that we cannot deny the fact that before an effective treatment or vaccine can be found, there is need to know the cause, how and where the disease actually came from. This would give a clue and enhance the approaches to treatment.

Having made these observations, there are different hypotheses and theories of the origin of HIV/AIDS. These can be classified into two categories: the natural theory hypothesis and the iatrogenic theory hypothesis. There are also two schools within the iatrogenic theory hypothesis: the accidental theory and the multiple conspiracy theories.

However, I shall only highlight these theories. I shall not go into a detailed analysis of these theories for two reasons. First is the fact that the scope of this thesis does not really permit detailed discussion. The origin of HIV/AIDS could be a thesis in itself. The second reason is the fact that these different theories are for now hypothetical, which thus make it difficult for any fruitful ethical discussion in the present circumstance.

5.1 *The Natural Origin Theory*

The human immunodeficiency virus (HIV) is considered to have evolved over a long period of years as a mutation from a family of a similar virus that is found in African primates, known as the simian immunodeficiency virus (SIV).[85] In other words, humans acquired the AIDS virus from the virus found in primates.

---

[85] Cf. M. GRMEK, *History of AIDS*, 146. Also M. ESSEX – P. KANKI – *al.*, «Antigens», 700-703.

Research by Beatrice Hahn and colleagues offers substantial evidence for a primate to human transmission of SIV as HIV-I.[86] However, this paper still does not answer the question of how the transmission occurred. It is on the basis of the primate to human conclusion that the writer of an unsigned article appearing in the *Economist* postulated thus:

> The human immuno-deficiency virus (HIV), which causes acquired immune deficiency syndrome (AIDS), is thought to have crossed from chimpanzees to humans in the late 1940s or early 1950s in Congo. It took several years for the virus to break out of Congo's dense and sparsely populated jungles, but once it did, it marched with rebel armies through the continent's numerous war zones, rode with truckers from one rest-stop brothel to the next, and eventually flew, perhaps with an air steward to America, where it was first discovered in the early 1980s.[87]

Again what the above position does is just to postulate and then describe factors that could aid the rapid spread of the disease. The writer did not substantiate this claim either scientifically or even historically.

In explaining the origin of HIV/AIDS, the natural theory simply says that humans acquired this primate virus through most «natural» of activities: eating of monkey meats, also the probability of monkey bites during hunting or people who keep monkeys as pets.

Interestingly, SIV is said to be natural to its host, that is, it causes no disease in monkeys but becomes a problem when it crosses species, namely from monkeys to humans. The conclusion therefore is that HIV is a result of a jump of monkey virus to human beings and this jump occurred in Africa.[88]

The question remains how does the cross breeding or transmission take place? If this is the case, why has there been a sudden reaction and breakdown of the immune system now, and not in the past?

It is claimed that this process of transfer involves a bizarre sexual practice, a kind of bestiality,[89] in which, to heighten sexual arousal, male and female members of tribes bordering the lakes of Central Africa introduce monkey blood into their pubic areas, thighs and backs.

---

[86] P. SHARP – D. ROBERTSON – F. GAO – B. HAHN, «Origins», 527-543; F. GAO – al., «Origin of HIV-1», 436-441.

[87] «AIDS in the Third World: A Global Disaster», in the *Economist*, January 2, 1999.

[88] Cf. J. GOUDSMIT, *Viral Sex*, 59-66.

[89] J. SLAFF – J. K. BRUBAKER, *The AIDS Epidemic*, 112.

It is also claimed that a possible explanation for the epidemic now is the combination of rapid urbanization in Africa, new travel opportunities as a result of independence, and even slavery etc.[90] These reasons, however, may not be sufficient.

For instance, during the era of slave trade, there was a mass movement of people from Africa to Europe and other parts of the world. Besides, at this time, there was also sexual contact between slave masters and slave girls. Furthermore, there was sexual activity among slaves themselves, who obviously came from different parts of Africa. These factors support the notion that there should have been an epidemic at that particular time, yet there was none.

Thus far, what we have are just hypotheses and propositions that cannot really be proven with substantial data. In any case, one thing seems to be true, that the monkeys may have played a crucial role, even though, the explanation for such a link is less than satisfactory. A recent article that appeared in the *International Herald Tribune* appears to justify my above conclusion.[91]

5.2 *Iatrogenic Origin Theory*

Iatrogenesis is the technical term for the epidemic of doctor-made diseases. It is derived from two Greek words: *iatros* for physician and *genesis* for origins. Hence iatrogenic disorder is one that results from the activities of the physician.[92] Iatrogenic theory implies that the physician or more accurately, scientist has unwittingly unleashed this disaster on the people he was seeking to protect.

The basic thesis of the iatrogenic origin theory is that the HIV virus and its resulting consequence AIDS, is due to the work of the human person, the scientist in the camp of medicine. Horowitz describes the iatrogenic theory of AIDS to mean the synthetic development of HIV-I, HIV-2, and a host of other killer viruses.[93]

There are two positions regarding the iatrogenic theory of the origins of HIV/AIDS, the accidental or unintentional hypothesis and the intentional or conspiracy hypothesis. The differences between the two positions has to do with whether this intervention of man was not intended to cause this disease, hence accidental, or whether it was intentional,

---

[90] M. GRMEK, *History of AIDS*, 149-150.
[91] G. KOLATA, «Origins of AIDS Remain Murky», 8.
[92] Cf. J. WALTON – P.B. BEESON – R.B. SCOTT, ed., *The Oxford Companion,* 574.
[93] L.G. HOROWITZ, *Emerging Viruses,* 134.

that is, whether the person or group of persons deliberately created the virus and then released it to humans.

5.2.1 The Accidental Hypothesis

According to this hypothesis, some of the vaccines used in the eradication of diseases like polio, herpes, adenovirus, yellow fever, small pox, etc. may be the cause of the present day AIDS epidemic. It is a known fact that some of the vaccines are made from the tissues taken from monkeys, especially the African green monkey, and the chimpanzee. As already mentioned in the earlier pages, these monkeys are believed to carriers of some kind of virus, the simian immune virus.

The accidental hypothesis origin of HIV/AIDS therefore is that there is the probability that monkey tissue used in the production of vaccine such as that of polio vaccine for example, could have been infected with simian virus, SIV.

The contamination of the vaccine with SIV therefore best explains the transmission of SIV as HIV. It is on this basis that we have the Oral Polio Vaccine (OPV), and the origins of AIDS theory.[94] This transmission is however considered as accidental.[95]

There is also another school of thought within the accidental theory hypothesis. For instance, Leonard Horowitz[96] argues that the iatrogenic theory of AIDS is not solely limited to polio vaccine, but to many other scientific alterations. His position is thus:

> The HIVs and SIVs most likely evolved from the «type-C» cancer viruses that were genetically altered and then cultured or inoculated into human tissues during cancer virus studies conducted by NCI researchers during the late 1960s and early 1970s. These studies were not limited to monkeys, cats, and chickens. Cow, sheep, horse, rodent, and human viruses were also hybridized and likely contaminated laboratory cell cultures and experimental vaccines. This theory best explains how HIV-2 / SIVmac' a

---

[94] Cf. L. PASCAL, «What Happens When Science Goes Bad». Also, W. KYLE, «Simian Retroviruses», 600-601. T. CURTIS, «The Origin of AIDS», 54-59, 61, 106 and 108; B.F. ELSWOOD – R.B. STRICKER, «Polio Vaccines and the Origin of AIDS», 347-354. The articles of Curtis and Elswood and Stricker can be found on the web: http://www.edu.au/arts/sts/bmartin/dissent/documents/AIDS.

[95] For a good literature of this hypothesis see, E. HOOPER, *The River*, especially p. 739.

[96] Leonard Horowitz is a Harvard graduate independent investigator, and a public health education scholar. Apart from the book, *Emerging viruses…* already cited, he is also the author of the critically acclaimed Florida dental AIDS tragedy exposé: *Deadly Innocence*.

simian virus found only in laboratory and not wild monkeys, was found by Max Essex in Senegalese female prostitutes.[97]

The picture the aforementioned depicts is that while it is quite certain that monkeys captured from the wild in Africa are carriers of different SIV viruses, that alone does not sufficiently explain the origin of AIDS. Rather, laboratory work appears to be a common denominator and experimental vaccines already contaminated were the most likely transmitter.[98]

5.2.2 The Conspiracy or Intentional Theory

This school of thought affirms that HIV/AIDS is not just iatrogenic, that is, man-made, but was created as a result of man's evil. The belief is that this deadly virus was purposely created and manufactured in the laboratory. There are two hypotheses put forward to justify this claim. These views basically allude to the fact that the HIV/AIDS virus was created to serve as biological weapons and also as an instrument or a means of population control.

The first position is one that sees HIV/AIDS as a deliberate effort by man to create a biological weapon. Under this position, one finger is pointed to the German scientists and the other to the American scientists.

It was claimed that Hitler's scientists created the virus in Germany as a secret biological weapon, meant for use during World War II. This allegation appeared in an American newspaper in 1989.[99]

The second position sees the HIV/AIDS virus as arising from the American laboratories. This position holds that the present epidemic is the result of work by scientists and generals in their laboratories of biological warfare. This thesis thus indicts some American scientists, the CIA and the US Army as those responsible. It traces the laboratory at Fort Detrick, Maryland as the probable place where the virus was created.[100]

---

[97] L. HOROWITZ, *Emerging viruses,* 133-134.

[98] Cf. L. HOROWITZ, *Emerging viruses,* 132.

[99] R. JACKSON, «Hitler's Lab Created AIDS Virus».

[100] Fort Detrick, Maryland is the site of American Army Biowarfare Laboratory called: United States Army Medical Research Institute for Infectious Disease /USAMRID/. This is believed to be the nation's, and likely the world's largest and most sophisticated BW testing center. Interestingly, this place is also close to Bethe-

One of the reasons for the above conclusion is the allusion made to the document obtained through the Freedom of Information Act which the proponents of this theory believe offers revealing evidence. This document for instance showed the desire of the United States Department of Defense to acquire or manufacture a virus to work as a biological weapon. In the document the intention to create a virus is stated as follows:

> Within the next 5 to 10 years,...(sic) a new infective microorganism which could differ in certain important aspects from any known disease-causing organisms. Most important of these is that it might be refactory to the immunological and therapeutic processes upon which we depend to maintain our relative freedom from infectious disease . . . It is a highly controversial issue and there are many who believe such research should not be undertaken lest it lead to yet another method of massive killing of large populations. ...[101]

With statements like this, one cannot but gasp for breath. Hooper who for instance believes in the accidental theory as seen earlier, concedes to the fact that the above quotation from the United States Department of Defense «superficially at least sounds like a description of HIV».[102] The synthetic biological agent to be created is said to be such that does not naturally exist and for which no natural immunity could have been acquired.[103]

Further evidence of government and scientific activities of the US Army is deduced from the view expressed by Han Swyter.[104] While addressing the National Academy of Sciences (NAS) assembly in 1970 he notes:

> Chemical and biological war is a grisly business. I am going to approach it

---

sada, where the National Institute of Health is situated. The reader interested in this theory can read: Cf. L. HOROWITZ, *Emerging viruses,* 35ff. See also E. HOOPER, *The River*, p.153.

[101] Department of Defense Appropriations for 1970: Hearings Before A subcommittee of the committee on Appropriations House of Representatives, Ninety First Congress, First Session, H.B.15090, Part 5, Research, Development, Test and Evaluation, Dept. Of the Army U.S. Government Printing Office, Washington, D.C., 1969. Quoted also in L. HOROWITZ, *Emerging viruses,* 18.

[102] E. HOOPER, *The River*, 154-155.

[103] The copy of the original classified document is published in the other work of Horowitz. L. HOROWITZ, *Deadly Innocence*, 124.

[104] Han Swyter was formerly with the Department of Defense. As an insider, he knows what was going on.

unemotionally; Unemotional analysis of the need for war-fighting (chemical and biological) capability goes on everyday. (Emphasis added) . . .The first kind of capability I will analyze is lethal biological. These are population killing weapons. In situations in which our national objective would be to kill other countries' populations, lethal biological could be used . . . If we want to kill populations, we can now do that with our strategic nuclear weapons – our B-52's, Minutemen, and Polaris. We keep the nuclear capability whether or not we have a lethal biological capability . . . A lethal biological capability would be in addition to our nuclear capability rather than a substitute for it.

... A decision to have capability, to have an option for that rare situation, requires weighing the uncertainties of non proliferation with the value of human life, perhaps of tens of thousands of Americans. If we decide today that we would be willing to sacrifice our soldiers in the situation I described, we do not need a capability. However, if we want the option to decide later, perhaps we need an incapacitating [as opposed to lethal] biological capability.[105]

The above quotation is seen as an indicator that led to the belief that HIV/AIDS was intentionally made, this time not just as biological weapon but also as means of population control. This hypothesis is buttressed and supported by the various US government population policy activities.[106] For example, in the United States National Security Memorandum, dubbed *NSSM 200*, it is stated «depopulation should be the highest priority of U.S. foreign policy towards the Third World». «Reduction of the rate of population in these states is a matter of vital U.S. national security».

The motivating factor for this conviction is said to be:

The U.S. economy will require large and increasing amounts of minerals from abroad, especially from less-developed countries. That fact gives the U.S. enhanced interests in the political, economic and social stability of the supplying countries. Whereas a lessening of population can increase the prospects for such stability, population policy becomes relevant to resources, supplies and to the economic interest of the United States.[107]

---

105 NATIONAL ACADEMY OF SCIENCES, «Symposium», 250-259.

106 For a better insight into the United States population measures, see S.D. MUMFORD, *The Life and Death*; E. LIAGIN, *Excessive Force*; J. KASUN, *The War on Population*.

107 NATIONAL SECURITY COUNCIL, *NSSM 200 - Implications of Worldwide Population Growth*. Declassified July 3 1989. The full text can be found in S.D. MUMFORD, *The Life and Death*, 433-558.

The case the conspiracy theory hypothesis is making is that a cursory look at the epicenter of HIV/AIDS is the third world, especially Africa, hence the suspicion that the virus of HIV/AIDS was intentionally made for the purposes enunciated above.

6. Concluding Remarks

In this chapter, we have tried to examine the meaning and understanding of this present human epidemic. Here we see that it has now been established that HIV evolved from the simian immunodeficiency virus, SIV. We also examined the clinical manifestations of this disease, where it is demonstrated that the asymptomatic stage poses a great danger in that the absence of test, the infected person is unaware and so could spread the disease to others if engaged in risky behavior.

However, it is also made clear that the disease could only be transmitted through specific means, for example through high-risk sexual contact, from sharing needles, from an infected mother to a developing fetus, from contaminated blood products. The most heartwarming point is that the disease is not transmitted casually. It is however important to add that the critical factor in the transmission of the disease is not the group to which one belongs, but the behavior in which one engages.

Finally, we highlighted the different theories of origin of the disease that have arisen. I only highlighted these different theories or hypotheses, as it is difficult to make any fruitful ethical discussion in this circumstance. It can only be said that if the virus was transmitted accidentally during the preparation of polio vaccines, then we are dealing with a historical event. Thus it does not easily yield itself to ethical discussion in the present, apart from efforts to avoid similar such mistakes from occurring.

As to the conspiracy theories, obviously if there was some intention to create a pathogen this would be morally reprehensible, but then, any exploration of this subject is purely hypothetical and is not subject to validation. Consequently, I did not pursue that in this thesis, which is meant to be a scientific, and a purely academic exercise. The question of how the transmission occurred could be a topic of dissertation in itself.

I shall conclude this chapter by affirming that HIV/AIDS remains an important human disease, which in one way or the other affects everyone, so it is not enough to think that as long as we do not belong to the risk group, it is not our problem. As John Seale warns, we should not be complacent, «infection with AIDS virus is potentially lethal to all men, women and children irrespective of lifestyle or sexual activity».[108]

---

[108] J. SEALE, «AIDS Virus Infection», 615.

CHAPTER II

Description of the HIV/AIDS in Nigeria

1. Introductory Remarks

In the previous chapter the meaning of HIV/AIDS was examined, as well as the issue of its origin, which remains unresolved. Also explored was, the various modes of transmission, where there is a general consensus of opinions. This second chapter examines the situation of HIV/AIDS in Nigeria. In doing so, the chapter is divided into four sections.

The first section gives a brief description and general location of the country. The second section is an overview of the HIV/AIDS in the country. It analyzes the HIV/AIDS situation in the country, including the statistics of each zone. In this section, one obvious fact is that there has been a rapid and an alarming increase in the number of infections, which makes the situation a cause of great concern.

The third section examines the factors for the rapid spread of the disease or, more accurately, it examines the specific problems that have contributed in no small way to the alarming spread of this deadly disease among the general populace.

The fourth section examines the effects that the epidemic is generating and will likely generate if adequate measures are not taken to halt the rapid spread of the disease. These effects range from economic, social and to political as well.

2. Location and Description of Nigeria

The amalgamation of the different components that make up Nigeria took place in 1914 by the British; Sir Lord Lugard was the Governor General. Nigeria remained a colony of the British till October 1, 1960, when she became independent.

Nigeria lies within latitudes 4°1' and 13°9' North and longitudes 2°2' and 14°30' East. The Republic of Niger borders it in the north, the Republics of Chad and Cameroon in the east and the Republic of Benin in the west.

Nigeria is said to have a total surface area of approximately 923,768 square kilometres, and as such is the tenth largest country in Africa.[1] It is, however, the most populous country in Africa. Nigeria is said to have a population of about 120 million people, which represents about one fifth of the total African population.[2] There are, however, more than 250 (three hundred and fifty) ethnic and linguistic groups.[3]

The country is divided into thirty-six States, with the Federal Capital Territory (FCT) of the country, being Abuja. While Abuja serves as the seat of government, Lagos, the former federal capital city, remains the capital of the Country's commercial activities.

The country is grouped into six geo-political zones, the North-East, North-West, North-Central, South-East, South-West, South-South. The breaking of the country into zones is largely for the sake of convenience, especially with regard to power sharing. It must be noted that these zones differ from one another in terms of geographical size, ecological characteristics, language and cultural variability, settlement patterns, economic opportunities and historical factors.[4] The HIV/AIDS study pattern in the country is modelled around the geo-political zones as well.

Nigeria, right from colonial times to the present, has practised a mixed public and private sector economy. Agriculture accounted for the high percentage of the gross domestic product (GDP) and employed most of the working population up to the middle 1970s; agriculture and industry now share 40 percent.[5]

Things however, changed drastically with the oil boom of the 1970s. The boom sparked considerable rural-urban migration, which led to the decline of agriculture, a situation that persists today. Today, the oil sector serves as the major source of the nation's economy. Nigeria in fact

---

[1] NASCP/FMOH, 11.

[2] FMOH/NACA, 1. The figure is now put at 126, 635, 626 according to July 2001 estimate. Cf. CIA, *The World Factbook-Nigeria,* 2001.

[3] Cf. CIA, *The World Factbook-Nigeria*, 2001. Cf. http://www.odci.gov/cia/publications/factbook.

[4] NASCP/FMOH, 12.

[5] Cf. CIA, *The World Factbook-Nigeria*, 2001.

is the sixth leading oil producing nation in the world. A recent report puts the country's oil reserve to about 26 billion barrels.[6]

3. Overview of the HIV/AIDS Situation in Nigeria

3.1 *History of HIV/AIDS in Nigeria*

Based on an examination conducted by a Japanese team, it was alleged that there were two cases of a positive HIV diagnosis in Nigeria as far back as 1966.[7] The general consensus, in Nigeria, however, is that unlike the East and Central African countries, where HIV/AIDS were first identified in the early eighties, the first case was identified and reported in Nigeria in 1986.[8] This first case was reportedly diagnosed in a foreigner, a Ghanaian prostitute, practising in the Ivory Coast.[9] Despite the fact that the virus carrier was a foreigner, the conclusion was that Nigeria has joined the ranks of countries with persons diagnosed as HIV positive. The country was nonetheless seen as having a low prevalence of HIV cases, and thus was not considered a high-risk country.[10]

3.2 *The Rapid Spread of HIV/AIDS in Nigeria*

At the beginning of the HIV/AIDS epidemic outburst in the Sub-Saharan Africa, the world focused its attention on countries like Uganda, Tanzania, Kenya, Zaire, Mali, and other parts of Central and East Africa. In the southern part of Africa, attention was focused on places like Botswana, Namibia, Swaziland and Zimbabwe, and lately, South Africa. These countries were said to hold the majority of the world's hard-hit HIV/AIDS cases, whereas West Africa in general was seen to be free from the epidemic.[11]

The general feeling at the beginning of the HIV/AIDS crisis was that Nigeria was seen to be one of the least affected countries. This is extraordinarily surprising to many, especially with her huge population.

---

6 CABLE NEWS NETWORK (CNN), «Nigeria's Oil Reserves Rise by 900 Million Barrels», (Lagos: XINHUA News Agency, May 21, 2000).

7 M. KAWAMUR – al., «HIV-2 in West Africa in 1966», 385.

8 O. RANSOME-KUTI, «The HIV/AIDS Epidemic in Nigeria», 20. Also NASCP/FMOH, 11; J.O. OKAFOR, «AIDS Campaign in Nigeria», 105.

9 O. RANSOME-KUTI, «The HIV/AIDS Epidemic in Nigeria», 20. Also NASCP/FMOH, 11; J.O. OKAFOR, «AIDS Campaign in Nigeria», 105.

10 C. HAG, «Data on AIDS in Africa», 17-19.

11 Cf. WHO – UNAIDS, *The AIDS Epidemic Update,* December 1998.

However, some have argued that the low level of HIV cases may be attributed to the expulsion from the country of about a million foreigners in 1983, when Nigeria also closed its borders.[12] In any case, Nigeria, the so-called «giant of Africa», has now come to a rude realisation of the fact that she is one of the epicentres of HIV/AIDS in Africa and in the world at large.

According to the released result of the November 1999 Sentinel report, it is estimated that currently 2.6 million adult Nigerians aged 15-49 years are HIV infected or carriers of the HIV virus.[13] With this figure, Nigeria then has 7.73 percent of the world's HIV cases (33.6 million) and 11.16 percent of Sub-Saharan Africa's HIV cases (23.3 million).[14]

This data in fact might not represent the true picture of HIV cases in the country. This is because the sentinel survey was conducted only among pregnant women, and as the report itself admits there are so many difficulties in interpreting the data from the sentinel survey. This is partly because the pregnant women tested are only those who attend public hospitals and clinics. Thus those who do not use these hospitals and clinics, for instance the wealthy and the very poor, are not included in the surveys.[15] In addition, commercial sex workers, long-distance haulage drivers and the hawkers at bus stops and lorry parks who constitute the «high-risk» group[16] in the country, are not included in the survey group. For instance Olikoye Ransome-Kuti notes:

> ...Between 1992 and 1996, the prevalence of HIV positive sera among commercial sex workers rose from 22.9% to 35.6%. Among sexually transmitted disease patients, it rose from 4.6% to 15.1%; among tuberculosis patients, it was 2.2% and 13.1% respectively and among women attending antenatal clinics, 1% in 1992, and 4.5% in 1996.[17]

Therefore, without discrediting those who worked tirelessly on the sentinel survey report, the data is not to be taken as an accurate reflection of HIV infection. In fact, WHO officials admit this with respect to the data upon which the Nigeria sentinel surveys is modelled. Data, as

---

[12] Cf. J.M. AMAT-ROSE – al., «La géographie de l'infection», 137-140.
[13] NASCP/FMOH, 10; also FMOH/NACA, I.
[14] Cf. WHO – UNAIDS, *Statistical Report* (1999).
[15] NASCP/FMOH, 17.
[16] I.O. ORUBULOYE, «Patterns of Sexual Behavior», 236.
[17] O. RANSOME-KUTI, «The HIV/AIDS Epidemic in Nigeria», 20.

deceased colleague Jonathan Mann opined «provide a broad yet extremely limited indication of the evolution of the pandemic».[18]

Therefore, these figures could be higher or slightly lower than what is given. In most cases, though, the tendency is to work towards a higher projection. This situation is not limited to Nigeria alone. It is a fact recognised in the developed countries as well.[19]

The conclusion that could be drawn from the sentinel report is simple, that is, with 2.6 million adult Nigerians living with the virus, one could see a steady and exponential increase in the number of infected. From the 0% of 1981-1985 to 1.8% in 1992 to 3.8% in 1994, to 4.5% in 1996, and to 5.4% in 1999.[20] For an accurate picture of this exponential increase, see the prevalence increase tables (Fig.1). Suffice to say that this exponential increase is alarming as a noticeable 3.6 increase occurred between 1992 to 1999.[21]

PREVALENCE INCREASE: 1992-1999

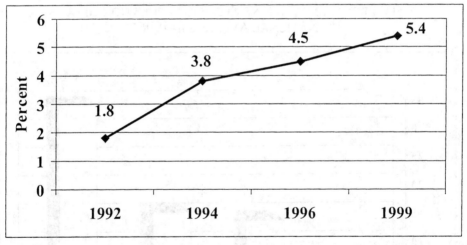

Fig. 1 – Source: Federal Ministry of Health. 1999

The implication of this is frightening as the erstwhile low seroprevalence country has now come to a rude realisation of an imminent, and if

---

[18] J. MANN – D. TARANTOLA, *AIDS in the World II*, 15.

[19] J. MANN – D. TARANTOLA, *AIDS in the World II*, 15. Also B. SCHOUB, *AIDS and HIV in Perspective*, 236-237.

[20] NASCP/FMOH, 10.

[21] FMOH/NACA, 3.

necessary actions are not taken, will become one of the epicentres of HIV/AIDS in Africa and in the world at large. Based on the present statistics, it is believed that Nigeria is now second of the worst hit countries in Africa behind South Africa. It is estimated that 4.2 million people are infected in South Africa, which are nearly 10% of its population.[22] This means that South Africa and Nigeria have surpassed epicentre countries (like Malawi, Zimbabwe) of HIV/AIDS in Africa.

It is essential to note that the huge population of Nigeria might make it difficult to unmask the real threat this epidemic poses for the country. If urgent steps are not taken to curtail the further spread, the country stands the risk of an AIDS explosion. The prevalence of HIV among specific population groups, according to the Federal Ministry of Health, shows that in 1996 alone, antenatal patients accounted for 4.5%, tuberculosis patients for 13.6%, sexually transmitted diseases patients 15.1% and commercial sex workers, a high prevalence of 34.2%.[23] (Fig.2)

HIV PREVALENCE AMONG SPECIFIC POPULATION GROUPS
(NATIONAL AVERAGE IN 1996)

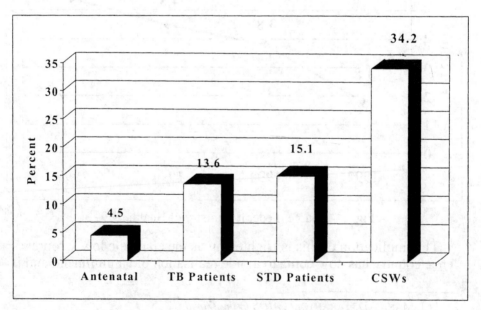

Fig. 2 – Source: Federal Ministry of Health. 1999

[22] EDITORIAL, «10% have HIV in South Africa».
[23] FMOH/NACA, 2.

Meanwhile, using the EPIMODEL, it is estimated that HIV will infect about 4.9 million adults in Nigeria by the year 2003,[24] whereas about 29.000 people are reported to have died of AIDS in the country since 1986, when the first case was identified.[25] (Fig. 3)

CUMULATIVE REPORTED AIDS CASES: 1990-1997

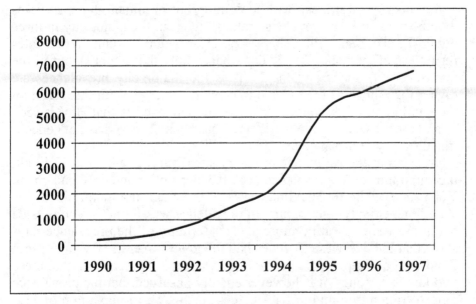

Fig. 3 – Source: Federal Ministry of Health. 1999

3.3 Estimated Summary of HIV Prevalence Per Zone

As mentioned earlier, the country is divided into six geo-political zones. The HIV prevalence study in the country is modelled on this zonal arrangement as well. The summary of each zone as reported by NASCP/FMOH can be seen on the appendix 1-6.

From the above summary, the first thing to note is that all the thirty-six states and the FCT has HIV positive persons. This means that there is no state or zone that is spared the epidemic. In addition, HIV in Ni-

---

[24] NASCP/FMOH, 41.

[25] The number above might be considered as modest based on the fact that not all cases are reported and in some cases, the true cause of death is not stated, as there is sometimes outright unwillingness to report AIDS death as a result of fear of stigmatization.

geria is predicated proportionally, that is, on urban to rural diffusion and rural to urban diffusion with slight variations.[26] The system used is that of Major City (MC) and outside major city (OMC). The capital or headquarters of each state serves as the major city, which is the urban area, while the outside major city sites (though not strictly rural in the real sense of the word) serve as the rural areas. The differences, if any, with the strict rural areas will be nothing but minimal. One also notes that the median HIV prevalence rate is higher in the major city in three out of the six zones. Thus, there is no clear pattern. Again, in the states regardless of the zone, it is evident that in only thirteen (13), out of the thirty-six (36) states and the FCT, is the major city prevalence rate higher than those of the outside major city-states.[27] With this situation then, unlike in other countries, where the tendency is that HIV is seen as an urban disease,[28] in Nigeria, HIV has been observed as not concentrated strictly in urban areas.

Also, from the estimated summary sites' survey, which is 73 in all, the minimum HIV prevalence was 0.5 percent found in Gendam, in Yobe state, while the maximum was 21.0 percent in Otukpo, in Benue state. Interestingly, the maximum prevalence was found in «an outside major city» site.[29] Furthermore, a clear scrutiny of the prevalence rates show that the two western zones had the lowest overall HIV rates, with Southwest at 3.5 percent and the Northwest at 3.2 percent. Within these two low HIV zones, it is however equally observed that the prevalence ranged from a minimum of 1.7 percent in Jigawa to maximum of 11.6 percent in Kaduna State.[30] The North central zone is reported to have the highest overall HIV prevalence rate at 7 percent. Within the zone, Benue state recorded the highest prevalence rate for the country, with the rate of 16.8 percent, which is three times more that of the national median, which is 5.4 percent.[31] Nasarawa State is another state contributing to the high zone rate with 10.8 percent. However, within the same zone, Kwara State has a rate of 3.2 percent, which is below the national median rate.[32]

---

[26] NASCP/FMOH, 42.
[27] NASCP/FMOH, 30-31.
[28] Cf. N. MILLER – R.C. ROCKWELL, ed., *AIDS in Africa*, xxv.
[29] NASCP/FMOH, 23.
[30] NASCP/FMOH, 30.
[31] NASCP/FMOH, 30.
[32] NASCP/FMOH, 30.

The deduction that can be made from the above is that some areas could be seen or considered as «hot zones» especially those areas where there is a high prevalence rate (Fig.4). Could this be because of differences in behaviour? The reason is unclear, but it is possible that many of those infected are those who were infected while outside these states but were constrained to return to their states as a result of being sick HIV positive. It will be interesting to find out the causes for the high prevalence rate in these areas.

HIV PREVALENCE BY STATE, 1999

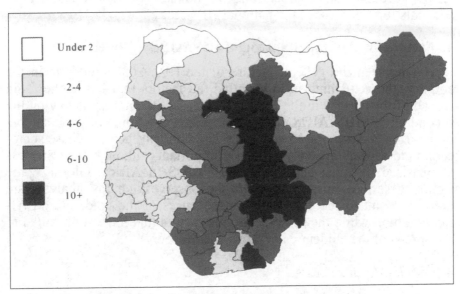

Fig. 4 – Source: Federal Ministry of Health. 1999

Another interesting feature of the HIV situation in Nigeria is that the high HIV prevalence rate is found among the age group of 20-24 years in all the zones except two. The figure ranges from 4.2 percent in the Southwest zone to 9.7 percent in the North central zone,[33] the majority of whom are women. Thus, the high prevalence is found among the group in the years of greatest sexual activity, or the peak time of sexual awareness. This portends a great danger for the country as the youth group stands the risk of being on the verge of an AIDS explosion. The impact this will have on the nation will be examined later.

---

[33] NASCP/FMOH, 32, 42.

3.4 *Distribution of HIV Types in Nigeria*

According to the NASCP/FMOH report, Nigeria has a distribution of the HIV types, that is, HIV-I and HIV-2 types. While all these different types are present, it is however revealed that HIV-I type is the most predominant in all the states except in Sokoto and Kebbi, where almost all the infections detected were said to be due to mixed HIV-1 and HIV-2.[34] HIV-1, the most diffused in Nigeria, is also the most diffused in the world, and it is the deadliest of all HIV types. HIV-1 type in fact accounts for 89 percent of all HIV cases in the country, while HIV-2 accounts for 4 percent and the mixed type HIV-1 and HIV-2 accounts for 7 percent of the national HIV cases.[35]

4. **Factors for the Rapid Spread of HIV/AIDS in Nigeria**

Having seen the general picture of the HIV/AIDS epidemic in the country, the next thing is to examine the factors that led to the rapid spread of the disease in the country, which put the nation as having the second largest HIV/AIDS population in Africa.[36] Some of these factors range from socio-moral to economic and political factors. These socio-economic aspects are very crucially important, although they are less emphasised by most analysts of HIV/AIDS in Africa. Gloria Waite rightly describes this point when she observes, «many analysts are quick to point to the economic consequences of the epidemic on Africa's future, while the socio-economic factors that have contributed to the spread of the epidemic are rarely mentioned».[37]

4.1 *Socio-Moral Factors*

Although HIV/AIDS has and knows no social status, ethnic group, race and religion, yet some conditions predispose some people to become more vulnerable to infection than others. This point becomes important as shall be seen shortly.

4.1.1 General Denial

At the onset of the outbreak of the disease and the recognition of the problem in Africa, especially in the east and central Africa, Nigeria was

---

[34] NASCP/FMOH, 34.
[35] NASCP/FMOH, 34.
[36] EDITORIAL, «Nigeria to Make Pre-Marriage HIV check compulsory».
[37] G. WAITE, «The Politics of Disease», 151.

considered a low sero prevalence country. Despite this fact, many people warned the country about the danger of complacency. Rather than
preparing the ground and informing people of the disease, there was an
official denial among many intellectuals, government officials and the
general populace about the presence of HIV/AIDS in the country.[38]

It is reported, for instance that, despite the claim of some health
professionals of having diagnosed symptoms similar to AIDS disease,
the Federal Health Authorities consistently denied the claims.[39] Even
the then Minister of Health, Olikoye Ransome Kuti was reportedly said
to have seen these claims as a distraction to his efforts in providing a
primary health care (PHC) system for the country.[40] Given this allegation, it is therefore surprising to note how the same Ransome Kuti now
claimed that it was the death of his brother Fela, in 1997 of AIDS that
convinced Nigerians of the existence of the disease in the country.[41]
The motive for the denial remains unknown. Perhaps it could be due to
the hostile and unfounded remarks and reports found in the western
media stigmatizing Africans as carriers of HIV.[42]

There was also a general lack of admittance that the epidemic was
real and that it could be contracted by anyone even with just one casual
incidence of genital intercourse involving either heterosexual or homosexual persons, either through vaginal or anal entry. This denial has led
to a passive attitude among a majority of the populace. Some even
think it is a disease of the west.

Finally, another aspect of the denial, perhaps the most dangerous, is
the refusal to know and accept one's status as sero positive on the part
of those who know that there is every likelihood that they have been
exposed to the virus. The general and official denial, which led to a
delay in appropriate action being taken as was done in other countries
around the world, no doubt aids the exponential spread of the disease in
the country.[43]

4.1.2 Inadequate Health Care System

To better appreciate this section perhaps it is important to know
what it means to be healthy. The World Health Organisation (WHO) in

---

[38] FMOH/NACA, 1, 9.

[39] J.O. OKAFOR, «AIDS Campaign in Nigeria», 106.

[40] J.O. OKAFOR, «AIDS Campaign in Nigeria», 106.

[41] O. RANSOME-KUTI, «The HIV/AIDS Epidemic in Nigeria», 20.

[42] Cf. B.O. OSUNTOKUN, «Biomedical Ethics», 129.

[43] Cf. FMOH/NACA, 1.

1958 defined health as «a state of complete physical, mental and social well being and not merely the absence or disease of infirmity».[44] Although this definition has been subject to a lot of criticisms,[45] the fact remains that this definition has something positive as it points out that human health is not to be restricted to physical concerns.[46] In this definition, we can see that human health extends far beyond mere biological function. Callahan, too, acknowledges the positive contribution as he thinks that it is difficult to talk meaningfully of health solely in terms of «the absence of disease or infirmity». The definition recognised the connection between the good of the body and the good of the self and in the context not only of the individual self, but the social community of selves.[47] Thus to be healthy, the person must interact with his or her environment and maintain himself or herself in the environment.

Applying the above definition of health, it is clear then that the social, economic and political malfunctions in Nigerian society relate also to illness and disease. This is particularly important as regards the rapid spread of HIV/AIDS in the country. While the structures for achieving complete well – being must be functional, in Nigeria the health care structures and system are nothing to boast about. From the late eighties to date, most of the hospitals have been reduced to mere «consulting clinics». The provision of basic health measures like health education, a clean water supply, components of primary health care such as maternal and child care, provision of essential drugs, adequate treatment of common diseases, adequate nutrition, etc. are lacking in most of the public hospitals.

The inadequate health care system can be seen for instance in the area of blood transfusion. It is a well-known fact that the transfusion of infected blood or blood related products has contributed to the spread of HIV/AIDS. In Nigeria, most hospitals cannot boast of kits for screening blood, because of the high cost of processing blood for transfusion.[48] It would not be surprising that contaminated blood could have been transfused to innocent and unsuspecting people.[49]

---

[44] D. CALLAHAN, «The WHO Definition of Health», 253. Also B.M. ASHLEY – K.D. O'ROURKE, Health Care Ethics, 3.

[45] D. CALLAHAN, «The WHO Definition of Health», 253-259.

[46] B.M. ASHLEY – K.D. O'ROURKE, Health Care Ethics, 3, 36.

[47] D. CALLAHAN, «The WHO Definition of Health», 259-260.

[48] F. ADEKEYE, «Before They Die», 42.

[49] Cf. O. RANSOME-KUTI, «The HIV/AIDS Epidemic in Nigeria», 21; also FMOH/NACA, 14.

In addition, there is also the problem of the inadequacy or lack of health care personnel who could attend to the health of the citizens.[50] For instance, in the area of maternal health care, it is reported that every 10 minutes, somewhere in the country, a woman dies from pregnancy-related causes simply because of limited skilled attendants attending to only 31% of deliveries in the country.[51] Consequently, some crude methods of deliveries often result in maternal and prenatal mortality, morbidity, and probably infection with diseases like HIV/AIDS. This possibility is high given that the HIV prevalence in pregnant women ranges from 0.5% to 21.0% with a median prevalence of 5.4%.[52] So HIV positive women face a double tragedy because of a lack of access to good health care and therefore have high chances of infecting others.

However, tied to the problem of an inadequate health care system, is of course, the issue of the economy. For instance, B. O. Osuntokun[53] argued for the importance of the economy on health, especially the connection between poverty and health; the effect the debt servicing of the developing countries is having not just on the economy but on all sectors.[54] Osuntokun believes that the poor economy makes it difficult for active support or pursuit of health and health research that can enhance development. Consequently, there is no such thing as health policy, which is necessary for health management research, and control of ethical issues in health care and health related research.[55]

The above position is true of Nigeria as all other developing countries. As a matter of fact health, which is an integral aspect of human need, is in a state of jeopardy in the country, as the past successive rulers did nothing to foster and promote health. For instance, between 1992 and 1998 when the country experienced a dramatic increase in the infection rate with HIV/AIDS, it is not a coincidence that the general chaotic situation of the country at this period aided the rapid spread of

---

[50] FMOH/NACA, 11, 26.

[51] G. EGUNJOBI, «Save the Mothers», 1 of 4. Article found on *The Guardian Online* http:/www.nrg guardian news.com.

[52] NASCP/FMOH, 9.

[53] B.O. Osuntokun is an acclaimed Professor of Medicine (Neurology). He has been for years a professor of Medicine, University of Ibadan, Nigeria and also a visiting professor (Neurology) at the Department of Psychiatry, Indiana University School of Medicine, Indianapolis.

[54] B.O. OSUNTOKUN, «Biomedical Ethics», 106. See also S.O. ALUBO, «Debt Crisis», 639-648.

[55] B.O. OSUNTOKUN, «Biomedical Ethics», 106. See also S.O. ALUBO, «Debt Crisis», 639-648.

the epidemic. Besides, in a situation where there is suppressed political freedom, it is not difficult to understand why ensuring that the right of citizens to have access to good health care is a non-issue.

Finally, apart from the inadequate health care system, there is also another important issue of affordability of the cost of health care services. Even where there is access to limited health care services, many could not afford the cost. Given all this, the conclusion is that the health care system in Nigeria is inadequate or fragile. Urgent steps therefore need to be taken to revamp the whole health care system.

4.1.3 Stigmatisation

Stigmatisation has contributed to the spread of the epidemic in the country as elsewhere in the world. Stigmatisation is based on prejudice in which case anyone known to be a carrier of the virus is condemned in many ways. The issue seems to be tied to sexuality rather that the disease itself. When a person is identified as HIV positive, questions are automatically raised about the sexual behavior of the person, as many who do not have the disease tend to blame, and even in some cases, condemn the behaviors of those that do. Why is it that HIV/AIDS is not regarded like any other killer diseases like heart problem, diabetes, cancer, etc., which do not carry any stigma? The is because in most cases, these diseases like diabetes, etc. are sometimes hereditary and are not acquired by the patients through direct action on their part – like HIV/AIDS.[56]

Stigmatisation is also tied to irrational fears and to a misconception and misconstruction of facts. Stigmatisation and the fear it engenders both fuel and spread the disease.[57] The danger here is very high as it makes a lot of people, especially those who are probably at risk unwilling to know about their HIV status. In addition, those who know that they are HIV positive are sometimes also reluctant to disclose this information. In this way they expose others to infection especially when they engage in activities that could endanger others, like having unprotected sexual intercourse.

Stigmatisation can and does occur in so many ways and forms. Although, there has not been reported cases of the extreme form of stig-

---

[56] We must not forget to note that some HIV patients acquired the virus not as a result of their direct action like the hemophiliacs, children through vertical transmission, etc.

[57] Cf. FMOH/NACA, 11.

matisation in the country, like the case of the South African woman, Gugu Dlamini, who was beaten to death in her village because she admitted she had AIDS.[58] Some other forms of stigmatisation, however, have been reported, for example, dismissal from work, and abandonment by relatives, friends and colleagues.[59]

A final point to note is that stigmatisation has to do more or less with cultural construction. Often, one notices that certain illnesses are tied to witchcraft; HIV/AIDS has not been an exception. This position is of course unfounded. Therefore, people who are HIV positive must be able to admit their positive status and see it like other life-threatening illnesses, seek treatment and live positively with such a human condition.

4.1.4 Growing Urbanisation

Urbanisation and the population movements that ensued have been seen as a contributing factor to the spread of HIV/AIDS in Nigeria.[60] In Nigeria, before the mid-seventies, agriculture was the predominant source of economy of the country. In fact, the country was as a rich exporter of cocoa, groundnuts, palm produce, timber, cotton, rubber, hides and skin, coal and tin. British colonialism also benefited from its gold. However, with the discovery of oil in large quantities, the economic focus changed dramatically.

While there is no doubt that movement had been ongoing for a long time, the oil boom brought an even larger mass exodus of people in search of greener pastures. This was also due to the construction of road networking linking the diverse parts of the country to one another. The mass movement was witnessed mainly among the males, some married, who, left their wives in the rural areas and had to travel back and forth. The result of this is that some tend to have relationships with other women in their new places of work, while others seek solace among commercial sex workers as an «outlet» for their sexual drives and desires.[61] Some form relationships with other women in their present work environment only to go back to the rural areas to infect the

---

58 Cf. J. CHRISTENSEN, «AIDS in Africa». Cf. http://cnn.com/SPECIALS/2000/aids/stories/overview.

59 O. RANSOME-KUTI, «The HIV/AIDS Epidemic in Nigeria», 21.

60 B.D. HARDY, «Cultural Practices», 1109-1119; M. EGBOH, «A Pathfinder to AIDS Cure».

61 M. EGBOH, «A Pathfinder to AIDS Cure».

wives left behind.[62] Although the sentinel report projects a balanced distribution of HIV/AIDS among the urban and rural areas, a lot of people still believe that large number of infections is located in the urban areas.[63] The percentage reported has to be considered in connection with the overall population of each state and zone. Besides, those already too sick as a result of the disease are normally taken back to their rural homes hence the rural areas become a receptacle for the spill over of urban problems.

In addition, not all those who migrated are able to find jobs. This is especially true in the case of women, who take to prostitution in order to survive. It is much more lucrative in the cities and urban areas, and with the crowded population, it becomes easier for the disease to spread vastly and easily.

4.1.5 Long Distance Truck Driving

Nigeria's land mass stands at about 913,073 sq. kilometres (356.666 sq. miles), four and a half times the size of Great Britain and Northern Ireland put together, thus movement is a thing of necessity. Thanks to the oil boom, however, the country was able to construct roads linking the different parts of the country to one another. For this reason long distance driving has been possible. Long distance haulage driving is a way of life in Nigeria, and it has become almost indispensable, as it is a major form of travel, linking the country's diverse regions to one another, not just in terms of people, but also in terms of goods and services.

This indispensable service has also been a major factor in the spread of HIV/AIDS in the country. In his studies, Orubuloye shows that there is a strong connection between the STD/HIV transmission and the Nigerian transport and commercial networks, especially with respect to truck and bus drivers.[64] According to him, because of the long distances these truck drivers have to make, they are inevitably forced to stop at some strategic locations for food and rest, both in the daytime and at night. At these stops, there are buildings and sometimes shacks, food and drinks, bars and clubs, with music and singing, and places to sleep. One also finds young girls and women who either work there or are there to sell their goods, mainly food items. In addition, the notice-

---

[62] See C. UWAKWE, «Socio-Cultural Factors», 40.
[63] M. EGBOH, «A Pathfinder to AIDS Cure», 1.
[64] I.O. ORUBULOYE, «Patterns of Sexual Behavior», 236.

able presence of some commercial sex workers is quite visible. Orubuloye, however, mentions that in most cases these girls are not only there to sell their goods, but they also provide company and sex to these drivers, who are mostly married but nonetheless are willing to make advances to these women.[65]

Long distance haulage driving, in Orubuloye's view, has contributed significantly to the spread of HIV/AIDS because in most cases, these long- distance truck drivers make up to three to four stops where they have at least one or more sexual partners. Thus in a lifetime, some of them have an average of sixteen partners.[66] The job, highly risky in itself, becomes even more dangerous by the practice of having multiple sexual partners along these routes because more often than not, they know little or nothing about the sexual history of their partners. Furthermore, in most cases, no method of protection is used. This explains the high incidence of venereal diseases among these drivers,[67] and by extension, one can safely infer too the possibility of HIV/AIDS infection.

4.1.6 Moral Relativism

The seemingly uncontrollable spread of HIV/AIDS is also due to the general lax moral attitudes in sexual behavior. While not making any moral judgement, moral relativism contributes to the spread of the epidemic. It is an undeniable fact that the low moral standard witnessed over the last few decades has had a significant impact on the spread of the disease. Different reasons have been attributed to this moral decline among which include, the taking over of schools from religious and private institutions by the government, and the lack of parental care and support in the area of sex and sexual matters.[68] There is also peer pressure which encourages young people to think that it is in the number of male or female partners they have gone to bed with that really shows how brave they are in sexual matters.

It is worth noting however that the above factors are not limited to Nigerian society,[69] hence it would be wrong to suggest that the people in this part of the world are more promiscuous that the rest of people elsewhere. There is no society that actively encourages promiscuity or

---

65 I.O. ORUBULOYE, «Patterns of Sexual Behavior», 239.
66 I.O. ORUBULOYE, «Patterns of Sexual Behavior», 239.
67 I.O. ORUBULOYE, «Patterns of Sexual Behavior», 239.
68 FMOH/NACA, 15.
69 Cf. G.D. COLEMAN, *Human Sexuality,* 271-272.

encourages its people to be immoral, yet promiscuity and immorality can be found in many societies.

a) *Pre-Marital Intercourse*

This is the practice of engaging in intimate genital intercourse before marriage. Some people have attempted to differentiate «premarital sex» from «preceremonial sex».[70] While the former refers to the state just described, the latter refers to the situation of those that are engaged without the marriage ceremony having been performed. Here it is believed that the two appear to be fully committed to each other and intend that commitment to be life – long. There are however those who disagree with such a distinction.[71] The fact also remains that such a commitment does not automatically lead to marriage.

A research carried out by *Girls Power Initiate* (GPI), a non-governmental organisation, in Cross River State of Nigeria shows that 150 out of every 1000 girls give birth before the age of nineteen.[72] This report, however, fails to mention whether these girls were married or not. One could safely assume that many are not married and that by the time they are ready for marriage, they probably would have had experiences of genital intercourse.

Regrettably, there are some conditions that indirectly encourage premarital sex. For example, poverty has forced some parents to send their girls to the street for sex in exchange for money. There is also the practice of hawking or street trading. These conditions will be examined separately later on.

Given the above the question may be asked, where is the virtue of chastity? Chastity is not a value taught only by the Christian religions. It is also found among some cultures in the country, for example, in the Yoruba traditional practice. The problem with the Yoruba perspective on chastity, however, is that while it stresses the importance of virginity among girls, it says little or nothing about their male counterparts. Today, however, no one is interested in the importance of such a value. In as much as the situation above is the true picture now, this is not to say that the older generations did not engage in premarital sex.[73] However,

---

[70] Cf. G.D. COLEMAN, *Human Sexuality*, 279.
[71] Cf. P.S. KEANE, *Sexual Morality*, 100-101.
[72] J. OKWE, «Research Reveals Rate of Birth». Article found on web at *Africa News Online*.
[73] Cf. B.D. HARDY, «Cultural Practices», 1112.

the problem now is that a new belief has been added, the belief that premarital sex is a sign of maturity.[74]

It is almost certain that once people begin to engage in premarital sex, they tend to continue the practice. The problem now arises, are they limited to the same partner? Is any precaution taken? With this in mind, the possibility of spreading STD/HIV/AIDS becomes high and probably explains why a high percentage of prevalence of HIV/AIDS is found among the 20-24 age groups,[75] which is about the peak of sexual awareness.

b) *Extra Marital Intercourse*

This is the case of a married person having genital intercourse with someone other than the person's spouse. The emphasis here is on those who are in concretely existing marriages, but engage in sexual intercourse with other persons apart from their spouses. This is different from a polygamous marriage. Thus a polygamous man cannot be accused of having extra marital intercourse. Neither can those who are remarried, even when they are not remarried in the church.[76]

Although no official survey that I know of has yet been done on this practice in the country, it is not difficult to see that such practice abounds in the country. This belief is reinforced by the attitude of our truck and long distances drivers,[77] the migrant workers, etc. This practice, unlike in the case of premarital sex, is less acceptable among the majority of the people yet, they still engage in it. When people engage in extra marital activity, the risk of contracting HIV/AIDS is high with the result that it spreads rapidly as these people go back to expose their innocent spouses to infections later. The problem can become worse if the male partner goes with commercial sex workers for instance.

c) *Multiple Sexual Partners*

According to Uwakwe, a survey of more that 5, 500 males and females aged 12-24 shows that there appear to be «sporadic and unstable» sexual intercourse in which many of these young people of both

---

[74] Cf. G.D. COLEMAN, *Human Sexuality*, 276.

[75] Cf. NASCP/FMOH, p. 32.

[76] Cf. P.S. KEANE, *Sexual Morality*, 104.

[77] I.O. ORUBULOYE, «Patterns of Sexual Behavior», 237; also M. EGBOH, «A Pathfinder to AIDS Cure», 3.

sexes have had more than one sexual partner.[78] This factor of multiple sex partners thus constitutes a high risk for STD/HIV/AIDS infection.[79]

4.2 *Economic Factors*

Some commentators[80] on the HIV/AIDS epidemic have come to agreement about the role of the economy in the spread of HIV/AIDS in general, and the effect this has on the developing countries in particular. The disease seems to be concentrated among people that are already marginalised socially and economically.[81] In a recent statement, Maria Minna, the Canadian Internal Development Minister, during a conference on AIDS in Toronto said, «(AIDS) is a huge economic issue, not just health issue».[82] How does this fact affect the situation of HIV/AIDS in Nigeria?

The Nigerian economy has deteriorated over the past two and half decades with negative and small annual economic growth, huge international debts,[83] with the attendant crippling repayment rate of international debts. The sudden downward economic turn is not just baffling but also embarrassing. The reason is that just about three decades ago, Nigeria had a vibrant and promising economy that even prompted the then Nigerian leader General Yakubu Gowon to make the famous declaration, «it is not the money», but «it is how to spend it» that is Nigeria's problem.

At the moment, less than thirty years later, the economy is in shambles. This has affected every fabric of the society as reflected in the low proportion of gross domestic product (GDP) allocated to health care services, for instance. However, till the recent past, the country had spent a high percentage on weapons and armed forces. Having made these preliminary remarks, we now turn to examine how the economic factor has contributed to the spread of HIV/AIDS in the country.

---

[78] C. UWAKWE, «Socio-Cultural Factors», 40.

[79] C. UWAKWE, «Socio-Cultural Factors», 40-43; also C. CAMERON – *al.*, «Female to Male Transmission», 403-407.

[80] Cf. B.O. OSUNTOKUN, «Biomedical Ethics», 106; S.O. ALUBO, «Debt Crisis», 640; N. MILLER – R.C. ROCKWELL, ed., *AIDS in Africa*, 150-151.

[81] NATIONAL ACADEMY OF SCIENCE, *The Social Impact of AIDS*.

[82] Reuters, «Canada to spend c. $120 Million on Global AIDS Fight», Ottawa, June 1, 2000.

[83] The Country's international debt as at of 1999 was put at $32 billion. Cf. *World Factbook OPEC*, 1999.

4.2.1 Poverty

The most glaring effect of the present economic hardship in Nigeria is that many people have been reduced to the poverty level. The widespread poverty is such that it is not just affecting only the peasants, but also those who were previously regarded as middle class. The Nigerian society is divided between the superbly rich and the poor, with an almost non-existent middle class. There is a wide disparity between rich and poor people. Because of this disparity, we see a gross inequality in the distribution of resources. The majority of people lack accesses to the most basic necessities of life – good nutrition, a clean water supply, housing, and education and health care services. Some of the effects of the hardship are that many cannot afford to pay their medical bills. Thus they do not even go to the hospitals. Some even send their children, especially young girls, to the streets, lorry parks, bars and hotels to do anything to earn money.[84]

The fact that many Nigerians have been impoverished is not news. What is interesting is that the situation reached an all time high between 1993 and 1998, under the late General Sani Abacha. It was during this period that the country also lost her international image. And also, during this period, Nigeria experienced a sharp increase in the number of HIV infection. This and other similar experiences have led many to believe that poverty plays a big role in the HIV/AIDS infection cases.[85]

An excellent article depicting this point appeared in the *Guardian*, a leading daily newspaper in the country, stating, «AIDS, harbinger of poverty in Nigeria».[86] It is with this in mind that one appreciates the view of Gloria Waite that «it is no coincidence that HIV/AIDS and poverty are found together».[87] This, however, is not to suggest that the rich are spared from HIV infection. There are a large number of rich people like the late Fela Anikulapo Kuti,[88] and the American basketball megastar, Ervin «Magic» Johnson, who have been infected with the

---

[84] Cf. I.O. ORUBULOYE, «Patterns of Sexual Behavior», 239; also C. UWAKWE, «Socio-Cultural Factors», 40.

[85] C. UWAKWE, «Socio-Cultural Factors», 40-43; FMOH/NACA, 15.

[86] L. SHOKUNBI, «AIDS, harbinger of Poverty», 15.

[87] G. WAITE, «The Politics of Disease», 150-151.

[88] Fela Anikulapo Kuti was a popular musician, the creator of Afrobeat, which is a fusion of highlife, soul and jazz. Through his music, he fought against political repression and injustice, founded his own community called, the Kalakuta Republic. He was notorious for having many wives and died of AIDS in 1997.

virus causing AIDS. These people have access to good medical care and can also afford the combination antiretroviral therapy.[89] The poor, however, cannot afford such treatment.[90]

This is another area in which poverty has contributed to the rapid spread of the disease in the Country namely, the cost of the treatment for those already infected. The combination antiretroviral chemotherapy is said to cost an average of $10. 000 (ten thousand dollars), to $15. 000 (fifteen thousand dollars), per year per patient.[91] With the exchange rate put at a modest N100 (one hundred naira) to the US dollar, means, the sum of N1m (one million naira) to N1.5m (one million, five hundred thousand naira) per year, per patient. Considering the fact that the minimum wage is N5, 500 (five thousand, five hundred naira),[92] means that the per capita income is N66, 000 (sixty-six thousand naira), which is equivalent to $660,00 (six hundred and sixty dollars) per annum. It is clear then that with this sum, an HIV positive person cannot afford the drugs necessary as he or she has other needs like food and housing to consider. What this means then is that there is no hope for HIV positive persons in the country. In addition, not everyone receives this minimum wage, as many receive even less.

The point, therefore, is that poverty plays a significant role in the spread of HIV/AIDS in the country. One fact that needs to be emphasized, however, is that poverty gives rise to powerlessness. Poverty and powerlessness create circumstances in people's lives that predispose them to the highest indices of social dysfunction, the highest indices of morbidity and mortality, the lowest access to primary care, and to little or no access to primary preventive programs.

4.2.2 Unemployment and Hawking

Again, economy is the key word here. The poor economic situation of the country has led to the loss of jobs especially in the unskilled labour sector as many companies and industries were forced to lay off their workers. Therefore, there are a vast and growing number of un-

---

[89] Cf. UNAIDS/WHO, *Report on the Global HIV/AIDS.*

[90] FMOH/NACA, 18.

[91] R. BAYER – J. STRYKER, «Ethical Challenges», 723.

[92] It is worth noting that the minimum wage was just increased by the present Obasanjo's administration as a Labor Day relief package for workers in May 1, 2000. It is important to note that this minimum wage does not cover everyone, like women who work as cheap labor.

employed people in the country.[93] Some of these unemployed people unfortunately happen to be graduates, with at least a first degree or more, who have had to struggle to pay for their education through the university, with the hope of getting good jobs, only to come out and be roaming about in the labor market.

Tied to the problem of unemployment is the growing phenomenon of hawking, which has become a major feature in most Nigerian cities. Hawking is the practice of selling goods, mostly items such as clothing, leather products, etc. This practice is common in the lorry parks, bus stops, on the major highways, in traffic jams and traffic lights, especially in the cities. These hawkers are mainly young girls, though not limited to them alone, the majority of whom have an average education or at least a primary school education.[94] A large number of others are dropouts from school, due to poverty and other reasons. These hawkers contribute to the spread of HIV/AIDS because these girls sell not only their goods, but «sell their bodies» as well in order to supplement for the little amount they earn from hawking.[95] In the hawking business, we also find married women, divorcees and widows. The study of Orubuloye is an eye opener as he says some of these people have «an average number of 2.3 sexual partners and 3.8 as life time partners».[96] Therefore, this case of short-term economic necessity, which is a stronger imperative, has now proved to be dangerous for long-term health and survival.

4.2.3 Prostitution

Prostitution, or to use the more accepted terminology, commercial sex work, is one of the world's oldest business and profession. Prostitution plays a key role in fuelling the HIV/AIDS epidemic in Nigeria in particular and Africa in general,[97] as these commercial sex workers have a high rate of changes in sexual partners.

Prostitution in Nigeria and other parts of Africa is practised not just for the fun of it or as preferred business rather, it is tied to an economic condition, that is, poverty. However it is worth noting that among the

---

[93] The 1992 estimates put the unemployment rate at 28 percent. Cf. CIA, *The World Factbook*, 2001.

[94] CIA, *The World Factbook*, 241.

[95] FMOH/NACA, 15.

[96] I.O. ORUBULOYE, «Patterns of Sexual Behavior», 242.

[97] Cf. W. HAYGOOD, «Prostitution», A 25.

sex workers there is a kind of distinction, as some are more sophisticated than others. For instance, we have the indigent female tertiary students, who practise part time commercial sex to make ends meet. These «attend to the needs» of some of the top government functionaries, business executives, etc.[98] The less sophisticated groups on the other hand just need money to cater for their immediate needs and that of their families. These do not have bargaining power like their sophisticated counterparts. One finds mainly deserted or divorced wives and mothers in this category, and of course the illiterate girls who come from the rural areas to practise in the cities.

Looking at these two groups, the first group, comprising the sophisticated commercial workers is more problematic in the spread of the virus as they are mainly migrants. These girls leave their schools and travel to other cities where they are not likely to be recognised. The fact, however, is that most of these girls have their regular boyfriends back on campus. More importantly, many are said to actually engage in unprotected sex as some are said not to believe in HIV/AIDS.[99]

The commercial sex workers are found mainly in major towns and cities of Nigeria. This is because these cities and towns have large, medium and small hotels, bars and nightclubs, where young women offer genital sex for money. The hotels also provide an excellent atmosphere for men, especially the rich and well to do of the societies, who bring in their «girl friends» for a short or long stay. The less sophisticated sex workers also use the environment to solicit for customers, but prefer to move to areas where they are not likely to be known for their profession.

There is, however, another dimension of prostitution that portends a great risk for the country in the spread of HIV/AIDS. This is the trafficking of Nigerian girls for prostitution in Europe and other overseas destinations. It has now been recognised that there exist prostitution rings,[100] «Mafia like» organisations where the traffickers procure these young women on the pretext of assisting them with jobs or even studies abroad. Once they have arrived at their destinations, these girls are constrained to work as prostitutes or worse still, as sex slaves do. Many of these girls can be seen everywhere in Italy, where they have established

---

[98] Cf. M. EGBOH, «A Pathfinder to AIDS Cure», 1.

[99] M. EGBOH, «A Pathfinder to AIDS Cure», 2.

[100] Cf. EDITORIAL, «Nigerian Authorities Worry». Also I. MODIBBO, «Vice-President Wife».

a strong base. It has even become something of a joke in some places that if one wants a Nigerian prostitute one should come to Italy! Bisi Olateru Olagbegi of the *Women Consortium of Nigeria*, a non-governmental organisation gave this point some credence when she said that, «between January and December 1999, more than 1,000 (one thousand) Nigerian girls were deported from Italy alone for prostitution and lack of travel papers».[101]

Apart from the high risk of contracting HIV/AIDS, which is a danger in itself, there are other risks involved as well. There have been reported incidences in which their «bosses» subjected these girls to inhuman conditions. Some were made to undergo some voodoo rituals, to swear oaths that they would never rebel nor reveal the identity of these traffickers. In addition, their travel document is seized until they are able to pay the stipulated amounts determined by the traffickers so that they could become free. Thus, these girls were not only prostitutes, they were normally held in bondage as well, with the risk of death should they refuse to compromise.

The dramatic condition and reality these girls face was brought to a new dimension recently, when during a general audience of Pope John

Paul II, a one time Nigerian prostitute, now sick with AIDS, had a brief yet dramatic face-to-face encounter with the Supreme Pontiff. This woman made a passionate appeal to the Pope to help intervene and liberate these girls from the bondage in which they found themselves.

It can however be argued that it is also true that some of these girls knew beforehand what they were coming to do. Due to poverty, some of them believe that the best way to make fast money is by getting a chance to come out of the country for prostitution abroad.

Meanwhile, different rates are charged for their services depending on the status of both the sex workers and the clients. Rates also depend on the season, as there are peak and low seasons. Higher fees are normally charged on weekends and festive periods.

Finally, it should be noted that prostitution in Africa is encouraged by the Westerners, a practice that dates back to the era of colonialism, and to the slave trade, etc. The clients of these Nigerian girls abroad are not Nigerians, but the indigenous people of the countries where they operate.

---

[101] EDITORIAL, «Nigerian Authorities Worry». Also I. Modibbo, «Vice-President Wife».

4.3 *Political Factor*

Just as socio-moral and economic factors have played a significant part in the spread of HIV/AIDS in the country, so also has the political. The political factor ranges from a lack of political will and commitment, to the influence of the military dictatorship, corruption, conflict and violence.

4.3.1 Lack of Political Will

Lack of Political will and commitment by our leaders can be seen right from the time the first cases were noticed. As mentioned earlier, there was reluctance by the government officials to admit the presence of HIV/AIDS in the country. Thus, the general populace were not prepared and informed on how to avoid the possible onslaught of the epidemic that had already taken roots then in other parts of the world.[102]

Once it was admitted in 1986, however, the government saw the threat of the epidemic as unworthy of serious attention. Different bodies were set up, for example, the *National Expert Advisory Committee on AIDS* (NAECA) in 1987, which was then succeeded by the *National AIDS Committee*, chaired by Olikoye Ransome-Kuti, the then Health Minister.[103] Despite the above, it was not until August 23, 1991 that the official campaign against HIV/AIDS was launched by the Federal Government. The question then is why the inaction between 1986 to the middle of 1991? A passive attitude permeated everywhere. It is therefore surprising to hear Olikoye Ransome-Kuti, the then Health Minister, who recently justified the commitment of the government in which he served.[104]

In addition, HIV/AIDS was seen just as a health issue. Thus there was no «multi-sectoral approach».[105] The seriousness to combat the disease was not well channelled. On the other hand, a multi-sectoral effort would have meant that the different ministries, apart from the ministry of health, would be active in the campaign against HIV/AIDS. It would also have involved an integral and enhanced co-ordinating effort between different government sectors at all levels, including the NGOs and even the academic community. Even when directives were given that HIV/AIDS education be incorporated into the curricula of all

---

[102] See J.O. OKAFOR, «AIDS Campaign in Nigeria», 107.
[103] Cf. T. ELOIKE, «AIDS Control in Nigeria».
[104] Cf. O. RANSOME-KUTI, «The HIV/AIDS Epidemic in Nigeria», 20.
[105] FMOH/NACA, 42.

schools,[106] the matter remained only at the level of direction, as nothing concrete was done to integrate HIV/AIDS education into the school curricula at any level.

It is based on the above that one sees the lack of political will and commitment. This lack of political will and commitment was in fact noted and stressed by the WHO, through its Global Program on AIDS. This world body warned Nigeria of her inaction and in fact emphasized that HIV was spreading quickly in the country.[107] This was during the regime of Ibrahim Babangida. In fairness to him though, he showed concern as reflected in his speech during the launching of «War Against AIDS (WAA)», where he noted that the disease is an issue of national emergency. He said that he was «under no illusion about the challenge facing the nation nor the burden of responsibility on leaders at every level to make effort now to stop the virus before further damage is done».[108] Nonetheless, one would have expected these words to be matched with actions. Thus, his commitment was inadequate and not sufficiently pursued.

If Babangida at least showed some concern, though insufficient, the Abacha regime showed no interest at all. It is not surprising therefore that there was a high rate of infection during his regime between 1993 and 1998.[109] Abacha was more interested in the consolidation of his despotic rule. He himself lacked the moral power and vision to lead by example. He was more interested in perpetuating himself as life president, and thus no serious attempt was made to look at the pressing need of the HIV/AIDS problem in the country.

Given the above, it is evident that political will and commitment is important and necessary in the fight against the spread of HIV/AIDS. This commitment, as Olikoye Ransome- Kuti rightly observed, must of course start from the leaders.[110]

4.3.2 Military Dictatorship

Since Nigeria's independence from the British in October 1, 1960, the military have dominated the nation's political life, thereby making it the longest serving regime in the country. The military ruled from1966 till 1979, then, from December 31 1983 till April 30 1999.

---

106 Cf. J.O. OKAFOR, «AIDS Campaign in Nigeria», 113.
107 Cf. W. OLADEPO, «AIDS Body Indicts Nigeria», 25.
108 Cf. O. RANSOME-KUTI, «The HIV/AIDS Epidemic in Nigeria», 20.
109 Cf. NASCP/FMOH, 10.
110 O. RANSOME-KUTI, «The HIV/AIDS Epidemic in Nigeria», 20.

Militarism is the governance of a nation by the military personnel. It is by its very nature authoritarian, since it is not based on the consent of the people. With authoritarianism comes exploitation and degradation by the rich minority, especially against the poor and defenceless, who are mostly in the majority. Militarism creates instability and underdevelopment

The effect of military dictatorship with respect to the spread of HIV/AIDS in the country is treated separately because it is the military rulers who caused a lot of havoc in the country. Some of the havoc done we have noted under the social and economic factors responsible for the spread of HIV/AIDS. The observations made under the section of political will and commitments are valid here as well. Some examples of the negative effects of the military dictatorship will suffice. For instance, Ibrahim Babangida, while launching the War Against AIDS (WAA), remarked:

...The implications are that unless urgent measures are taken, the havoc done by this deadly pandemic will obliterate the gains made over the years in the field of maternal and child health services. Similarly, the tremendous benefits of our primary health care system will be severely eroded, if not completely nullified.

Should we fail to check the spread of HIV/AIDS, the gains resulting from the collective sacrifice of the people of this great nation for the establishment of a sound economic base for future generations will be in vain.[111]

Despite this seemingly encouraging rhetoric, it is not a secret that the primary health care of the country started to deteriorate under the same Babangida. Many of the nation's finest doctors and nurses began a mass exodus from the country to Saudi Arabia and other parts of the world, in search of greener pastures. This reflected the lack of job satisfaction caused by measures and policies initiated by Babangida's administration. The health care system started to dwindle as a result of the «brain drain syndrome» and many of the hospitals that were in the past functional and reputable for good care became mere «consulting clinics», due to a lack of drugs and no incentives for research, etc.

In addition, Babangida spoke of a sound economic base, yet the economy of the nation collapsed under his regime. The collapse of the economy was as a result of the infamous Structural Adjustment Pro-

---

[111] I. BABAGINDA, «AIDS Patients Need Care», 10. Also cited by O. RANSOME-KUTI, «The HIV/AIDS Epidemic in Nigeria», 20.

gramme (SAP), which was widely condemned by the populace and which even led to loss of lives during the ensuing national strike and protest. Again, the Babangida regime spent a huge amount of money on unending and eventually futile transitions» programmes, whereas, on the other hand, meagre amounts were spent on health in general, and, an even lesser amount on the fight against HIV/AIDS.

With Abacha, however, the already bad situation was aggravated and became worse. His regime was marked by anarchy and terror, as witnessed by the number of mysterious deaths recorded in the history of the nation through Government sponsored and funded assassinations and arsons. There was a general lack of political stability. Tyranny and oppression were everywhere in the country.

The press, which could have played an active role in the information and in the enlightenment campaign against the menace of HIV/AIDS, was constantly harassed, under attack and surveillance. Some journalists disappeared mysteriously while a large number were imprisoned or forced to quit their jobs.

Based on these facts and other reasons, we can then better appreciate why and how the military dictatorship contributed to the spread of HIV/AIDS in the country. As a result of the general oppression and authoritarianism, many people sought refuge in sexual pleasure as an escape from the reality of the country. The result is the alarming number of those living with the deadly virus.

It is therefore a well-established fact that authoritarianism only represses development and is a means of maintaining the status quo – the rule of minority over the impoverished majority. The incursion of the military into the political life of the country created instability that in turn aided in a significant manner to the spread of HIV/AIDS.

4.3.3 Corruption

Corruption has long been the bane of the country. It has become an embarrassing phenomenon that has come to be associated with the country, so that as Peter Enahoro says, «to some, a report on Nigeria that excludes at least passing mention of corruption would be disdained as reactionary and incomplete».[112] Corrupt practices are found almost everywhere from the leaders to the young school children. The effects have been great and are reflected in the crumbling infrastructures in all sectors, especially in the health sector, and the fact that the majority of

---

[112] P. ENAHORO, «The Ugly Nigerian».

the population remains mired in abject poverty. Corruption is not limited to the leaders alone, but if the leaders were to show a good example, it might be possible to eradicate this phenomenon. Unfortunately, the whole problem lies with the leaders both past and, sadly enough, even the present leaders.[113]

A recent report by the American Jack Blum, made to the United States Congress, showed that «from independence to the present time, past leaders in Nigeria have either stolen or misappropriated state funds estimated at N400 billion ($40 billion)».[114] This huge amount was said to involve funds received on behalf of the country by key government officials in the form of international assistance, loans from international financial institutions, kick backs to government officials and special arrangements for currency conversion. This figure is not only embarrassing but it is also destabilising, considering the poverty that abounds in the country.

Ironically, corruption was the excuse given by the military juntas for re-entering into Nigeria's political arena in December 31, 1983 when the civilian administration of Shehu Shagari was ousted from power. However, the military juntas did not fare better. For instance, from the late Sani Abacha's family, a whopping sum of $900 million has been reportedly recovered.[115]

In addition, Ibrahim Babangida has been linked to various corrupt malpractices. According to the recent news, Babangida is said to have misappropriated about $3.4 billion meant to fund the Nigeria Liquified Natural Gas Project (1993). This money could not be accounted for by the then President. The same is said of the 12. 4 billion-oil windfall during the nine-month (1990-91) Gulf War between Iraq and Kuwait, with the allied nations.[116] Also unaccounted for is $1.4 billion from Ajaokuta Steel Plant, $765.45 million for an aluminium smelter plant, and the annual $50 million, which went into the Babangida's family coffers through the diversion of 100.000 bpd of the country's petroleum to the former president's personal marketing company.[117] Meanwhile, an earlier $6 billion debt buy-back scam had been attributed to the former president through a finding made by the British born Nigerian soc-

---

[113] Cf. EDITORIAL, «Lawmakers Loot Nigeria».
[114] P. NWOSU, «Nigeria Leaders».
[115] EDITORIAL, «Beaming Light on Recovered Loot».
[116] T. DAVID WESt, «Obasanjo's Problem is Obasanjo».
[117] T. OGUNJIMI, «Out to Recover IBB's Loot».

cer star, John Fasanu. Babangida and his cronies between 1988 and 1993 perpetuated this $6 billion debt buy-scam according to Fasanu.[118]

The foregoing and other official corrupt practices aided the spread of HIV/AIDS as these amounts could have been used to alleviate the sufferings of the people. In addition, even the allocation made to the fight of HIV/AIDS through the special Petroleum Trust Fund (PTF)[119] was allegedly mismanaged.[120]

Given all these revelations, it is thus amazing that programmes designed for the control of HIV/AIDS could not be executed for lack of funds.[121] Besides, in most public hospitals and sometimes private hospitals, drugs and other medical equipment meant for the use of these hospitals are diverted by some of the medical personnel or the administrators into their private projects as a good number of them own clinics and operate paramedical services. Thus, they boost their own projects whereas these hospitals are left in ruins.

It is on this basis that one sees corruption as an alibi for the spread of HIV/AIDS in the Country. Therefore, to fight the spread of HIV/AIDS in an effective manner, there is need for a change in orientation and in attitude at all levels.

4.3.4 Conflict and Violence

Since the end of the Nigerian civil war in the early seventies, the country has not engaged in any war. The memories of this bloody clash are still fresh in the minds of many, and the wounds are yet to be healed completely.

Nigeria has, however, had to contend with sporadic conflicts and violence in the last couple of years. The sporadic violent protests during the adoption of the Structural Adjustment Programme of Babangida regime left many dead, and properties worth millions of naira destroyed. Then there were violent protests after the annulment of the June 12, 1993 elections, which continued up to 1998. Apart from the loss of life and property, many women and young girls suffered a lot as a large number of them were raped. Unfortunately, these rape cases

---

118 T. OGUNJIMI, «Out to Recover IBB's Loot».

119 The PTF was an agency set up in October 1994 to utilise excess accruals from an increase in the pump price of petroleum products for the development of the country.

120 EDITORIAL, «No tears from AIDS workers», 1-2.

121 FMOH/NACA, 15.

went unmentioned and unreported. In such a situation, it is easy to spread the disease, as a lot of people seek solace in sexual activity.

Besides, the Nigerian soldiers who were on peacekeeping missions in Liberia between 1990 and 1998, had reportedly been accused of having indiscriminate sexual affairs with the women in Liberia, and were said to have fathered some 25, 000 children who were abandoned after their mission work ended.[122] The same allegation has been levelled against our soldiers who were on peacekeeping missions in Sierra Leone. It is therefore almost certain that these soldiers possibly acquired the HIV/AIDS infection during the war, and spread the infection when they returned home.

Thus, conflict and violence no doubt will enhance the rapid spread of HIV/AIDS, as women make easy targets for sexual predators, some of whom carry virus-causing AIDS. It must be also stressed that sustainable development cannot take place in a situation of war, violence and political instability. In such situation, there cannot be any meaningful control programme to curb the spread of HIV/AIDS.

4.4 *Cultural Practices*

There is no doubt that there are some cultural practices that are harmful and may aid the spread of HIV/AIDS in the country. For instance it has been reported that the use of the same blades or knives in cutting the genital area of girls in the traditional therapy of female circumcision is a possible route.[123] Through this practice and with the contact of blood, it is easy for contamination and infection to take place. These practices not only help the spread of HIV/AIDS, but they sometimes lead to reproductive health infections, infertility, and sometimes death.

Another harmful cultural practice is the myth in some parts of the country concerning the cure of sexually transmitted diseases (STD). It is believed that if a male person with a sexually transmitted disease, has sexual intercourse with a virgin girl, he will be cured of the sexually transmitted disease.[124] The fact is that rather than being cured, not only is the disease transmitted and spread, but that condition itself is an ave-

---

[122] This was reported by the Pan African News Agency of September 21, 1998.

[123] Cf. FMOH/NACA, 15.

[124] FMOH/NACA, 9. See also K.O. ALAUSA – A.O. OSABA, «Epidemiology», 239-242; C.S. BELLO – J. D. DADA, «Sexually Transmitted Disease», 202-205. This practice is reportedly found among the Yorubas and the Hausas.

nue for the spread of HIV/AIDS, especially in the situation of genital sores. It must be emphasised that this myth is not only harmful, but it could also be tied to the already perceived male sex dominance behavior.

Another harmful cultural practice is polygamy.[125] Polygamy is the state in which a man has more than one wife at the same time. The strict terminology for this condition is «polygyny».[126] In the case of a woman with many husbands, it is referred to as polyandry.[127] The practice of polygamy is found in many cultures in Nigeria and has the blessing of some religions like Islam. Although this practice has existed for a long time, it is not an ideal practice. It has to be emphasised that it is not only Christianity that has praised monogamy. Some of the cultures of Nigeria held monogamous practice as an ideal. This could be seen in the traditional Yoruba culture, for example.

It could be argued that some of the people who entered polygamy did so for economic reasons. At the time most people were still oriented towards agriculture, many believed that having large families would produce enough hands to cultivate the land and thus avoid the need of having to hire paid labourers. With the focus now shifted from agriculture to white collar jobs, and with the economy now at a low level, it is difficult to a sustain large family, and with HIV/AIDS, the practice needs to be reconsidered as it has no doubt hastened the rapid spread of HIV/AIDS. In addition to polygamy there is also the practice of wife inheritance.[128] This is like the leviratic practice.[129] This practice arises from the desire to protect the woman socially and economically after the death of her husband.

However, it should be stressed that these practices per se have not caused HIV/AIDS. Rather they have only hastened the rapid spread of the epidemic. Besides, if we look at the situation of the developed countries, though technically polygamy does not exist, there are however some practices close to that like divorce and remarriage, prostitution, etc.[130] as Macquarrie rightly points out.

---

125 FMOH/NACA, 9.

126 J. MACQUARRIE, «Polygamy», in J. MACQUARRIE – J. CHILDRESS, ed., *A New Dictionary of Christian Ethics*, 485.

127 This situation is almost non – existent. There are only cases of divorce and remarriage.

128 FMOH/NACA, 19.

129 Cf. Dt. 25:1.

130 J. MACQUARRIE, «Polygamy», in J. MACQUARRIE – J. CHILDRESS, ed., *A New Dictionary of Christian Ethics*, 485.

Finally, another important cultural factor is the place of women in Nigerian society. To some extent, many Nigerian women have proven to be as capable as their male counterparts in the different fields of human endeavours. This gain is however not well diffused in the country as some parts of the country still see women as «second class» citizens. This is seen more in the northern part. The result is that there is a high level of illiteracy among women in this region.[131]

There is also a general lack of empowerment and thus a majority of the women lack knowledge about reproductive health issues, consequently, they are not able to make positive, life-saving choices and protect themselves from male dominance. C. Uwakwe rightly describes the reality as he says «our women lack assertiveness in interpersonal and social relations».[132] These practices, whether we like to admit them or not, place many people at risk with the HIV/AIDS infection.

4.5 Other Factors: Border Movements

We have earlier mentioned the fact of growing urbanisation and migration as some causes for the spread of HIV/AIDS. Another area that cannot and should not be ignored is the fact of border closeness and movements along the border areas.

A careful look at the 1999 sentinel report shows that some of the states sharing borders with countries like Cameroon, Niger, Chad and the Republic of Benin have a high HIV infection rate. It cannot be completely ruled out that because of the movement of people within and across these boundaries, cross border infection cannot and does not occur. Cameroon, for instance, has a high rate of HIV infection. Again, the border dispute between Nigeria and Cameroon over the Bakasi Peninsula could have fuelled HIV infection as well.

5. Effects of HIV/AIDS in Nigeria

As rightly mentioned in the Situation Analysis Report, there has not been a documented report on the impact of HIV/AIDS in the Country.[133] Therefore, some think that the effects are yet to be seen. The fact however remains that one does not need to look far before seeing the effects of this epidemic and the implication for the nation. It is enough to look at the experiences of the other African countries that have been

---

[131] FMOH/NACA, 19. Also, G. EGUNJOBI, «Save the Mothers», 1-2.
[132] C. UWAKWE, «Socio-Cultural Factors», 40.
[133] FMOH/NACA, 4.

hit by the plague to realise the magnitude of the effects that this epidemic will have on the nation. These effects will be examined on the economic, social and political levels.

5.1 *The Economic Impact*

Just as economic considerations played a great role in the spread of HIV/AIDS, so also the impact of this disease has its economic consequences. As already mentioned, it is the economically active adults that are being hit by the disease. These are the people upon whom the economic growth and development of the country lies, hence it is obvious that there will be a negative economic impact, collectively as a nation, and individually as well. Some of these economic impacts include the following.

5.1.1 Decline of Labor Force

The HIV prevalence is said to be high among the age group of 15-49 years, but particularly high among the 20-24 years age bracket.[134] Given this, we see a threat to the economic survival of the nation as the Labor sector depends on these people for productivity. With many already HIV positive, and probably a great number still in the incubating stage, many of these people will become sick as they progress to full blown AIDS, granted the fact of a lack of money to purchase drugs that could help them to live longer and relatively healthier. Consequently, national productivity will gradually decrease as these workers – teachers, business men and women, artisans civil servants, bank officials, etc., succumb to AIDS and eventually die.

What does this hold for the nation? There is bound to be a loss of trained and experienced workers. The next concern then is how do we replace these people especially as infection is still continuing at an alarming rate on a daily basis. Perhaps we may have to start importing expatriate workers as the country's skilled powers diminish. Where do we get the money to pay expatriate workers? Would they even be willing to come to a place that could become a disaster zone?

In addition, another issue is that the economic base of the country relies on the availability of cheap, unskilled labour, especially in the private sector and in the area of agriculture and agricultural products,[135] etc. The problem then would also arise in the area of food production.

---

134 NASCP/FMOH, 32.
135 Cf. CIA, *The World Factbook-Nigeria*, 2001.

Besides the problem of low productivity, demand for goods will certainly be reduced as well, as those who are potential buyers eventually die.

5.1.2 Increased Poverty

Poverty had been earlier identified as contributing to the spread of HIV/AIDS. However, with AIDS comes also the result and burden of increased poverty. The fact is that many will become poorer as the breadwinners are lost to AIDS, and the already scarce resources will be put into burying the dead. It has already been reported that in some areas, about four or more persons are buried in a day because of AIDS.[136]

The consequence of the HIV/AIDS epidemic is that it becomes more difficult for those who are already at a disadvantage economically, so that these people might never get the chance to rise beyond the poverty level.[137] Unfortunately, children who are AIDS orphans may bear the crunch more severely.

This increased poverty will become more worrisome when one considers the fact of corruption, mismanagement and lack of accountability on the part of the leaders. As Shokunbi rhetorically observes, «what is left to be seen – a badly managed economy crippled by HIV/AIDS?»[138] There is therefore the need to take urgent and drastic measures to halt the further spread of the disease. This is necessary before the situation will metastasize into a disease whose progression is no longer measured solely by the depletion of a patient's T-cell but increasingly by every percentage point that is shaved from the nation's gross domestic product.

5.1.3 Deterrent to Potential Investors

HIV/AIDS may also prove to be a bad omen for the country economically as it could scare away potential investors, especially foreign investors from the country. This is based on the fact that these investors would have to contend with the possibility of not getting local workers and the fact that their goods or products may not sell, as the demand for goods will go down. People will be thinking more about survival and having to care for the dying.

---

136 Cf. L. SHOKUNBI, «AIDS, harbinger of Poverty», 15.

137 In 2000, the estimate of population below the poverty line is said to be 45 percent. Cf. CIA, *The World Factbook-Nigeria*, 2001.

138 Cf. L. SHOKUNBI, «AIDS, harbinger of Poverty», 15.

However, it must be pointed out that this will create a problem not only for Nigeria, but also will affect foreign investors, mainly from North America and Europe, who are expecting a peak in their economies and so need to turn to the developing countries for profits. There is no doubt that Nigeria represents a potential economy base for world investors despite her many problems. Therefore, the HIV/AIDS crisis in Nigeria will have a destabilizing effect on the global market economy.[139]

5.2 *The Social Impact*

Just as we have the economic crunch as a result of HIV/AIDS, so also we have the social effects. Society too bears the crunch on different levels. The social impact would be seen in the following ways:

5.2.1 Overstretched Health Care System

With HIV/AIDS, the little gains made in the area of health care would be eroded. This is a point Babangida referred to in his inaugural address during the launching of the War against AIDS in August 1991.

The issue is that by the time the situation becomes explosive, which is already happening in some parts of the country,[140] «the already fragile health care delivery system [will be] overloaded».[141] The hospitals will have to grapple with the problem of beds to keep the patients; the cost of drugs again will become emblematic. The health personnel available definitely will not be sufficient to handle an explosive situation caused by HIV/AIDS.

Furthermore, the country's resources in fighting other health problems like malaria, cholera, tuberculosis, etc. may have to be diverted to HIV/AIDS, leaving these health problems to ravage the population at will. As the existing health structures are not sufficient to cater for the needs of the people, there is bound to be a double tragedy.

In addition, the epidemic is bound to cause an increase in mortality rate. Infant mortality rate (IMR) will be drastically increased, as the possibility is high that some infants born to HIV positive mothers will be infected. On the other hand, those who are lucky not to have been infected have their own risks as well since they have to grapple with life's cruel reality. The same is expected in the area of maternal mortal-

---

[139] Cf. J. JETER, «AIDS Cripples Economies», 1, 6.
[140] Cf. L. SHOKUNBI, «AIDS, harbinger of Poverty», 15.
[141] FMOH/NACA, 4.

ity rate (MMR), as this will be reduced drastically. Already many lives are lost either through pre-natal maternal death or antenatal death.

Therefore, the life expectancy (LE) of the population which is modestly put at 52[142] at the moment, may be drastically reduced to about 35 if not less, as a result of HIV/AIDS, given the fact that the high prevalence is found among the 20-24 age groups.

5.2.2 AIDS Orphans

It has now been established that AIDS is causing huge deaths rates among young adults in the country, those who are just starting to form new families. The attitude of denial earlier mentioned still permeates our society, as many deaths due to AIDS are described as due to «brief illness»,[143] especially amongst the relatively well to do. In the meantime, the effect of the epidemic will be felt more by children. The effect touches children mainly in two ways, as a disease that kills their parents (as either mother or father, or even both die of AIDS), leaving them orphans, and as a disease that infects children themselves.

As regards AIDS orphans, the UNAIDS reported that as at the end of 1999, the cumulative number of children estimated to have been orphaned by AIDS at the age of 14 or younger is 11.2 million.[144] Of this figure, Sub-Saharan Africa has 10.7 million.[145] The consequence of this is that the number of AIDS orphans will continue to grow.

Orphans in Nigeria, and in other parts of Africa are not new. These people are traditionally absorbed into extended family networks. With the advent of AIDS, however, the extended family is becoming overextended, as the survivors of the AIDS victims are becoming too numerous for the extended family to support. Besides, with the poor economic condition of the country, and coupled with imitating western styles, the extended family system is becoming more a thing of the past.

Therefore, with AIDS, the future looks bleak for the orphan children and inevitably for the nation, as there would be more cases of juvenile delinquency and crime. This is a likelihood since orphans are less likely than other children to be able to go to school or to have access to ade-

---

[142] Cf. CIA, *The World Factbook-Nigeria*, 2001.

[143] It seems that «brief illness» is another form of health problem in the nation now. This is because most deaths announced in the pages of newspapers seem to be due to «brief illness».

[144] UNAIDS, WHO, Cf. http://www.unaids.org.

[145] UNAIDS, WHO, Cf. http://www.unaids.org.

quate health care. In addition, they are more likely to live in poverty and to be malnourished. They will also suffer psychologically which can lead to developmental problems. In fact, orphans in general will be more vulnerable.

5.3 *The Political Impact: Threat to Peace and Stability*

The HIV/AIDS impact is not limited to the economic and social levels alone, it will also be felt on the political front as well. For now, the epidemic has taken on a political, as well as a diplomatic dimension, as seen recently.[146]

That HIV/AIDS is not just a health issue or even economic issue cannot be overemphasized. It has now been recognized at the highest International level that HIV/AIDS constitutes a «global security threat».[147]

The above affirmation was made recently by the then Vice President Al Gore of the United States, while addressing a sitting of the United Nations Security Council Meeting. According to him, «for the nations of sub-Saharan Africa, AIDS is not just a humanitarian crisis, it is a security crisis».[148] He goes on to say that the threat is not just to be understood in terms of war and peace; rather, he opined that the havoc wreaked by HIV/AIDS and the toll it exacts threatens security. Thus he argued that HIV/AIDS belongs to a group of new scourges including terrorism, drugs, corruption, environmental degradation and weapons of mass destruction threatening the security of the world.[149]

The above is true and relevant to Nigerian society because with the continuous spread of HIV/AIDS, which is taking its toll in all fabrics of the society, namely, among military personnel, civil servants, professionals in different fields, etc. There is likely to be frustration and thus instability, especially as many are already frustrated by the poor economy and mismanagement. Also with the increase in AIDS orphans who are faced with uncertainties and the lack of home, there likely could be mass insurrection and violent reactions. Thus if the spread of the epi-

---

146 M. DEL CORONA, «L'AIDS divora l'Africa», 14. Il virus è diventato una questione politica e diplomatica.

147 C. LYNCH, «AIDS is security Threat»; also M. DEL CORONA, «L'AIDS divora l'Africa», 14.

148 C. LYNCH, «AIDS is security Threat»; also M. DEL CORONA, «L'AIDS divora l'Africa», 14.

149 C. LYNCH, «AIDS is security Threat»; also M. DEL CORONA, «L'AIDS divora l'Africa», 14.

demic is not quickly arrested, it is likely that more lives will be lost. These portend badly for the country.

6. Concluding Remarks

From the explanation of the situation of HIV/AIDS in Nigeria, and the reflections on the causes for the rapid spread of the disease and its effects, it is now certain that the epidemic of HIV/AIDS infection long predicted in the country has come to pass. This means that within the next ten years or even less (as long as there is no effective cure), the people already infected will go on to develop AIDS and eventually will die of it. This of course will be a huge loss to the families of these people in particular and the whole country in general. Against this background I suppose the warning of Olikoye Ransome-Kuti, while delivering a paper as guest speaker at the United Bank for Africa medical lecture in Lagos. may already be too late. He says:

> The world is holding its breath in horror and in anticipation of the disaster that will befall Nigerians if we do not take effective steps to stop the spread of AIDS in our country. .:.Slowly, but surely, holes are being made in the fabric of our society the way termites reduce the hardest wood to rubble . . .[150]

What needs to be done now is how to halt its rapid and further spread. The Situation Analysis Report document is a welcome step but there is need to move beyond the level of directives alone as was done in the past. HIV/AIDS is not just a health issue but an all encompassing problem that requires a multisectoral approach. The observation of Kennet Prewitt must be taken seriously in the country:

> The crisis presented by [HIV/] AIDS in Africa [Nigeria] extends beyond its toll as a viral epidemic. ...It is far more complex than that as: «it disrupts the economic and social personnel – the loss of trained resource, the deflection of scarce resource, the strain on public health and education systems, the reduction of tourist revenue and the potential political unrest resulting from a pressing social problem.[151]

The task therefore is to begin to take concrete steps in preventing the spread before further harm is done to the fabric of our society.

---

[150] O. RANSOME-KUTI, «The HIV/AIDS Epidemic in Nigeria», 21; F. ADEKEYE, «Before They Die», 41.

[151] K. PREWITT, «AIDS in Africa», ix. Emphasis added.

CHAPTER III

Towards the Prevention of HIV/AIDS in Nigeria

1. Introductory Remarks

In this chapter, attention is focused on ways to prevent the further spread of HIV/AIDS in Nigeria. The importance of prevention of this disease cannot be overemphasized. At the time of writing this work there is no known vaccine to block the virus from infecting humans, nor is there a cure for those already infected. While efforts are being made to find an effective vaccine and cure for this dreaded disease, which will be significant for prevention strategy, it is, nonetheless, important that every effort should be made to prevent infection in the first instance.

This chapter seeks to look precisely at the issues related to the prevention of the HIV/AIDS, bearing in mind the particular situation of Nigeria. This does not however suggest that this preventive approach is limited to Nigeria alone.

The preventive strategy that I am proposing here is that which examines where we are at the moment as a nation in the fight against this deadly disease. What we need to do to confront the causes of the spread of the disease, issues in the preventive strategy, hence, the need for a moral vision. I shall then proceed to look at the responsible agents for carrying out this vision and how we can achieve these goals. To achieve the set objective, this chapter is divided into four sections.

The first section is where we are at the moment in the fight against the disease. In my judgment, I think we are not doing enough as a nation to prevent the spread of the disease.

The second section therefore examines what must be done, that is, the response needed. The emphasis is on the need to have a moral vision, stressing three basic principles, which I believe, can be of great importance in the fight against the spread of the disease. These principles are that of responsibility, non-discrimination, and confidentiality. This section also examines the issue of justice, especially, economic and social justice, and the gender power relations.

The third section deals with the responsible agents in the prevention strategy. Here I want to deal with the role of the government, the role of the non-governmental organization, the role of the religious bodies, and the role of the developed nations.

The final section focuses on how to achieve the objective of the prevention of the disease of HIV/AIDS. The issues here are that of information and enlightenment campaign, Testing for HIV, Counseling and the renewal of the traditional moral values and custom. This will be followed with the conclusion of this chapter.

2. HIV/AIDS Prevention: Where We Are Now

A cursory look at the situation of HIV/AIDS in Nigeria reveals a lot of interesting but embarrassing facts. In the past there had been great emphasis on the family, and family life was a strong component in the day-to-day life of the Nigerian people. The disease of HIV/AIDS is changing that fast; the impact on the family has been great to the extent that some families are being destroyed as a result of this disease. Despite this ugly reality, the effort to combat the disease collectively and individually has not been sufficiently pursued. The consequence of this lack of focus and commitment to combat the disease as mentioned earlier will be very devastating for the country. This is the reason that everything possible to curtail the spread must be done so as to save the country from the avoidable disaster.

3. The Response Needed

I am of the opinion that as a nation and individually, the way we have been acting and reacting to the HIV/AIDS epidemic is inadequate. This is too big to explore. I have tried to show that in the previous chapter. This is why we have to speak in the way that addresses the reality of our people now. I believe we can do that in a number of ways, and specifically through the following ways.

3.1 *The Need for a Moral Vision of HIV/AIDS Prevention*

The Spanish moral theologian Marciano Vidal proposes what he believes should be the basic criteria of the ethics of AIDS.[1] These are what he calls «responsibilization» and «non-discrimination». I would like to add «confidentiality». Hence, in what I propose as a moral vision of HIV/AIDS prevention, I will be looking at the principles of responsibility, non-discrimination and confidentiality. These principles in my opinion can guarantee a better way of handling the epidemic in the country.

3.1.1 The Principle of Responsibility

If one looks at the history of the disease in Africa in general, and Nigeria in particular, one discovers that the infection occurred as a result of irresponsible choices and ways of acting, both on the individual and collective levels, as well as a result of ignorance. It is as a result of this fact that one is convinced that the prevention of HIV/AIDS requires a great responsibility. Here, one thinks of the individual or personal responsibility, and the social responsibility that involves the community, the religious group and the government. The principle of responsibility makes a moral imperative on all in this time of AIDS. There is a moral imperative for those infected, as well as the non-infected persons.

The moral imperative for those infected is to accept their condition, and to do all they can, not to spread the disease. The moral responsibility on those already infected is seen in the following remarks of Noerine Kaleeba. Although she writes on the need to «live positively with AIDS», the need to live responsibly, too, is emphasized. She writes:

> To the person who is infected it calls on them to live responsibly with the HIV infection in their blood, to face up to the infection as a starting point. It calls on them to recognize their responsibility to society, the responsibility to retain the amount of virus they have in their blood, and not to spread it around, by making the effort not to infect others. It also calls upon people who are infected to look after themselves better, and preserve themselves until a cure comes. It calls to people who are infected to remain actively involved in society, and in social activities within society.[2]

---

[1] M. VIDAL, «The Christian Ethic», 89-98.
[2] N. KALEEBA, *We Miss You All,* 79-80.

This means there is a need for responsible behavioral action on the part of these people at all times. Responsibility in sexual behavior makes it clear that those already infected must exercise control over their sex lives, especially by not exposing others to the virus.

The principle of responsibility on the part of those who are free of infection writes Kaleeba, is «to support people with HIV infection so that they can fulfill their obligations…Acceptance of people with HIV or AIDS within our community is the starting point for dealing with the problem».[3] Here we can talk of the moral imperative this principle makes on the government. On the government level, the principle of responsibility calls for the provision of basic health care facilities to cater for the people living with the virus, to protect their rights as citizens, with dignity, thus making sure that they are in no way discriminated against. That is why one cannot but agree with Ronald Bayer, Carol Levine and Susan Wolfe when they conclude:

> We believe that the greatest hope for stopping the spread of HIV infection is the voluntary cooperation of those at higher risk - their willingness to undergo testing and to alter their personal behavior and goals in the interest of the community. But we can expect this voluntary cooperation — in some cases, sacrifice — only if the legitimate interests of these groups and individuals in being protected from discrimination are heeded by legislators, professionals and the public.[4]

The above quotation is basically calling attention to the responsibilities of the infected individual not to infect others, but more than that, it is a challenge to and the responsibility of the public authority in the prevention of HIV infection. The chief concern of the public authority, especially the public health officials, must therefore be to ensure that the rights of the infected persons are defended and promoted, so that each one may strive to live a responsible life.

One can also think of the responsibility on the religious level, that is, on the Church's level. It is important to note that when we talk about responsibility we are not just talking about secular ethics, but this is a principle that is well rooted in the Catholic tradition, and especially Catholic Social Thought. In *Mater et Magistra*, John XXIII stressed that responsibility is a basic demand of human nature, a concrete exercise of freedom and a path to development.[5] The Church therefore will

---

[3] N. KALEEBA, *We Miss You All*, 79-80.
[4] R. BAYER – C. LEVINE – S. WOLFE, «HIV Antibody Screening», 1774.
[5] Cf. JOHN XXIII, *Mater et Magistra*, May 15, 1961, no. 54.

be fulfilling her responsibility by becoming visibly present to those who suffer, that is, to the people living with this unfortunate disease through a loving and caring attitude, to their families and relatives. The Church will also be living out her mission responsibly when she can stand up for these people in demanding social justice for them where that is lacking. The English theologian Kevin Kelly has even gone further to point out what he perceives as an element of responsibility on the part of the Church by calling for a renewal and enrichment of the Church's sexual ethics.[6]

The principle of responsibility as a moral vision of HIV/AIDS prevention can, and does eliminate fear and help to transform behavior, which is a sure guarantee of a preventive approach.[7] I shall deal with this again when I get to the morality of condoms and needle exchange programs. It is my conviction that proper education and the awareness for responsibility can bring about behavioral changes — like reducing the number of partners, abstinence, etc — among people, especially the young adults who are sexually active. It may be foolish to just place our hopes on medical wonders that as of now remain illusory.

From the foregoing, we could see that the principle of responsibility is of practical importance in the area of prevention, transmission, and that of care, or healing.[8]

3.1.2 The Principle of Non-Discrimination

While the principle of responsibility deals with both the infected and non-infected in the society, the principle of non-discrimination specifically seeks to safeguard and protect those who are infected and as such, suffer as a result of this disease. The aim of this principle, as Vidal points out, is to «put forward a project of humanization in the dehumanized and dehumanizing situation of AIDS».[9] The attempt is to reorientate and restore the dignity of the persons who face a double tragedy namely, the tragedy of the disease, and the tragedy of social discrimination and prejudice.

The principle of non-discrimination calls attention to the fact that it is morally wrong to discriminate against the HIV/AIDS persons simply because of their social condition. This principle essentially flows from

---

[6] Cf. K.T. KELLY, *New Directions in Sexual Ethics*, especially 137-176.

[7] See J.H. PELÀEZ, «Educating for HIV Prevention», 148.

[8] See M. VIDAL, «The Christian Ethic», 93.

[9] M. VIDAL, «The Christian Ethic», 93.

the fact of our personhood. The notion of person in the Christian vision
means, the fact that human beings are created in the image and likeness
of God. As Gula explains, «Image of God» says «we all share in a
common human condition, which has a common end, namely, God. It
also says that human dignity does not depend ultimately on human
achievements (perfection), but on divine love».[10]

Therefore, each individual, male or female, young or old sick or
healthy, HIV positive or negative, morally mature or otherwise is in the
«image of God». Thus, each human person is a being with dignity and
worth. Therefore, whatever the human condition, the person is not just
a mere object, rather, the person has something of value, of resem-
blance with the being of God.[11]

Discrimination normally occurs because of the social stigma already
associated with the disease. We need to also understand that discrimination entails denying the person his or her basic rights. To discriminate against a person or to deny a person his or her inalienable rights
based on the person's physical condition is to go against the demands
of justice.[12]   This is, of course, morally wrong and unacceptable.
HIV/AIDS is, and should be seen as a disease like every other human
disease, like cancer, influenza, malaria, etc. What is at stake therefore
«is the recovery and raising of the integral well-being of those impli-
cated».[13]

Meanwhile, there are many areas or contexts in which discrimination against HIV/AIDS persons take place. We see this in the area of
housing, employment, access to health care, movement, vocation — the
obligation to take the antibodies test as a condition for admittance, or
the condition for obtaining a scholarship to study for those already or-
dained, especially those coming from Africa. Discrimination is also
seen even in the use of language like, the label «groups at risk».[14]

Discrimination sometimes occurs from those who are supposed to
ensure and guarantee individual rights, that is, from government, especially in the area of mandatory test for immigrants, prostitutes, prison-
ers, those applying for marriage licenses etc. Also, we see discrimina-

---

[10] R. GULA, *Reason Informed by Faith,* 65.
[11] See VATICAN II, Pastoral Constitution of the Church in Modern World, *Gaudium et Spes*, nos. 26, 29. Also M. VIDAL, «The Christian Ethic», 93.
[12] See C. CAMPOS, «A Catholic Hospital in India», 208.
[13] M. VIDAL, «The Christian Ethic», 93.
[14] M. VIDAL, «The Christian Ethic», 95. Here one thinks of the prostitutes, drug users and sometimes homosexuals, as in the developed nations.

tion from professionals, like the health officials calling for quarantine in hospitals or clinics.

Discriminatory practices cannot be justified for whatever reasons. Besides, taking discriminatory actions would not prevent the spread of the disease. It rather would enhance a rapid spread, as those who are infected would want to keep their seropositive status secret for fear or repercussion of disclosing such vital information.

Finally, the principle of non-discrimination though important yet appears to be negative. Its positive dimension, as Vidal rightly says, should be «solidarity and inclusion».[15] According to this vision, the starting point is the acceptance of the «other» (the HIV/AIDS sufferer), and incorporating this 'other' to the dynamic of solidarity of human actions. The principle of non-discrimination thus entails guaranteeing the HIV/AIDS persons the basic rights of every citizen.

3.1.3 The Principle of Confidentiality

This is another important principle in the area of HIV/AIDS prevention. The duty of medical confidentiality is well established in the practice of medicine and the expectations of patients. This, in fact, is one of the central expressions of ethical practice. With HIV/AIDS, there is need to confront the difficult tensions that arise in the attempt to achieve this confidentiality in reality. HIV as we know is a transmissible disease, and it is one that is transmitted in private (genital or anal intercourse) settings, or even in clandestine setting as in the injection of drugs. This raises issues about the duties to protect the public's health, while at the same time privacy and individual autonomy are not compromised or hindered.

The question is: can the threat of the common good justify the curtailment of rights such as confidentiality and privacy? Or, to put it in another way, how should the patient's right to privacy and confidentiality be balanced against the need to inform others (caregivers, epidemiological investigators, public health officials and sexual partners) of the presence of AIDS or exposure to HIV? These are issues of debates that are not that easy to resolve and as such call for greater attention.[16] The fact remains that patients have a legitimate interest in seeking to keep their sexual orientation or medical status confidential especially, when

---

15 M. VIDAL, «The Christian Ethic», 94.

16 Cf. J.J. FERRER, *Sida y Bioetica,* 149-194. See W.J. WINSLADE, «Confidentiality», 451-459.

disclosure could lead to undesirable results like loss of employment, eviction from house, social isolation, etc. Confidentiality is an important principle that should be kept and respected especially in this time of AIDS.

Confidentiality as Winslade says,

> ...concerns the communication of private and personal information from one person to another where it is expected that the recipient of the information, such as health professional, will not ordinarily disclose the confidential information to third persons. In other words, other persons, unless properly authorized, have limited access to confidential information.[17]

It is important to note the phrase «will not ordinarily disclose the confidential information...» This phrase will be useful in understanding the subsequent analysis of this principle. Confidentiality has its linguistic roots in the two Latin words: «cum» and «fides» which means «with fidelity».[18] From this etymology confidentiality thus assumes a relationship based on trust or fidelity. It is not surprising then to see why some people tend to opt for the word fidelity, of which confidentiality is seen as an expression.[19]

The principle of confidentiality is not a novelty in the Catholic moral teaching. This principle is found in the Catholic moral tradition, though; it was treated under the heading of secrecy.[20] It is seen as the moral duty of not divulging to anyone what is known or received in confidence.[21] Secrecy is said to have its basis in the dignity of the human person hence, it has a good that is personal, a bonum privatum.[22] There is also the social dimension to it, thus bonum commune, the common good.[23] The third dimension is theological in nature.[24]

The theologians spoke of various kinds of secrecy. These distinctions are relevant in understanding the level of obligation that this principle imposes. G. Taliercio gives four of these distinctions.[25]

---

[17] W.J. WINSLADE, «Confidentiality», 452.

[18] W.J. WINSLADE, «Confidentiality», 452.

[19] See J.F. KEENAN, «Notes on Moral Theology», 142-159. Also G. GLEESON – D. LEARY, «When Fidelity and Justice Clash», 221-230

[20] G. TALIERCIO, «Segreto», 987-993; L. PADOVESE, «Segreto», 1205-1212; J.J. FERRER, *Sida y Bioetica,* 150.

[21] G. TALIERCIO, «Segreto», 988.

[22] G. TALIERCIO, «Segreto», 987.

[23] G. TALIERCIO, «Segreto», 987.

[24] G. TALIERCIO, «Segreto», 987.

[25] G. TALIERCIO, «Segreto», 988. Jorge Ferrer on his part lists five distinctions. See J.J. FERRER, *Sida y Bioetica,* 151-152.

The first is the «natural secret». This type of secret by its nature forbids a person to reveal what has been made known to him or her. A good example is issue relating to sentiments. The obligation to keep the secret is based on the demands of justice and charity. Charity demands that we do not do unto others what we do not want done unto us. As a result, this kind of secret imposes an obligation of not revealing information known about a person that can damage his or her integrity. Justice on the other hand, demands that we respect the good name and the dignity of the person. The obligation to keep the secret in this first aspect can either be grave or light, depending on the piece of information known.

The second type is «promised secret». As the name shows, this is a situation in which the receiver of important information promises to keep as secret the information received. Here the intention of the person making the promise is very important. The obligation to maintain the secret is derived from the nature of the promise. The obligation to keep the secret could either be on the demands of justice or simply as a duty to be faithful to the promise. It is, however, said that one cannot presume the obligation of justice hence, we are dealing with the need to be faithful to the demands of our relationship, in this case, the keeping of the promise as agreed upon.

The third is «confided secret». This is a type of secret that is based on agreement. The agreement could either be implicit or explicit. Taliercio gives three types of confided secrecy. First is that which is confided in a friend for the sake of seeking consolation. The second is that confided in a competent friend for the motive of receiving sound advice. The third grade is that which is shared with a professional, otherwise known as «professional secrecy».[26] Professional secrecy is a secret shared with another person based on his or her professional competency. In this situation we are talking about the relationship between doctors and patients, lawyers and their clients, etc. The obligation to maintain a secret here is more rigid than the obligation that the earlier two levels impose. It is however necessary to distinguish between what is made known to the professional from what he or she deduces based on his or her professional knowledge. The obligation to maintain confidentiality is tied to the information received from the client. The exercise of professional prudence nonetheless calls the professional to be

---

26 Jorge Ferrer treated this kind of secrecy differently from confided secrecy. See J.J. FERRER, *Sida y Bioetica*, 152.

cautious about the things he or she discovers based on his or her professional knowledge.

The fourth and the last type of secret found in the Catholic tradition deals with «confessional or sacramental secret». This is the secret that is linked with the sacrament of reconciliation. The Catholic teaching in this regard is that under no condition does human law permit its violation. As a result, all Catholic priests that have the faculty to administer the sacrament of reconciliation are forbidden from disclosing whatever is revealed to them in the sacramental confession. Therefore, the secret here is absolute.[27]

One important justification of confidentiality is to preserve human integrity and to allow the formation of close human bonds. It is important to also note that confidentiality depends not just on the information, but also on the context of the disclosure as well as on the relationship between the person disclosing the information and the recipient of that information. I wish to limit myself to confidentiality between health personnel and their patients, as regard the HIV/AIDS patients.

Confidentiality in the context of medicine and its practice is built on a covenant relationship between doctor and patient. It is the covenant that causes the need for confidentiality. This bond is important for the diagnostic process because the patient knowing that there is this bond of trust will share his or her life history accurately and correctly. If that is not the case, that is, where this trust is suspected to be lacking, accurate information cannot be secured and necessary preventive precaution will be lost.[28] H.T. Engelhardt is more blunt in this regard as he says, «the more one has grounds for suspecting that such disclosures prevent individuals from seeking treatment… the more one will suspect that the requirements of disclosure will do more harm than good».[29]

However, it has also been recognized that confidentiality is not absolute.[30] There are occasions when we have conflict of rights and values,

---

[27] G. TALIERCIO, «Segreto», 988-989; J.J. FERRER, Sida y Bioetica, 151-152; L. PADOVESE, «Segreto», 1205-1206.

[28] Cf. J. ELIZARI, «Segreto professionale e Aids», 240-242. He says that this principle is important in this time of AIDS: «Il segreto e anche come una garanzia efficace contro L'Aids. Fra le misure per contenere l'epidemia si considerano essenziali il counseling e il test volontari. E ci sono buoni motivi per temere che molte persone a rischio rifiuteranno, senza la protezione del segreto, di andare da un medico per farsi consigliare e prendere cosi le misure necessarie per evitare di contaminare altri» (p. 241).

[29] H.T. ENGELHARDT Jr., The Foundations of Bioethics, 299.

[30] See Sir D. BLACK, «Absolute Confidentiality?», 172-176; G. TALIERCIO, «Segreto», 989-993; J. ELIZARI, «Segreto professionale e Aids», 241.

hence, there are exceptions to the principle of confidentiality.

For clinicians, the most substantial tension has been in the potential or perceived conflict between the duty to an individual patient and the duty to protect others. The basic question is how far should a doctor go in attempting to protect others from HIV risk from his or her patient? This question could be elaborated with a case study.

The case:[31] Johnson has been diagnosed as HIV positive. He continues to have unsafe sex with Jacqueline, his girlfriend, yet he is unwilling to inform her of his HIV status. The doctor knows the girlfriend, too, and also that she is ignorant of Johnson's HIV status, what should the doctor do?

The answer to the case above is not an easy one. It is not a question of mathematical calculation but that of values. As a result of the complexity of this case and other similar cases, it has been suggested that the principle of confidentiality must not be treated in isolation but in relation to virtues.[32] There is thus the need to examine the different issues involved to be able to arrive at mature decisions.[33]

As a rule, confidentiality or secrecy has to be maintained. However, it has been recognized that the disclosure of information could be justified by recognition of legitimate exceptions or by conflict between principles.[34] The Catholic teaching on secrecy is that (outside the sacrament of reconciliation), there are exceptions to this rule.[35] In the Catholic moral tradition, there are four legitimate exceptions that are usually accepted. These exceptions: the common good, informed consent, threat to innocent third party, and imminent threat to the professional.[36]

The first exception is that which seeks to protect the common good. This exception is one that seeks to protect the societal good against the individual good especially in a situation of conflict. An instance of this will be in regard to infectious diseases. It is recognized that the common good must be protected especially when it entails taking measure

---

[31] The names are imaginary thus there are no known persons with these names in the situation described here. For a similar case see J.C. BERMEJO HIGUERA, «A Spaniard», 239-246.

[32] See G. GLEESON – D. LEARY, «When Fidelity and Justice Clash», 221-230.

[33] See J.F. KEENAN, «Notes on Moral Theology», 142-56. He gives useful insight on the issues to be considered.

[34] Sir D. BLACK, «Absolute Confidentiality?», 172-176. See J.J. FERRER, Sida y Bioetica, 160. He sees the moral community as occupying an important position.

[35] Cf. G. TALIERCIO, «Segreto», 989; L. PADOVESE, «Segreto», 1206-1207.

[36] G. TALIERCIO, «Segreto», 989-992.

for the public health safety. The breaking of confidentiality in a situation like this nonetheless has been recognized to be justifiable when it is done within the confines of laid down procedure. This could happen in the case of private good versus common good.

The second exception to the rule of confidentiality is that of informed consent. The obligation to maintain confidentiality by the health care professional ceases when the patient freely gives his or her consent, thus allowing the information about his or her to be divulged. In this situation, it is presumed that the divulging of such information is for the benefit of the patient.

The third exception is when there is a threat to innocent third party. It is considered to be legitimate, or even, a question of duty for the health care professional to break the rule of confidentiality in order to safeguard a third innocent party whose interest may be jeopardized if the secret is kept. It must be noted however that there have been diverse opinions regarding this exception. It is for the health care personnel to use his or her prudential judgment in determining when confidentiality should be maintained or not. There are some prudential rules given to help determine when to maintain secret or to break it:

If the secret is made known to someone whose duty towards the public is of great importance to the third innocent party as well, then, he or she has a duty to inform those who could intervene and save the innocent party. In a situation where there is a great danger to the third innocent person but where the danger has nothing to do with the information confided in the professional, it is recommended that the professional should maintain the secret.

If on the other hand, there is a strict connection between the confided secret and the threat to the third innocent party, the professional has to persuade his or her client to inform the third innocent person. In a situation where the client refuses to disclose the information despite persistent encouragement from the professional, then, the professional is obliged to divulge the secret.

In the first case of the exception to the exceptions, the professional's knowledge of the secret is just an occasion of the danger to the third party, while in the second place the knowledge could be described as the cause of the danger to the third party.

It is not right for the client to attempt to hide under the cloak of confidentiality while purposely doing harm to an innocent person. In a situation where the harm has already been done to the third party, the professional is bound to maintain the secret because there is no harm to prevent again.

The last exception to the rule of maintaining confidentiality is when there is an imminent threat to the professional, like there is threat to his or her life. This exception is based on the notion of legitimate self – defense.[37] An exception to this exception could occur when this is excluded contractually and in advance.

Having stated the principles, I now return to the point of departure, that is the case study of Johnson and the girlfriend. The first thing is for the doctor to encourage Johnson to summon the courage to disclose his HIV-status to the girlfriend if he truly loves her. There problem comes in a situation where it could be ascertained that she has not been infected, and Johnson the boyfriend is still adamant in not disclosing his HIV-positive status to her. There are divergent view points here as we have those who maintain that even in this case the patient confidentiality must be maintained because the covenant relationship is between Johnson and the physician and not with the patient's girlfriend. There are, however, those who maintain that the physician has a duty to warn the girlfriend of the danger.[38]

General Medical Council guidance allows the physician to breach confidentiality or to maintain it so long as the physician is able to justify his or her actions. In all, the insight of Morton Wiston is helpful. Talking about the duty to treat and maintain confidentiality he says, «in general, the duty to protect should be discharged in the way that is least invasive of the patient's rights while still effectively serving to protect potential victims».[39]

While the foregoing seems to be the general consensus in the discourse on confidentiality, some even think it is impossible to maintain confidentiality in the practice of modern medicine. Mark Siegler, for instance, says confidentiality is a «decrepit concept».[40] According to him, modern high-technology health care does not permit medical confidentiality as was traditionally conceived. Most hospitals, he notes, now have health care teams, who in one way or the other have legitimate interest and duty to know the patients' record hence the information that previously had been held in confidence by an individual phy-

---

[37] G. TALIERCIO, «Segreto», 989-992.
[38] L. FLECK – M. ANGELL, «Please Don't Tell», 216-219; R. BAYER, «Public Health Policy», 1500-1504.
[39] M. WISTON, «AIDS and A Duty to Protect», 23.
[40] M. SIEGLER, «Confidentiality in Medicine», 169-171.

sician will necessarily be disseminated to the health team members. Thus, he thinks that we can only talk of medical confidentiality in the non-bureaucratic, non-institutional medical encounters — that is, in the doctor — patient encounters that take place in physicians' offices.[41]

The fact is that in this time of HIV/AIDS, confidentiality remains an important principle, especially in the area of prevention This is be cause there is real danger if the doctor starts to act beyond the compass of his or her role with his or her patient. If patients perceive that physicians will breach confidentiality to protect others, such information will no longer be forthcoming. Therefore, the (physician or health official) must be able to influence the patient for the wider benefit of all and so exert influence to protect others.

I wish to conclude this section on the need for the principle of confidentiality in the time of HIV/AIDS with the conviction that confidentiality can still be maintained in a large-scale health sector, like in the teaching hospitals and the big hospitals. The patient's medical record or information should be provided or made available to those who have a need to know. The basic need to know is legitimate when this enables the health care providers to serve the patients' interest.

3.2 The Demands of Justice

The point I wish to emphasize here is, for the preventive program to be meaningful in the country, there is need to effectively to tackle the broader predisposing economic and social factors, such as poverty, inadequate health care facilities, malnutrition, the low status of women, etc.

As already mentioned in this work, there is a great deal of inequalities both in the areas of access to, and in the distribution of the country's resources. This inequality also extends to the access to health care programs and facilities. This is why I believe that the principle of justice is of great importance in order to effectively deal with the imbalance and inequity that are visibly seen in the country.

The issue of justice is of great importance if HIV/AIDS epidemic is to be addressed holistically. One writer who has given thought to this dimension is Lisa Sowle Cahill. In her own contribution to the recent book entitled: *Catholic Ethicists on HIV/AIDS Prevention*, she emphatically states, «AIDS is a justice issue, not primarily a sex issue».[42]

---

[41] M. SIEGLER, «Confidentiality in Medicine», 170.
[42] L.S. CAHILL «AIDS, Justice, and the Common Good», 282.

However, it must be noted that the concept of justice is a big issue, as there are the philosophical and biblical dimensions of justice. The concept of justice is an issue with more than two and half millennia of history, hence, I am not going into the details in this work.[43] I wish to examine only the aspects of economic and social justice in the fight against the further spread of HIV/AIDS in the country.

Meanwhile, it is pertinent to note what Pope John XXIII said with regard to justice. He says:

> Justice is to be observed not merely in the distribution of wealth, but also in regards to the conditions under which men engaged in productive activity have an opportunity to assume responsibility and to perfect themselves by their efforts.[44]

3.2.1 HIV/AIDS and Economic Justice

One of the ways of resolving the present rate of the HIV/AIDS epidemic is to address the economic structures existing in the country.

The view of the US Catholic Bishops' Conference in their pastoral letter, «Economic Justice for All…,» emphasized this point:

> Economic arrangements can be sources of fulfillment, of hope, of community — or of frustration, isolation and even despair. They teach virtues — or vices — and day by day help mold our characters. They affect the quality of people's lives at the extreme even determining whether people live or die.[45]

The above view describes accurately the situation in Nigeria. Therefore, the role that poverty plays in the spread of the AIDS epidemic in Nigeria and in the developing nations in general needs to be repeated again and again, as it renders people powerless. Powerlessness is a structural problem that is embedded in and reinforced by the fabric of our social institutions.

The challenge, therefore, is the need to have institutional responses to address these economic and social dysfunctions and inequalities, and bridge the gap that the disparities have caused. This is why I agree with Gloria Waite when she said that instead of looking at the «aberrant cul-

---

[43] See for instance J.C. HAUGHEY, ed., *The Faith That Does Justice*; R.L. COHEN, ed., *Justice: Views from the Social Sciences*; E.C. GARDNER, *Justice and Christian Ethics*; A. SARAT – T.R. KEARNS, ed., *Justice and Injustice in Law*.

[44] JOHN XIII, *Mater et Magistra*, May 14, 1971, no. 82.

[45] NCCB, «Economic Justice for All», 34.

tural traits» of Africans» as regards HIV/AIDS, it is more important to look into, and focus on the «aberrant nature of the African econo- mies».[46]

The government in general, and the Catholic Church in particular, can play a pivotal role in this regard. There is, therefore, a dire need for commitment to eradicate poverty, and to guarantee all the citizens the right to share in the blessings of the land.

It is heartwarming to note the effort of the present Administration's commitment to eradicate poverty through *The Poverty Alleviation Pro- gram Scheme*. Certainly the task of poverty alleviation may be complex and demanding, but it is not insurmountable. The situation calls for radical steps as opposed to goodwill and inspiring words. Radical changes must be made in order to have a lasting solution. Hence, the structural injustices we mentioned cannot be remedied without radical structural changes.

The first step in any structural change entails an honest and serious effort to bridge the gap between the rich and the poor. A critical look at the situation of the country reveals that many of the rich, who are in the minority, acquired their wealth from what was meant to belong to the vast majority. This wealth was accumulated through contracts that were either inflated or contracts that were awarded but not executed, or even through an outright looting of the public treasury at all levels of gov- ernance. Actions such as these violate the principle of the common good. These corrupt practices must be addressed in order to heal the wounds of the people, as well as to heal the memories of the wasted opportunities.

In addition, there is need to build and sustain a healthy economy.[47] This fact was also stressed at a National Symposium to mark the coun- try's 40th Independence anniversary. Speaking on the occasion, Umar Abba Gana[48] stressed the need for sustained macro- economic stability, fiscal transparency and political stability to engender foreign invest- ment in the economy.[49] He also urged the country to borrow ideas from successful countries, and to experiment with them until a time comes when Nigeria is able to create her own formula.

---

[46] G. WAITE, «The Politics of Disease», 151.

[47]Cf. NCCB, «Economic Justice for All», 51.

[48] Alhaji Umar Abba Gana is the Managing Director of African Petroleum Plc. AP is one of the leading oil companies in the country.

[49] C. OGBU – C. OZOR, «Utomi, Gana, Akingbola».

One of the ways of building a healthy and sustainable economy is through the creation of job opportunities and employment for all. There is no denying the fact that poverty is closely related to the issue of employment. In a country where millions are unemployed,[50] where those who are currently working lack job security, and wages are too low, poverty is bound to exit.[51] A critical look at the present situation in the country reveals that a large number of people who are fortunate enough to have jobs, are locked into jobs with low pay, poor working conditions and little or no opportunity for career advancement. It must also be noted that unemployment leads to low productivity. It is becoming an increasingly well-known fact that achieving a more just economy anywhere in the world depends in part on increasing economic resources and productivity. Unemployment and dehumanizing conditions of employment also go against the demands of justice. The demands of justice entail more than just providing help to the poor and the vulnerable members of the society. Rather, it entails economic participation through employment and widespread ownership of property. Therefore, creation of job opportunities and employment for all should be a priority. With the creation of job opportunities, the young and able bodied women and men will spend their time and energy in building the society positively, instead of having to spend their time in dangerous activities and behavior that could only enhance the spread of HIV/AIDS.

Another important step that needs consideration is the need to empower people to be self-reliant, and become self-sufficient. If people lack empowerment, they will be perpetually dependent on the government and on others. Lack of empowerment can only create a situation of powerlessness, which as earlier mentioned, is an offshoot of poverty. Hence, there is a need to design programs that encourage and stimulate initiatives such as small-scale businesses. This will ultimately enable those who are presently poor and dependent to participate in the ownership and control of economic resources. Thus, there is the need to educate and encourage programs such as credit unions, farmers' cooperatives, etc., at the community level. These programs will not only benefit the poor, but will serve as an instrument of empowerment, especially for women who are often marginalized and have had to depend on their

---

[50] The 1999 estimate put the labor force of the country at 66million and 1992 estimate put the unemployment rate at 28%. Cf. CIA, *The World Factbook-Nigeria*, 2001.

[51] CIA, *The World Factbook-Nigeria*, 2001. The population below poverty line in the country is said to be 45 percent.

husbands or male partners. In this task of empowerment, it has to be stressed that corporations, private organizations and the public sector are all needed to provide the education and the basic assistance needed to make such programs viable.

3.2.2 HIV/AIDS and Social Justice

Social justice seeks to ensure that persons fulfill their obligation to be active and productive participants in the life of society, and that society has a duty to enable them to participate this way. Social justice, as a matter of fact, stresses the need to do everything for the promotion of the common good. Pope Pius XI states, «it is of the very essence of social justice to demand from each individual all that is necessary for the common good».[52] The purpose of common good is to enhance the well being of every single member of the society, as well as of society as a whole.[53] This aspect of justice is very crucial and important in this time of AIDS. As Lisa Cahill rightly points out, «the framework of the common good is incompatible both with the rejection of HIV infected persons in their local communities and with the economic greed that creates the conditions in which AIDS thrives».[54]

The need for the common good makes a demand on the government to design programs that cater for the welfare of the citizens, especially the elderly and the poor. A good Medicare program for example, will enhance the life expectancy and health status of the elderly and the poor. So also will Medicare look after infants and expectant mothers; thus, infant mortality will be reduced and access to health care for all will be available. The implementation of these programs will demonstrate the country's commitment to social justice and the ideal of a decent life for everyone. The consequence, of course, will be the reduction of those factors that contribute to the rapid spread of HIV/AIDS in the country.

3.2.3 The Gender Power Dynamics

Gender relations have been defined as «the processes, structures, and institutions by means of which societies order sex differences and invest them with cultural meanings for the people who act them out in

---

[52] PIUS XI, *Divini Redemptoris*, March 19, 1937, no. 51.
[53] Cf. L.S. CAHILL, «AIDS, Justice, and the Common Good», 288.
[54] L.S. CAHILL, «AIDS, Justice, and the Common Good», 289.

daily life».[55] As seen in the last chapter gender inequality and injustice play significant roles in the spread of HIV/AIDS in the country. It was emphasized that gender relations are characterized by an unequal balance of power, which creates a situation where women have less power or control in the area of sexual decision making, as well as by economic inequality, which places women in a disadvantaged position.[56]

In the fight against HIV/AIDS it becomes imperative that this inequality and oppression of women be addressed. The permissiveness of violence against women and even within marital relationships must be addressed. This is where gender power dynamics comes to play, or what has been described as a «gender solution».[57] Lisa Cahill described it simply as «a commitment to equal personal respect and equal social power for women and men».[58] Basically, the issue is not an attempt to deny or eliminate the differences that exist between women and men. Rather, it is an understanding of the fact women are not subordinate or inferior to men, but also are equal in dignity and respect as human persons.

Therefore, it becomes necessary to dismantle the structures on which this inequality thrives. As some writers on the HIV/AIDS epidemic have rightly shown, it is a sheer illusion to think that behavioral changes alone will bring about a halt to the spread of HIV/AIDS.[59] For instance, Geeta Rao Gupta and Ellen Weiss argue for the need to provide women with economic opportunities, especially for women for «whom bartering sex is a matter of survival». Where this is not possible, messages such as «stick to your partner» or «love faithfully» are inappropriate to motivate behavior change.[60]

Kevin T. Kelly has given some direction in this matter of gender equality. After highlighting various ways in which women are at a disadvantage in the rapid spread of HIV/AIDS, he concludes:

> In the light of the picture presented above, it would seem unrealistic and even harmful to suggest that the only real solution to the HIV/AIDS pan-

---

[55] B.G. SCHOEPF, «Gender, Development, and AIDS», 53-85.

[56] Cf. R. BURGGRAEVE, «From Responsible to Meaningful Sexuality», 306-307.

[57] It must be stated that different writers have used different terminology like «feminism», «gender analysis», etc. to describe this reality of gender crisis. See for example L.S. CAHILL, Sex, Gender and Christian Ethics, 1; K.T. KELLY, New Directions in Sexual Ethics, 34.

[58] L.S. CAHILL, Sex, Gender and Christian Ethics, 1.

[59] See L.S. CAHILL, «AIDS, Justice, and the Common Good», 282-285.

[60] G.R. GUPTA – E. WEISS, «Women's Lives and Sex», 267.

demic lies in the traditional «faithful to one partner» sexual ethic. That offers no help to many women. For them, what is lacking is the very foundation without which such sexual ethic is virtually meaningless. As long as
their full and equal dignity is not accepted in theory and in practice, many
of the norms of this traditional sexual ethic are likely to work against the
well-being of these women and may even prove to be the occasion of their
becoming infected by HIV. It would seem obvious that there will be no
substantial alleviation of the plight of women oppressed in these various
ways until there is a cultural shift to accepting the full dignity of women
and adapting cultural norms so that the relationships of women are able to
be lived out in true equality and mutuality.[61]

The challenge of Kevin Kelly is worth noting, especially when one
considers the fact that the injustice against women is even prevalent in
the male defined religious doctrine.[62] A critical look at the different
religious groups and bodies, with regard to their teachings and practices, portray a disturbing picture of discrimination and injustice against
women. For instance, with due respect to the Islamic religion, the recent introduction of Sharia laws in some parts of the country makes one
wonder about the role and position of women in these areas. It is not
the Sharia laws in themselves that pose the problem, but rather the
manner in which such laws were introduced. How many women were
involved in the decision making-process? How many women are members of the Sharia courts that decide cases concerning women in their
relations with their husbands? These and many other examples are in-
stances of oppression and injustice against women, which make them
vulnerable and leave them open to exploitation economically, socially,
politically, biologically, psychologically and also in the field of religion, by their male counterparts.

4. The Responsible Agents for the Prevention of HIV/AIDS

The prevention of the spread of HIV should be the concern of everyone since it is a human disease, and anyone could be infected. However, there are those who should show greater interest in this struggle
on behalf of the populace, such as the government, religious leaders,
etc.

---

61 K.T. KELLY, *New Directions in Sexual Ethics*, 8-9.
62 I refer here to the different religious faiths. Later, however, my focus will be on
the Catholic Church.

4.1 *The Role of the Government*

The role of the government is that of showing political will and commitment in the prevention of the spread of HIV/AIDS infection. There are so many ways in which this political will and commitment is needed.

The first point is for our leaders to see the current epidemic as a threat not just to some individuals but to the whole society. This epidemic tends to pose a great danger to the growth and development of the country. Therefore our leaders should strive to be at the forefront of the crusade to curb its further spread. The effort of the present administration of President Obasanjo needs to be commended in this regard. However, a lot can still be done. The commitment should not just be at the federal government level alone, but also at the state and local government levels.

In addition, some of the activities needed to curb the spread of the disease, such as information and enlightenment campaign, testing for HIV, etc., that will be highlighted later on, can be successfully carried out only when there are sufficient resources and funds. The fight against HIV/AIDS cannot be won without sufficient financial resources. For instance, in the Sentinel report produced by the Federal Ministry of Health, lack of funds was one of the reasons given for the government's inability to track the situation of HIV/AIDS in the country.[63] To this end therefore, the government has to make funds available.

It is also important and necessary to make funds available in the area of health care systems, so that health care is made accessible and affordable to all those who need it. As a matter of fact, if the amount allocated for the defense and security in the last fifteen years were spent on health and fighting HIV/AIDS, perhaps the high prevalence rate that we have in the country could have been averted. (See appendix b tables demonstrating the Federal Government Budget allocations). Funds are also needed in the area of research, which at the moment is not encouraging. If we are to effectively prevent the further spread of HIV/AIDS, it is important to prevent illness and disease through the improvement of the health care systems both in the urban and rural centers. The importance of good and improved health care systems cannot be over emphasized. The reason is that with good health care systems, there can be

---

[63] NASCP/FMOH, 11.

early diagnosis or detection, and early treatment of infectious diseases such as tuberculosis, sexually transmitted diseases, etc., which are associated with, and can enhance the rapid spread of HIV/AIDS. This then calls for improved health care systems. This means that when illness does occur, there is need to provide care, and particularly to prevent the disarray in the health care systems that would threaten the quality of available medical attention. Thus as HIV and related illness begin to strain existing health care services in the country, access to treatment is critical.

Also, the government must collaborate with religious groups and the non-governmental organizations to effectively prevent the spread of disease. This need for cooperation and collaboration may be difficult, especially when there are conflicting values, for example, in the area of the effectiveness of condoms to contain the spread of infection. This is why political will and commitment are also necessary in the areas of objective information and communication. For instance, the populace should be enlightened about the nature of the virus and how it is transmitted; how it can be contained, especially by abstaining from indiscriminate genital intercourse.

Political commitment also calls for legislation that will outlaw social discrimination such as the refusal to treat HIV patients, discrimination from work or housing, etc. This will equally involve having legislation making the transfusion of blood without screening an offense in the public and private hospitals and clinics. This is to ensure that infected blood is not transfused to uninfected patients. However, this legislation is to be backed with genuine action because it is meaningless to have legislation that will not be implemented and enforced.

Legislation of laws will also be necessary, for instance, in the disruption of the infrastructure of our public health system and health care facilities. A situation where health personnel divert whatever goods or equipment meant for the welfare and maintenance of sound health of the whole public to their private enterprises, is not only unjust, but also gravely immoral, since such action jeopardizes and threatens the wellbeing of the whole society. For the above reason, the government needs to enact laws and be ready to enforce these laws. In this way, public health will be safeguarded.

Political will and commitment is also crucial for making the hard political choices involved in the prevention of HIV/AIDS, like the possibility of needle exchange programs for drug users, sexual health education in schools, etc. In this regard, there is need for political prudence: that is, what is the actual situation in the field, namely, the HIV/AIDS situation of the country, the level of its awareness, then, what is it that could be done.

Finally, the government role in the fight against the spread of HIV/AIDS will ultimately be tested in the ability of the leaders to eschew personal ambition and corrupt practices and show themselves as true leaders. This conviction is based on the fact that the social, economic and political problems of Nigeria as described in the second chapter have largely been due to lack of true and committed leaders. To this effect, I find the view of Chinua Achebe to be prophetic. He says:

> The trouble with Nigeria is simply and squarely a failure of leadership. There is nothing basically wrong with the Nigerian land, or climate or water or air or anything else. The Nigerian problem is the unwillingness or inability of its leaders to rise to the responsibility, to the challenge of personal example, which are the hallmarks of true leadership.[64]

The result of this pathetic plight is the multiple crises the country is now facing, of which HIV/AIDS is a major issue.

4.2 *The Non-Governmental Organization*

The task of fighting the spread of the HIV/AIDS epidemic is not, and should not be, left to the government alone. It must involve every sector and fabric of our society. This is why and where the non-governmental organizations (NGOs) have pivotal roles to play.

Either individuals, groups or corporate bodies can form the NGOs. For instance, the Justice Development and Peace Commission (JDPC) of the Catholic Church is an example of an NGO. Through this department of the Catholic Church, the social support and social identity of the rural communities in particular are enhanced and catered to.

Here, the preventive strategy would focus on HIV/AIDS as a rural community issue rather than urban issue. A concrete example is the needle exchange program, which is more of an urban issue rather than a rural issue. The transmission of HIV in Nigeria is mainly through heterosexual intercourse, hence, to focus on a needle exchange program in the rural areas where many are not aware of the hard drugs, would amount to waste of resources and time. Also in the rural area, it will be useless to focus on the commercial sex workers since those who are in this business live and work mainly in the cities and towns. Thus,

---

[64] C. ACHEBE, *The Trouble with Nigeria*, 15.

through personal contact with the people in the rural areas, the message of HIV/AIDS prevention could bring about positive community responses.

The strategy must include not only basic information about AIDS, but also must challenge individuals to examine and confront their fears and biases, to reduce community hysteria and discriminatory acts toward people living with AIDS and their families. The positive outcome of this approach would be that people would see the HIV/AIDS prevention project as their own and not just coming from the government, hence, more community HIV/AIDS ownership.

In addition, individuals and corporate organizations are needed to work for the prevention of HIV/AIDS. This could be done in terms of care provided for those already infected so that they do not go on infecting others. A good example of non-governmental organizations running supportive services for those infected with HIV in the country is the *Networks on Ethics and Rights and Support and Care of HIV/AIDS*,[65] at Badagry, Lagos. This organization provides succor for poor people living with HIV. The need to support initiatives such as the above, and to have more people and corporate bodies to follow in this line cannot be over emphasized. To say that the government alone cannot do it is to say the obvious. Femi Soyinka rhetorically emphasizes that the Non-Governmental Organizations are indispensable for HIV/AIDS prevention, in an interview. He says:

> If those whose duties and responsibilities are to protect the rights and provide the basic needs and care for the welfare of the citizens, do not care if institutions are not provided with necessary tools to care, if health-care givers renege on their professional oath and fail to care, then who will care for the millions of Nigerians including children with the virus and stand the risk of getting infected.[66]

The above is the motive for which his organization was founded, that is, to provide succor for these unfortunate people.

In addition, the NGO is needed also in the area of funding. The government alone may be unable to provide and fund all HIV/AIDS projects, for example, in the area of research. I believe that there are many brilliant and gifted Nigerians who are capable and could come up with effective vaccine to block the virus, but for lack of funds are un-

---

[65] This organization is founded and owned by Femi Soyinka, Professor of Venereology, Obafemi Awolowo University Teaching Hospital. Ile-Ife, Osun State.

[66] F. SOYINKA, in F. ADEKEYE, «Before They Die», 41.

able to optimize their talents and gifts. There are abundant examples to justify this claim. Therefore, corporate bodies and wealthy individuals in the country are indispensable and are needed to rise to the challenge of making funds for research available. The time is ripe for us to act as individuals and corporate bodies to fight the disease. I therefore agree with Aylward Shorter and Edwin Onyancha in their view that «to peg the AIDS research to the marketing strategies of Euro-American pharmaceutical companies is ultimately short – sighted».[67]

Finally, though subject to debate, another effective way of prevention is to encourage those people whose behaviors put them at risk to come together as a body or an organization. They should be encouraged and trained so that they, too, in turn can be peer educators. In this way, they will be protecting themselves, as well as the wider society. This vision has been embarked upon in some parts of the country. Sex workers were trained to be peer educators to work with clients and other sex workers.[68] Their work, for instance, is specifically to educate their peers to insist on using the condoms for both vaginal and oral sex and its correct use. These people should not be stigmatized; rather they must be encouraged until they are able to arrive at mature decisions, when they will quit their present lifestyle. Practices such as the training of sex workers in the campaign against HIV/AIDS, as William and colleagues point out, have been shown to be effective for the prevention of the disease.[69]

4.3 The Role of Developed Countries

It is an undeniable fact that the HIV/AIDS epidemic is a global issue. This epidemic has taken a sad toll already in many countries, though, with varying effects. Unfortunately, the developing nations in general, and Sub Saharan Africa in particular, have a large proportion of the cases of infection.

Consequently, there have been discussions about the role of the developed nations in the fight against the further spread of the disease.[70] For instance, the general consensus in the United Nations Security

---

[67] A. SHORTER – E. ONYANCHA, The Church and AIDS in Africa, 140.

[68] See E. WILLIAM – al., «Implementation», 229-230.

[69] E. WILLIAM – al., «Implementation», 229-230.

[70] This issue was featured during the United Nations Security Council Meeting in New York on Monday January 10, 2000. See C. LYNCH, «AIDS is Security Threat». See also other world newspapers.

Council is that the developed nations have an important role to play in preventing the spread of this disease in the developing countries.

The issue, however, is what role should the developed nations play in assisting the developing nations to halt the diseases spread? Is it a question of moral obligation based on common human history or should it be what we can get in return for what we give? For instance, when the developed nations are giving economic assistance to the developing nations through an agency like the World Bank, the practice has always been to give specific conditions, which in the long run have always proven to be detrimental to the receiving nation.[71] These are big issues to be resolved. This is where one finds the thinking of James Keenan instructive. He called on all to examine how we understand and look at the Continent of Africa. He writes, «Do we see Africa as it actually is, a land where business, industry and farming can prosper? Do we see the future of Africa as reasonably and potentially economically sound? Or do we imagine Africa as an «elective' Charity case».[72]

In the first place, the fact that the human race is a single family makes it imperative for the developed nations to assist. This is the challenge of human solidarity. What happens to one and one's concern should be the concern of all. Thus, the challenge is for «a global mind-set of nations for a commitment to the single family of humankind».[73] Human solidarity reminds us of our power to overcome disaster; hence, we cannot lose the focus that our strength comes from solidarity as members of one human family.[74] Therefore, human solidarity calls for human compassion. This compassion could be expressed in diverse ways. For instance, on the scientific level, the effort to find effective vaccines, drugs etc. Although no cure has been found, yet, important biomedical advances have been made in the treatment of HIV infection with antiviral therapies. The problem, however, is that the majority of the people who are infected cannot afford these medications because of the high cost. To this end, the developed nations who are manufacturers

---

[71] A concrete example is seen in the situation of Nigeria when she applied to the World Bank for a loan in 1986. One of the conditions that was given was the deregulation of the local currency. From that moment to the present time, the local currency has become extremely valueless. Prior to the reception of the loan, the Nigerian currency was at par with the US dollars. Today, the exchange rate is One hundred and twenty Nigerian naira to One US dollar.

[72] J.F. KEENAN, «Making a Case for Casuistry», 185.

[73] B.D. SCHOUB, *AIDS and HIV in Perspective,* 253.

[74] See JOHN PAUL II, «Pope Addresses Vatican AIDS Conference».

of these drugs can help to lower their prices and render them accessible to the vast majority who could benefit from them.

Finally, the assistance to combat the spread of HIV/AIDS should be done not just with a short-term political imperative because quite apart from any moral perspective, there is the economic dimension that must be considered, based on the increasing awareness of global economy. Because of the global economy, the HIV/AIDS crisis will eventually affect investors around the world. Thus, investment in a global response will in the long term, protect the health and economic prospects of the developed nations themselves. Therefore, one would hope that the international interlinking of economies would increase the rest of the world's awareness of the crisis and lead to a shared sense of responsibility to assist those who suffer from this human tragedy.

4.4 *The Role of the Religious Bodies*

It is true that Nigeria is a secular state, yet religion and religious activities are part and parcel of the people's activities. It as a result of this fact that I am convinced that in the fight against HIV/AIDS, the different religious groups that are found in the country can, and should be involved. This could be achieved through their teachings and the correct observance of the demands of their doctrines. In this work, I will limit myself to the Catholic Church and the Islamic religion alone.

4.4.1 The Catholic Church in Particular

The HIV/AIDS crisis presents a number of challenges to the Catholic Church, which therefore has a great role to play in the control of the spread of HIV/AIDS. There are a number of reasons for this conviction. The opening words of Vatican II's document *Gaudium et Spes*, gives the setting. It says: «The joys and hopes, the griefs and anxieties of the people of this age, especially those who are poor or in any way afflicted, these, too, are the joys and hopes, the griefs and anxieties of the followers of Christ».[75] The HIV/AIDS epidemic fits the situation described in this document.

In addition, the epidemic challenges our faith as individual members of the Church and collectively, to realize what God is saying to us in a particular situation. Therefore, the Church has to be authentic sign of Christ's presence in the world and she needs to demonstrate that

---

[75] VATICAN II, The Pastoral Constitution of the Church in Modern World, *Gaudium et Spes*, no. 1.

both in words and actions as Christ did. As already shown in this work, those who are infected with the virus not only experience suffering, but there is also loneliness, abandonment, guilt and shame. It is in the face of this dramatic situation that the Church must move decisively both to help halt the spread of the disease, as well as to show care and support to those who are already infected.

It is heart warming, for instance, to read in the statement of the Administrative Board of the U. S. Catholic Conference «The many Faces of AIDS – A Gospel Response», where the bishops of the United States say, «Jesus has revealed to us that God is compassionate, not vengeful. That every person made in God's image is of inestimable worth. All human life is sacred and its dignity must be respected and protected».[76] That document further says:

> The Gospel acknowledges that disease and suffering are not restricted to one group or class. Rather, the history of the human condition is such that in one way or the another all will face pain, reversal and ultimately the mystery of death itself. Through sharing in the cross of Christ, human suffering and pain have redemptive meaning and goal. They have the potential of opening a person to new life. They also present an opportunity and a challenge to all, calling us to respond to suffering just as Jesus did – with love and care.[77]

It is against this background that I believe that the Church in Nigeria, too, must move and act. There are a number of ways in which the Church can contribute positively in the prevention of this deadly disease. Her role will be basically pastoral, educational and social, which involves training counselors and home – based care workers, etc.

She needs to pay particular attention to the right presentation of her theology of human sexuality if she hopes to make her impact felt in the fight against this deadly disease.[78] I will elaborate on this point under the section on human sexuality in the next chapter. It must be added, though, that it is important to integrate courses on the topic of HIV/AIDS in the seminary curriculum, for instance. This is important so as to inform and educate her future ministers, who will be in the field, to enlighten people on how they can avoid being infected, as well as care for those already afflicted with the disease.

---

[76] USCC ADMINISTRATIVE BOARD, «The Many Faces of AIDS», 483.
[77] USCC ADMINISTRATIVE BOARD, «The Many Faces of AIDS», 483.
[78] Cf. J. BACKE, «AIDS: A Serious and Special Opportunity», 252-253.

In addition, the hierarchy must see this moment as a «kairos» time to exercise their authority as shepherds, by establishing an office for HIV/AIDS affairs on the national level to liaise with the government and other agencies that are working for the prevention of the disease. It will also be desirable if each diocese can create a department or ministry for the HIV/AIDS patients that will coordinate the activities of the care and support groups.

The epidemic of HIV/AIDS also challenges the Church to review her pastoral approach and mission in our changing world. To this end, the Church must make use of her theologians to discern ways and manners to meet with the fresh and sometimes crucial challenges that the epidemic is posing, like in the case of a marriage between HIV-positive persons or intending HIV-discordant couples.

The importance of compassion and not judgment need to be stressed, too, in order to deal with the problem of stigmatization and isolation that the carriers of the virus and their families encounter in the communities.[79] In this way, there will be more awareness and openness about the disease, which will definitely help people. Openness will help relieve the heavy burden of guilt people feel. I strongly believe that beginning to accept HIV/AIDS as human brokenness and as a reality that we have to live with, will go a long way toward healing the disease in the sense of being spiritually able to cope with it, something that at the moment is absent.

4.4.2 The Islamic Religion

The Islamic religion is one of the major religions that is practised in the country, thus it is necessary to devote a section of this work to the role the Islamic religion can and should play in the fight against the spread of HIV/AIDS in Nigeria.

One of the areas that I perceive that the Muslims should look into in the effort to fight the spread of HIV/AIDS will be the issue of polygamy. It is true that the Islamic religion is not opposed to polygamous practice, yet with the enormous problem of HIV/AIDS and the risk of transmission, it will be desirable that members of this religious affiliation should be encouraged to opt for monogamy.

---

[79] Cf. N.J. WERT, «The Biblical and Theological Basis», 231-242; B. ZION, «The Orthodox Church», 243-248; J. FILOCHOWSKI, «A Measure of Our Humanity», 262-272.

5. How to Realize the Goals of HIV/AIDS Prevention

As seen in chapter two, one of the difficulties of AIDS prevention programs is the tendency to see the disease as that of other people. Also, the continuing tendency of describing some people as belonging to «high risk groups» does not help this situation. The foremost barrier to effectively integrating HIV/AIDS education is the fear and stigma that individuals and, even entire communities experience, when people disclose their HIV status. It is on this basis that any approach to preventing the spread of HIV/AIDS must make educational campaigns a priority. This educational approach can be achieved in the following ways:

5.1 *Information and Enlightenment Campaign*

Given the history of low seroprevalence HIV rates in Nigeria at the beginning of the outbreak of the epidemic in the world, it is only recently that the country has been confronted with the complex psychosocial realities, which accompany HIV/AIDS. As earlier noted, HIV/AIDS was identified historically as a disease of homosexuals and hard drug users, especially in the developed world, whereas, in Nigeria, it was historically seen as a «white man's» disease. These are false assumptions and were so proven by the current epidemiological trend. The fact remains that this denial has facilitated a corresponding lack of ownership of HIV/AIDS as a public health threat in the country. To this effect, therefore, information and enlightenment campaigns become a necessary tool in the fight against the further spread of the disease.

The first step in the information and enlightenment campaign is to attempt to decrease the fear and stigma about the disease, while at the same time, it must seek to increase a sense of community ownership of the epidemic. In other words, information and enlightenment campaigns make the disease and its prevention everybody's concern. This is necessary given that there is ignorance and misinformation about the transmission of the disease. As a result, proper and right information will serve to eliminate the false assumptions that those who are HIV positive are infected because of their lifestyle or sexual orientation, or even as a result of divine punishment.[80]

---

[80] Richard McCormick makes this point too. He calls for separating the medical problems and conditions from value judgments about the lifestyle that may have caused it. See R. MCCORMICK, *The Critical Calling,* 318.

As a matter of fact, information and enlightenment have to focus on, and should target the population that is not yet infected, so that they can stay uninfected and at the same time they can become less hostile and more tolerant towards those already infected. This of course does not imply complete exclusion of those already infected or those at the risk of infection. Thus, information and enlightenment campaigns should strive to bridge, and perhaps, to eliminate the dichotomy created between the «ill» and the «well», or what has now been socially reconstructed as between the «good» and the «bad».[81]

In addition, information and enlightenment campaigns are also important because there is a tendency to maintain that the disease is only for a certain class of people. The fact, however, is that there is no individual or social group that cannot contract the disease. It has been demonstrated that even professionals in the medical field are not immune from the disease.[82] Thus our social class or status, or even our knowledge, is not a guarantee of being free from the HIV/AIDS infection.

The next issue is to determine and formulate the right content for the information and enlightenment campaigns. As with any good project, if the right choices are not made at the right time and to the right audiences, the desired goal may not be met. Consequently, the contents of the information and enlightenment campaigns are to be formulated in such ways that must respect the cultural values and norms of the people they address. At the same time, they must seek to correct whatever false cultural beliefs exist. The following remark of J. Stephen McDaniel, et al. drives home the point:

> ...The educational AIDS message must be delivered in a culturally competent manner that makes effective use of skills, resources, and knowledge that are pertinent and responsive to the cultural values and norms, strengths, needs, and self-determined goals of the audience.[83]

While cultural values must be taken seriously, information campaigns must also endeavor to correct and challenge cultural values that could be obstacles to the successful fight against HIV/AIDS. Some concrete examples are wife inheritance and polygamy.

---

[81] L. MORRISON – S. GURUGE, «We Are a Part of All That We Have Met», 198.

[82] This fact is brought out in the story of a young Professor, a specialist in infectious disease who became infected himself. See J.H. PELÀEZ, «Educating for HIV Prevention», 144-145.

[83] J.S. McDANIEL – D.J. ISENBERG – D.G. MORRIS – R.Y. SWIFT, «Delivering Culturally Sensitive AIDS Education», 174.

Apart from the content, another important factor will be to find the right language. As a country colonized by the British, Nigeria maintains English as the official language. Yet there are over three hundred and fifty indigenous languages. Given this factor one of the difficulties the information and enlightenment campaigns will face is how to develop their messages in these various local languages. Although the literacy level in the country is relatively high,[84] yet, the need to develop the messages in the local languages is necessary. If this is not done one cannot expect any meaningful achievement. The message must reach the grass root levels. The reason for this is not far-fetched. A good number of those already infected are those of low education, so also are those who are at risk of infection. Besides, the messages will be well accepted and assimilated if they are developed in the local languages, using the cultural sayings and idioms of the people.

However, for the information and enlightenment campaigns to be successful, there is the need to train the people who will do this job. These people need to acquire the necessary skills, as well as to be well informed about the nature of the disease. So, there is need for «communication skills». As Jorge Pelàez observes, «prevention campaigns require highly professional knowledge of communication regarding messages, motivations, and image management».[85]   In my opinion those who do this work may not necessarily be geniuses or intellectuals. However, they need some basic skills and training in the diverse areas of human endeavors like education, psychology, theology, communication and human relations, and of course, some medical understanding of the nature of the disease is equally necessary.

In addition, other materials would also be used for conveying this information — films, television documentaries, and radio shows, workshops and seminars that could also be used in the classroom. In this regard one notices that this is already in place in the country.[86] Besides, another important area where this could be achieved, but often times neglected, is through a one – to – one meeting with one's doctor, even when the encounter is not related to the problem of the AIDS disease.[87]

---

[84] See N. ONISHI, «Against Tough Odds», 1, 18.

[85] J.H. PELÀEZ, «Educating for HIV Prevention»,146.

[86] See L. SHOKUNBI, «AIDS, harbinger of Poverty», 15.

[87] Flynn strongly suggests that AIDS education should not be left to parents and schools alone, but that the doctor's office provides an excellent setting also. E.P. FLYNN, *Issues in Health Care Ethics*, 133-134.

Finally, it must be stated that information and enlightenment campaigns are important and necessary. It is, however, important that detailed and objective information must be the hallmark, especially as regards the preventive measures to be taken to avoid being infected. This point must be emphasized in order to counteract, and to avoid a situation of using information as a tool of advocating «safe-sex» in a way that promotes promiscuity.[88]   An information and enlightenment campaign, important as it is in my opinion, will be a secondary preventive measure.

5.2 *Testing and Screening for HIV*

As this sub-title shows, we can only talk of testing and screening for HIV. There is no such thing as «AIDS test». This is because the underlying disease is HIV infection, with AIDS only representing the manifestations of the disease.

The term «screening», according to James Childress, usually refers to testing groups, while the term «testing» usually refers to testing individuals. It is, however, admitted that there is no sharp distinction between the two terms.[89]

The presence of HIV in an individual is diagnosed by a series of tests performed on the person's blood sample, to check for the presence of antibodies to the virus. Testing for HIV antibodies that are currently being employed involves two steps: an initial screening test, and a more specific confirmatory test. The first test is known as ELISA (Enzyme-Linked ImmunoSorbent Assay). In the ELISA, blood from the individual is placed in a test tube containing a HIV antigen preparation. If antibodies against HIV are present, the serum will become attached to the HIV antigens. The excess serum is washed away and a chemical is then added. If the chemical is colored, it indicates the presence of human antibodies.[90]

The second test, which is the confirmatory test, is the Western Blot (WB) assay. In the WB, HIV antigens are placed on filter paper, which is then subjected to a strong electric current. Then, blood from the person being tested for HIV is placed on the paper. If the individual's immune system has made antibodies directed against viral antigens, they will stick to the paper at the location of their target antigen. The final

---

[88] See R. McCormick, *The Critical Calling,* 321.
[89] J. Childress, «Mandatory HIV Screening and Testing», 745.
[90] Cf. J. Fuller, «HIV/AIDS: An Overview», 25. Mimeographed article.

step of this procedure is that the blood sample being tested is washed away and markers are added to the paper to detect the presence of human antibodies, showing a characteristic «fingerprint» of HIV in the person who has been infected.[91]

It must be noted that the combined tests are not 100% accurate, as there is possibility for false positives or false negatives.[92] The accuracy (or the predictive power) of the test result depends upon the risk for HIV infection in the individual being tested. A positive test in someone with a high-risk history has a low chance of being falsely positive.

On the other hand, a negative test in someone with a high-risk history has an appreciable chance of being falsely negative.[93] The fact that a negative test in someone with a history of high-risk activity could be falsely negative should never be interpreted as absolute proof of one's inability to transmit the virus, or as a justification for engaging in irresponsible sexual or needle-sharing activity. This is the problem of having a false negative test result as it provides a deceptive and illusory comfort. False positive test results, on the other hand, could be a bedrock for psychological and social problems. For instance, on the psychological level, it could lead to worry, suffering, and sometimes, suicide.[94] On the social level, the risks include discrimination, stigma, breaches of confidentiality, etc.

The moral justification for testing individuals or screening populations for antibodies to HIV has been extensively debated.[95] These debates have been more pronounced in the developed countries, especially in countries that recognize and protect individual rights and liberties.

The issue at stake, according to Childress, is to resolve the difficult question of when the public health justifies overriding these rights and liberties.[96] The protection of public health is a legitimate concern or even a moral imperative based on fundamental moral principles, like

---

[91] J. FULLER, «HIV/AIDS: An Overview», 26. See also, CENTERS FOR DISEASE CONTROL, «Interpretive Criteria», 694-695.

[92] J.P. PHAIR – S. WOLINSKY, «Diagnosis of Infection», 13-16.

[93] Cf. J. FULLER, «HIV/AIDS: An Overview», 26-27; K.H. MAYER – al., «Human T-lymphotropic Virus», 194-196; D.S. BURKE – al., «Measurement of False Positive Rate», 961-964.

[94] P. MARZUK – al., «Increased Risk», 1333-37; J. FOREMAN, «Suicides Raise Questions», 17.

[95] INSTITUTE OF MEDICINE – NATIONAL ACADEMY OF SCIENCES, Confronting AIDS, 112-130.

[96] J.F. CHILDRESS, «Mandatory HIV Screening and Testing», 741.

beneficence, nonmaleficence, justice, and respect for personal autonomy.[97]

To clearly understand the ethical issues around screening and testing, a further distinction is necessary. James Childress proposed a helpful taxonomy of screening and testing programs. According to him, screening and testing may be consensual or compulsory, and universal or selective.[98] The debates on screening and testing center mainly on whether testing should be mandatory or voluntary, universal to all or selective to some identified groups, such as prostitutes, homosexual persons, hemophiliacs, etc.[99]

Mandatory screening and testing refers to the obligation imposed on the one to be tested or on the tester or on both. For example, in the context of screening blood donated for transfusions, the term «mandatory» here refers to the obligation imposed on organizations collecting blood.

Furthermore, in the ethical consideration on mandatory screening and testing for HIV, there is a distinction between persons and objects – such as blood, organs, sperm and ova, etc. In the context of screening of objects, mandatory testing could be morally justifiable for two reasons. First, screening and testing would help to serve the purpose of universal precaution against infection from HIV. The second justifying reason is that the recipients of these objects cannot take other measures to protect themselves.

The problem with mandatory screening and testing comes with regard to persons. In this instance, the debate is on the universal mandatory screening and testing. James Childress lists five ethical conditions that he considers necessary to justify mandatory screening and testing.[100] These conditions, which he called «justificatory conditions», are effectiveness, proportionality, necessity, least infringement, and explanation and justification to the parties.

---

[97] For these principles, see T.L. BEAUCHAMP –J.F. CHILDRESS, *Principles of Biomedical Ethics*, 120-394; T.A. SHANNON, *An Introduction to Bioethics*, 22-27.

[98] J.F. CHILDRESS, «Mandatory HIV Screening and Testing», 745; also, J.F. CHILDRESS, «Mandatory HIV Screening and Testing», in F. REAMER, ed., *AIDS and Ethics*, 56.

[99] J.F. CHILDRESS, «Mandatory HIV Screening and Testing», 745. See also, L. WALTERS, «Ethical Issues», 708-718.

[100] J.F. CHILDRESS, «Mandatory HIV Screening and Testing», 743. For similar reasons, see R. BAYER – C. LEVINE – S.M. WOLF, «HIV Antibody Screening», 1768-1774. C. LEVINE – R. BAYER, «The Ethics of Screening», 1661-1667; L. WALTERS, «Ethical Issues», 708-718.

According to Childress and most commentators, mandatory screening and testing is not an effective policy in protecting the public health. It needs to be repeated at regular intervals to monitor changes in antibody status. The cost of such a program is too high and so the money could be diverted to another program in education. It is not a necessity since the outcome of the result does not translate into cure and care; hence, it is incompatible with the principle of beneficence. The identification and disclosure to the individuals who are seropositive do not translate into benefits for others, without additional interventions like counseling. The policy of mandatory screening and testing involves a violation of the principle of the respect for autonomy, and would also be an offshoot for discriminatory practices.[101]

As for selective screening and testing, there are different ethical issues. Some of the main concerns for such programs are the questions of who should be encouraged to be tested or who should be selected? What will be the consequences of such actions on the target groups or individuals? Is there any justification to support the singling out of particular individuals or groups? Who will bear the costs? These are fundamental questions and are of legitimate concerns.

There has been the suggestion for selective testing and screening of certain groups: the «high–risk» groups, such as commercial sex workers, homosexuals, intravenous drug users, hemophiliacs, etc. The problem is that to think this way already entails some bias and a kind of stereotype attitude.[102] For example, while people differ with regard to homosexual practice, it is not necessarily true that a homosexual person is a likely or potential carrier of HIV. It is true that if homosexual persons engage in indiscriminate and unprotected sex, they are exposing themselves to risk, but this is equally true and applicable to heterosexual persons. The fact then is that it is not one's sexual orientation that makes one a potential target for HIV infection rather, it is one's behavior.

In addition, some suggestions have been made, and even in some cases, some policies have been introduced for mandatory selective screening. For example, the Federal Government of Nigeria has proposed to make HIV test compulsory for couples intending marriage,

---

[101] J.F. CHILDRESS, «Mandatory HIV Screening and Testing», 743. For similar reasons, see R. BAYER – C. LEVINE – S.M. WOLFE, «HIV Antibody Screening», 1768-1774. C. LEVINE – R. BAYER, «The Ethics of Screening», 1661-1667; L. WALTERS, «Ethical Issues», 708-718.

[102] Cf. M. ANGELL, «A Dual Approach», 181.

that is, those applying for marriage license.[103] I think this proposal is ethically not sound, and as such is unacceptable for various reasons, some of which have been mentioned earlier under the ethical considerations for mandatory testing. The cost of implementing such a program will be too high for the country; thus it is an economically unsound proposal. There is also the issue of privacy and personal autonomy. The proposal, if approved, could drive many away from applying for marriage license or from marriage entirely. In addition, the fact that those tested prove negative does not mean they cannot be infected in the future. Hence, I do not think that enacting a law that makes premarital testing for HIV is a step in the right direction. Information about the risk of HIV and education to avoid infection are viable alternatives.

The proposal for premarital HIV testing makes the concern expressed by Bayer a justified one. He says:

> The threat of AIDS may elicit Draconian measures and an unreasoned reliance upon coercion that could, while justified in the name of the public health, actually subvert the prospects of effective public health policy.[104]

However, I disagree with Bayer on the fact that Draconian measures such as compulsory HIV testing can be justified even in the name of public health.

Given all that has been said about mandatory screening and testing, whether it is selective or universal, I believe that the best thing to do at the moment is to encourage voluntary testing for HIV.

5.3 Counseling to take the HIV Test and Counseling Those Already Infected

I wish to address the issue of counseling as a preventive measure under these two categories, namely: counseling to take the HIV test and counseling that focuses on those already infected. While information and enlightenment campaigns target the larger society in general, especially those who feel they are not at risk, counseling to take the HIV test as a preventive strategy, targets those who are HIV negative but whose behavior is risky enough to make them easy targets of the virus. It also targets the asymptomatic HIV – positive persons identified through HIV testing centers, hospital inpatients, clinic outpatients, etc. The importance of counseling the asymptomatic HIV positive-persons,

---

[103] EDITORIAL, «Nigeria to Make Pre-Marriage HIV Check Compulsory».
[104] R. BAYER, *Private Acts*, p. 4.

in my view, should be given serious attention, as they constitute the greatest risk group of infecting others. It is necessary to note that there is need for counseling before testing and also after testing. This is why commentators on this issue speak of pre- and post - test counseling.[105]

The goals of counseling are to stop the spread of HIV and limit the pain it causes. A critical look at these goals would reveal that they are preventive and supportive. Sometimes, though, these goals overlap and are not easily distinguishable. The emphasis on one or the other depends on the target population, the program providing the service, and the population served. The aim is to let people, especially those who know or feel that they have exposed themselves to risk, come to know if they are HIV positive or HIV negative. If the result of the test comes out negative, through post test counseling, these people would be encouraged not to use their HIV negative status as a license to live careless or carefree lives. In counseling they would be encouraged to stay uninfected. On the other hand, counseling, as a preventive strategy that targets those already infected, aims to encourage these persons of their duty not to expose others to the infection. For instance, the counselor will point out the need to abstain from having sexual relations and where that advice is seen as not a good option, then the need to use prophylactics. There is also the supportive dimension of counseling as already mentioned.

Learning about a positive test for the virus would normally be a shattering experience no matter the kind of lifestyle that an individual lives. The discovery could be accompanied by a sense of guilt, anger and rage, fear, etc. These feelings are fueled by the fact of a hostile environment. That is, environments in which people are ready to blame, condemn, isolate or ostracize those who are seropositive.[106] There is also the thought of imminent death despite the fact that HIV-positive persons could still live healthy and relatively prolonged lives.

How well the HIV positive persons are able to come to grips with their new situation and accept their seropositive status will determine how they will live their lives thereafter. It is possible that some might deliberately go on to infect others out of rage and anger. Some might even go on to be involved in criminal activities that are not only un-

---

[105] S.A. ALLEN – E. KARITA – N. N'GANDU – A. TICHACEK, «The Evolution», 89. Also, L. SHERR, «Counseling and HIV Testing», 42.

[106] This is the point Stuart Bate tries to emphasize when he opines that social isolation of HIV/AIDS persons make their situation more «sickening» than the clinical symptoms themselves. S.C. BATE, «Differences in Confessional Advice», 218-219.

healthy for them, but can also be detrimental to the well-being of the society.[107] For sure, to willingly and knowingly infect others with a fatal disease is a grave matter. But good counseling will point out the obligation one has to avoid this act of deliberately infecting others.

Besides, when these HIV positive persons are reassured through good counseling, then they would know that they are not alone, that the society, their communities, their families, friends, religious groups etc. will care for them, then they will be able to take a positive approach to their «new» life. For instance, there is the need to have good eating habits – eating nutritious foods, then basic hygiene, etc. These positive attitudes are necessary and important especially where medications are not available. In fact, it is believed that counseling, prior to testing as well as immediately upon the receipt of results, could provide the initial point of good therapeutic relationships.[108] This counseling approach aims to help the HIV carriers find meaning and sense of purpose in their situation. This type of counseling bears similarity with what Pelàez calls «accompaniment processes».[109]

In addition, counseling, like information campaigns, should take the cultural dimensions of the peoples' lives into consideration. At the same time, negative counseling skills or oppressive traditional wisdom must be discouraged in the light of our experiences and the challenges that have come from gender conflict situations.[110] A concrete example is the need to counsel seropositive male persons not to coerce their sexual partners to having genital intercourse without first disclosing their seropositive status, and obtaining the consent of their spouses. Then they should be informed and advised to take necessary precaution not to expose others to the virus.

It is therefore necessary that the counselors must be properly trained and should include a team of experts, that is, specialists in some basic areas of human endeavor like medical personnel, psychologists, ethicists, social workers, religious leaders,[111] legal personnel, etc. These people are expected to be sensitive to human needs and problems.

---

[107] See G. GLEESON – D. LEARY, «When Fidelity and Justice Clash», 221.

[108] L. SHERR, «Counseling and HIV Testing», 43.

[109] J.H. PELÀEZ, «Educating for HIV Prevention», 146-147.

[110] See K.T. KELLY, New Directions in Sexual Ethics, 16-17.

[111] Presently many of the religious leaders in the country are not well equipped in this area. By religious leaders we mean both Christian and Moslem leaders and even the traditional healers. The situation described by Stuart Bate in South Africa abounds in Nigeria too. See S.C. BATE, «Differences in Confessional Advice», 213.

The medical personnel are to explain the nature of the disease to the patients, the treatment options and the need to live healthy lifestyles including eating habits, recreational activities, and above all, the need to minimize the viral load in the already troubled immune system of the body.

Psychologists will be expected to provide the psychological framework the people need to cope well with their situation. This aspect will help to reduce or eliminate any unhealthy behavior.

Religious leaders on their part will provide the necessary spiritual dimensions to the people living with HIV, their families, friends and partners. The idea is to show the healing dimension that is needed to cope with the epidemic. Religious leaders, when well equipped, are also in the position to offer sound advice concerning various moral dilemmas posed by the disease.[112] A good example is seen in the case described by Maurizio Faggioni of an HIV infected couple seeking to have children.[113] Whether this couple and those who might read Maurizio's analysis agree with his insight is another story entirely.

Ethicists on the other hand must give the necessary moral framework and support, helping the HIV infected persons to resolve difficult life decisions about their behaviors. Through their sound advice, they will be helping these people to arrive at a mature level of decision-making, resolving the conflicting issues of conscience, etc.

Social workers serve as a bridge between the sufferers and the wide society. They serve to reassure the infected persons that they are not alone in the situation. They rekindle hope, love and acceptance in the infected persons who are like any other persons with a medical problem.

Legal personnel will be of assistance in ensuring that the fundamental human rights of these people are respected and enforced. They are to provide legal counsel and services when the need arises, especially in the issue of discrimination in the areas of employment, housing, insurance, even in access to health care facilities, etc.

Therefore, the counseling approach, unlike information and enlightenment campaigns, requires the services of well-trained counselors and experts. In a situation where the counselors are ill prepared, they may be doing more harm than good to those they seek to help.[114]

---

[112] See S.C. BATE, «Differences in Confessional Advice», 218.
[113] See M.P. FAGGIONI, «An HIV – Infected Italian Woman», 246-254.
[114] S.C. BATE, «Differences in Confessional Advice», 219.

The counseling approach must take cognizance of the essential counseling skills like openness, mutual respect, confidentiality etc. These will help the infected persons to open up to the counseling team in a free manner more than they would normally do to any other person. It needs to be stressed, however, that counseling is meant to aid the person seeking it to have a clear vision of the options available. Counseling is meant to help people take responsibility for their own decisions, to decide for themselves what is best and the most responsible thing to do. Hence, the responsibility to decide and to act ultimately rests on the person seeking counseling. The counselor cannot and should not impose his or her ideas on the person seeking counseling.

Another important area of counseling as a preventive strategy is in the area of vertical transmission prevention. As noted earlier on, the provision of counseling should facilitate, allow, and even promote individual decision – making. Decision – making about treatment to prevent vertical transmission of HIV is even very crucial and necessary. This is necessary, as there is no cure yet, and medical interventions are also still subject to debate, and prophylactics have side effects that ought to be weighed clearly in terms of advantages and disadvantages. It is true that there are a number of advances in interventions; yet, these interventions are subject to questioning. For instance, a trial study showed that the administration of Zidovudine to women during pregnancy, labor, and to the infant for six weeks reduced vertical transmission from 25 to 8.3 per cent.[115] It is, however, unclear which element of the protocol was effective: whether the results generalize to all women with HIV, what are the long – term effects of AZT on the unborn,[116] and the effect of monotherapy on the women's future drug resistance and combination therapy.[117] Counseling, as a preventive strategy in this situation should aim at providing the basis for «informed decisions to help prevent perinatally acquired...(HIV)».[118] Counseling on this level can prove to be difficult. This is because the counselor is not faced with the issue of protection against transmission of HIV via sex (e.g. the adoption of condoms) but a case where the counselor has to wrestle with the need to advise against HIV-infected women from

---

[115] E. CONNOR – al., «Reduction of Maternal Infant Transmission», 1173-1180.

[116] P. ROWE, «US Expert Panel», 258; P. TOLTZIS – al., «Zidovudine», 1212-1218.

[117] For a detailed discussion, see H. MINKOFF – M. AUGENBRAUM, «Antiretroviral Therapy for Pregnant Women», 478-489; also J. LAURENCE, «Zidovudine in Pregnancy», 74-76.

[118] CENTERS FOR DISEASE CONTROL, «Recommendations», 721-726, 731-732.

becoming pregnant or bearing children. This is why it is important to have counselors that are well prepared to meet some of these challenges that the HIV/AIDS epidemic pose.

One final point here is that the country should be able to develop these methods to suit the reality of the situation there. At the same time, she could borrow examples from other places, like having free telephone lines for anonymous calls, information and counseling.[119]

5.4 *The Renewal of Traditional Values and Customs*

In the second chapter I mentioned some cultural practices that endanger peoples' lives and thus make the risk of HIV/AIDS infection high. It is, however, equally true that there are traditional values and customs that can contribute positively to the prevention strategy. The issue then is to find ways and means to reconcile these conflicting values in a way that will be culturally sensitive and at the same time, culturally acceptable to people.

One of the ways of reconciling the conflicting traditional values and customs, for instance, is in the «leviratic custom». This is a common practice in many traditional African customs. This is a situation where the widow of a dead man is «inherited» by the surviving brother of the deceased husband. Some modern African writers are contesting this interpretation of «widow inheritance». They argue that the correct interpretation is the «care of the widow». [120]

The purpose of this custom about widows is to care for them, both for the material needs as well as sexual needs. It is believed that in this way, the widows are not left alone to fend for themselves and their children without adequate care and support. Also, through this practice, widows are not exposed to behaviors that are considered inimical to the values of the community. To better appreciate this, one must understand the fact that in the traditional African society, «sexuality and sexual activity are directed to one end, procreation and continuity of the family, clan or community».[121] What happens in the case of «care of widows», therefore, is that there is no new marriage involved hence it cannot be justly called marriage. At the same time it is said that it is unjust to call it «adultery» or «concubinage». It is not seen as strictly

---

[119] See N. MICHEL, «Fighting AIDS», 156.

[120] See B. KISEMBO – L. MASEGA – A. SHORTER, *African Christian Marriage*, 101.

[121] L. MASEGA, «Recognizing the Reality», 77.

polygamous marriage, nor is it a question of sexual relations outside marriage. It is rather seen as «a marital adjustment in a continuing marriage in which a brother-in-law substitutes temporarily for a deceased legal husband».[122] This practice is also strengthened by the belief in life after death. A critical look at this practice shows that there are some good values inherent therein; hence it will be wrong to dismiss it outrightly. By the same token, good sex educational programs, especially in the time of AIDS, could also point out the negative sides, especially if the risk of transmission exists.

While in the African traditional society the practice of polygamy flourished, based on the desire to have a large family,[123] yet there are still African customs that praise monogamy and encourage people to be monogamous.[124] While the advantages of the practice of polygamy should not be dismissed outright, education can also let people realize that times are changing, and the wisdom of the old about monogamy should be reawakened, especially in this time of HIV/AIDS.

Furthermore, in the aspect of educational programs for HIV/AIDS prevention, the traditional values and customs have a positive contribution that must be tapped. For instance, strong nuclear and extended family was a common feature of the traditional African society; as a result, education of children in the traditional African society was the collective responsibility of the community. The education of children is not just the task of the immediate family but also that of the extended family and, indeed, of the whole community. As a result, it was difficult for any child to misbehave even when the immediate family was not present. The family unity is now under threat as mothers or both parents die from AIDS[125] and the grandparents may be too old, and sometimes too poor as well, to look after their grandchildren. It is therefore necessary to strengthen the extended family system again where

---

[122] B. KISEMBO – L. MASEGA – A. SHORTER, *African Christian Marriage*, 102. See pp. 101-103 for full details of this leviratic custom.

[123] Polygamy in the traditional African Society had a number of well-defined social functions and advantages. There is for instance the socio-economic advantage of the large family in the labor-intensive subsistence economy. Unfortunately, there are no written documents as the reasons are transmitted orally.

[124] This claim, for instance, is found in Yoruba traditional oral saying, that the beauty of married life is experienced in a monogamous marriage.

[125] The situation in Nigeria has not reached that level yet but examples can be seen from other African countries. See A. SHORTER – E. ONYANCHA, *The Church and AIDS in Africa*, 85-92.

where children can enjoy support and care, thereby becoming responsible adults in the future.

In the areas of sexual conduct, even though talk about sex in an explicit manner was a taboo, yet the traditional custom encourages children to live chaste lives, and to abstain from genital intercourse before marriage.[126] People adhered strictly to these instructions not just because of the values inherent in them but because failure to keep them would be discovered not just by the family but the whole community. This in turn means bringing shame not just to oneself but also to the family and community at large. It is, however, important to emphasize that the call for renewal of traditional values is not to be perceived as a means of repressive and negative morals of control;[127] rather, it should be seen as a value that leads to responsible growth in relationship.

What do we find now? With the increasing collapse of the extended family, the responsibility of educating children has fallen now on the immediate family, especially parents. It has to be stated that even at this present time, teachers and school officials do not concern themselves again with the religious and moral formation of their students. The emphasis now is on the need to respect pluralism of opinions and individual liberty. Based on this fact, therefore, it is my conviction that some of the traditional values and customs could contribute positively to the prevention of HIV/AIDS.

In addition, it is important at this time of HIV/AIDS, for parents and community once again to take up the roles they once exercised. This must be done not in an oppressive way (as that may have adverse effects), but in ways that direct and encourage the young people to live responsible lives as youths in order to be able to occupy their places in the larger society as responsible adults.

6. Concluding Remarks

From all that has been said in this chapter, one obvious fact is that everyone agrees that there is need to find an effective way to prevent the further spread of the disease. This preventive effort requires the participation of all and sundry. In a special way, it challenges the government at all levels: national, state, and local government, to act decisively. Some of the ways by which the government is challenged to action are the reduction of poverty, more budgetary allocation to the

---

[126] There are several oral sayings that praise virginity until marriage.
[127] Cf. R. BURGGRAEVE, «From Responsible to Meaningful Sexuality», 308.

health sector, and increase in public awareness. It has also been shown that the Church, that is, the Catholic Church in particular, must see the preventive effort as a challenge as well as a task, especially in the area of her sexual teaching.

Finally, it was pointed out that HIV transmission, like many health problems, is the product of factors operating at multiple levels. In addition to personal behavior, relationships with family and friends, community norms, access to health care, and local laws can affect HIV infection rates. For HIV prevention to make the biggest difference, programs are needed that address all levels of risk: individual, familial, community, medical and legal.

CHAPTER IV

Specific Moral Issues in the Prevention of HIV/AIDS

1. Introductory Remarks

In the last chapter I tried to look at basic principles and approaches that I believe are necessary in prevention strategy against this deadly disease. This chapter deals with some specific moral issues in the prevention strategy. Some have been the subject of lively debates and discussions, namely, the use of prophylactics (condoms) and the needle exchange program. It is not likely that these debates will be laid to rest in the near future.

The aim of this chapter is to examine and engage some of this divergent viewpoint and see what could be learnt in the struggle to curb the rise in the number of infections that occur on a daily basis.

This chapter is divided into three sections. The first section confronts the Church's theology of sexuality by contrasting the manualist's understanding of sexuality that some people still follow, with the contemporary approach to sexuality, and figure out the implications of the contrasting methodologies in relations to HIV/AIDS.

The second section examines the prophylactics debate, that is, the arguments against the use of prophylactics as a preventive measure and the reasons for such a stand. Then, I examine the arguments in support of prophylactics and the reasons for such support.

The third section examines the Needle Exchange Program. Like prophylactics, there are those who argue in favor of it and those who argue against it.

2. Confronting the Theology of Sexuality

In the many diverse cultures in the country one thing appears to be common, namely, attitudes to sex, sexuality and gender roles. These are issues that are not normally discussed openly within these various cultures. It is assumed or even taken for granted that each person will normally and automatically learn what sex is all about.[1]

Consequently, and unfortunately, parents do not discuss sex at home with their children. As a result, many young people's experience of sex talk is from peers who know little or nothing about sexual discourse and the dynamics of human sexuality. In addition, many depend on information from television, print media, internet, etc., where they get information that too often is not clear. Therefore, there is need for meaningful sex education for preventing HIV/AIDS. This is where the Church's teaching on human sexuality is important. Nonetheless, the same teaching, if not properly exposed can be an obstacle in the fight against the epidemic. This is what I seek to deal with in this part of this work.

2.1 *Meaning of Human Sexuality According to Catholic Thought*

There has been a lot of discussion on human sexuality in both secular and religious circles, with the view of expressing what it is and how it should be understood. In this section, the focus is just on the Church's understanding of human sexuality. The conviction is that a thorough understanding of human sexuality and its dynamics can help to prevent the spread of HIV/AIDS.

It is important to note that the way human sexuality was understood and described in the Catholic sexual ethics about four decades ago is not the way it is understood now. Nonetheless, one still finds that there are some Church leaders and even theologians who still present the sexual ethics that was seen in the moral manuals of that era. Therefore, I will examine the two approaches that one sees in the treatment of human sexuality as seen in the Church's sexual ethics. One approach is that which is described as the manualist approach while the other approach is the contemporary. The understanding of these two approaches and methodologies for treating human sexuality has a significant effect on the way human sexuality is to be understood, especially in this «time of HIV/AIDS».[2]

---

[1] It is worth noting that the attitude that each person independently would learn about sex is not limited to the various Nigerian Cultures alone. It is found in some other cultures like the Asian American. See B. AOKI – C. P. NGIN – B. MO – D. T. JA, «AIDS Prevention Models», 290-308.

[2] This is an expression that has been rendered famous by the Irish theologian Enda McDonagh. See E. MCDONAGH, «Theology in a Time of AIDS», 81-89.

2.1.1 Manualist Treatment of Human Sexuality

In the manuals of moral theology, one discovery about human sexuality is that there was no explicit treatment or a clearly defined theology of human sexuality. The question then is what is this traditional approach to the understanding of human sexuality?

The treatment of human sexuality as espoused in the moral textbooks and treatises of the manualist tradition regarded human sexuality as finding its exclusive meaning and purpose only among married couples. From this perspective, the exclusive meaning and purpose of human sexuality is procreation, understood as reproduction.[3] The exclusive meaning and purpose of human sexuality is based on, or limited to, a «simple biological function», that is, the capacity to rear children. The whole idea of manualism is the physical notion of male depositing the semen into the woman's body for fertilization and the reproduction of a new offspring.

A good example of this understanding is seen in the moral treatise of Edwin Healy:

> God, our Creator, has endowed all living creatures with a sacred and wonderous gift, the faculty of generation. Moreover, He has given to each human being a certain vital urge for placing acts belonging to the generative faculty that are conducive to the reproductive species. This vital stimulus is important, for without it the species would be in a grave danger of extinction. This stimulus is called sex urge because it inclines man and woman toward that union which is necessary for procreating children.
>
> …Reason makes it clear that one may yield to the prompting of the sex urge only in the married state, for it is only that state that procreation of children can be achieved according to the design of nature.[4]

The extensive quotation above gives us the insight on how human sexuality is viewed in this manualist approach. The focal point of emphasis is the reproductive aspect as the exclusive meaning and purpose of sexuality. And as mentioned, it is believed that the sex urge is created in the human person for achieving this exclusive primary finality of human sexuality- procreation. Thus, in the manualist tradition, it is

---

[3] The use of procreation in this sense of reproduction is too restrictive because this is just an aspect not the totality of the meaning of the word. Procreation is more than reproduction. I think that procreativity in a broader sense entails sharing of love, intimacy, responsibility, etc. It is because human sexuality is more than reproduction that differentiates our sexuality from that of animals.

[4] E. HEALY, *Moral Guidance*, 188.

believed that the sex urge is natural in human beings because it is for the generation of new life; and the manner of bringing about this purpose finds its true meaning and expression in the married state. This is why Healy concludes that the use of the generative faculty outside the married state is contrary to the demands of nature. The presentation of Healy is a broad representation of human sexuality in this traditional approach.

It is, however, equally true that some theologians in the contemporary period still subscribe to the view in this traditional approach. For instance, Henry Peschke, with specific reference to sexuality writes:

> Sexual love has as its purpose the propagation of mankind through procreation of children. Any unprejudiced evaluation of sexuality will have to agree with the traditional sexual ethics in this affirmation. Procreation of children is the innate, ultimate purpose of man's sexual faculties. The whole sexual structure and inclination indicates the child as its aim. The creator's ultimate intention in providing man with the sexual faculties is the propagation of mankind. The urge for sexual union and the sexual organs themselves would not exist without the necessity of procreation.[5]

This way of looking at human sexuality leaves room for some inherent problems. Does it mean that it is the capacity to reproduce that make one a sexual being? Or is it the totality of human sexuality? To look at sexuality this way, does that not imply negating the sexuality of the celibate or, even the sexuality of the sterile persons? The celibate does not cease to be a sexual person even when he/she freely embraces to be celibate for a perceived value other than the married state. Celibacy does not imply that the celibate will not have sexual urge rather, the celibate person is expected to control his/her urge and channel his/her energy towards living in harmony with the free choice he/she made. As for the sterile persons, they still have sexual urges even though they might be lacking in the capacity for procreation. Sterility is not and would not be an impediment to having genital intercourse.

In pursuance of the exclusive meaning and purpose of human sexuality as reflected in the «manualist» approach, we have further insights given by theologians of the «traditional» era that even in the married state, the sexual instinct is social, directed to the good of the race, rather than personal. It is believed that the sexual difference between man and woman is in view of the ultimate sexual union of man and

---

[5] H.C. PESCHKE, *Christian Ethics*, II, 379.

woman, and the sexual union is for the purpose of offspring.[6] On this, Healy says, «the sex urge is intended not for the good of the individual, but for the good of the human race; that is, the conservation of the species».[7] From this, we see that even the expression of the sexual urge in the married state is not for personal satisfaction but for the multiplication and conservation of the human species. Consequently, in this approach, sexual pleasure, even among married couples is viewed as a manifestation of sin. It will be venial sin if it occurred among married couples; it is seen as mortal sin if it happened outside of marriage.[8]

In showing that human sexuality is seen and treated exclusively in relation to marriage, the whole treatment of sexuality in the manualist approach is presented in the context of the sixth and ninth commandments. In the thinking of these theologians, these commandments are directed toward helping achieve the objective meaning and purpose of sexuality, procreation, which finds proper realization in the married state. Thus, the sixth and ninth commandments are guides to help attain the ends of marriage. The sixth commandment says, «You shall not commit adultery».[9] The ninth says, «You shall not covet your neighbor's wife».[10] These two commandments are part of the Decalogue given by Yahweh to Moses on Mount Sinai. These two commandments, like all the others, are concerned with regulating the conduct of married couples in accordance with the demands of their covenant relationship to God. Commenting on these precepts, Davis writes:

> By the sixth commandment, adultery alone is forbidden explicitly, but all actions which are intended to lead or which naturally lead to it, and all actions contrary to the orderly propagation of the race are implicitly forbidden. By the ninth commandment all lustful thoughts and desires are forbidden.[11]

From this quotation, one notices that both commandments treat the same subject matter, that is, whatever is opposed to the orderly propagation of the race according to the dictates of nature. The dictates of nature are carried out in a manner «permitted» as «legitimate» in the married state only. Any contrary attitude is seen as wrong and sinful.

---

[6] See F. CUNNINGHAM, ed., *The Christian Life*, 173.

[7] E. HEALY, *Moral Guidance*, 188.

[8] See H. JONE – U. ADELMAN, *Moral Theology*, 1.

[9] Exodus 20:14. Citation from the Revised Standard Version, Catholic Edition.

[10] Exodus 20:17.

[11] H. DAVIS, *Moral and Pastoral Theology*, II, 172.

As already noted, in the traditional approach, sexual expression and sexual pleasure are licit in marriage when they do not in any way interfere with the possibility of generation of new life. In this approach, however, there is another important element in the treatment of human sexuality, that is, the role of pleasure. The regulation of the sixth and ninth commandments can be said to explicitly forbid adultery and impure desires, while implicitly, however, they command the practice of chastity.

According to Davis, chastity is «the moral virtue that controls in the married and altogether excludes in the unmarried all voluntary expression of the sensitive appetite for venereal pleasure».[12] He goes on to say:

> The rational motive of the virtue of Chastity is the reasonableness of controlling sexual appetite in the married and excluding it in the unmarried, as also of seeking and expressing it in marriage in a rational way, unless the exercise of some higher virtue or more pressing duty justify complete continence, temporary or perpetual, without prejudice to the rights of others. Chastity is a virtue for every state of life. There is chastity of the married and of the unmarried. Perfect chastity is abstinence from all expressions of the sexual appetite, both in the external act and internal thought, desire and complacency. This virtue connotes a great victory over an imperious appetite. Few persons of adult age are immune from this appetite. The practice of virtue is usually arduous, is highly meritorious, gives a man great mastery over himself in this respect, and is pleasing to God.[13]

In this long quotation, the role of pleasure as the determining norm for making moral evaluation of human sexuality is noticeable.[14] Although it is true that pleasure occupies a place of importance in making moral evaluation of human sexuality in this approach, it is nonetheless important to clarify the issue. The question that could be raised is, is pleasure the determinant of morality, or is the marital state the determinant of the morality of pleasure? I think the latter is the focus of this manualist approach. In this thinking, venereal pleasure is «permitted» as «legitimate» in the married state when it does not interfere with the possibility of generating new life, but it is «grievously sinful» outside wedlock. This is the reason that Davis, like the other representatives of this approach, concludes:

---

[12] H. DAVIS, *Moral and Pastoral Theology*, II, 172.
[13] H. DAVIS, *Moral and Pastoral Theology*, II, 173.
[14] Cf. C.H. POULIN, «The Theology of Human Sexuality», 5.

It is grievously sinful in the unmarried to deliberately accept even the smallest degree of venereal pleasure; secondly, that it is equally sinful to think, say, or do anything with the intention of arousing even the smallest degree of this pleasure.[15]

The primacy of pleasure as a determinant of sexual morality is also clearly illustrated in the following way:

All directly voluntary sexual pleasure is mortally sinful outside of marriage. This is true even if the pleasure be ever so brief and insignificant. Here there is no lightness of matter. Even the individuals in whom the sex urge is abnormally intense (sexual hyperesthesia) can and must control themselves. Indirectly voluntary sexual pleasure is a mortal or venial sin or no sin at all according as the action causing it by nature exercises a great deal or slight influence or none whatsoever upon the stimulation of the sexual appetite.[16]

The attitude in the manualist tradition from the foregoing is that which focuses attention from the beginning on the human person's sexual behavior and then formulates principles to guide that behavior. The exclusive meaning and purpose of human sexuality in the manualist approach is the procreation of children that is realized in marriage. Any sexual act, which does not fulfill this exclusive finality of sexuality or carried out outside of wedlock, is «gravely sinful».

As shall be shown shortly, there are cases that challenge this manualist view of human sexuality. More so, at this time of HIV/AIDS, there are some grave practical implications that must be resolved. For instance, in a situation where we have an HIV – discordant couple, the emphasis should not be on the need to maintain perpetual abstinence; the concern rather should be how do we help the uninfected partner to remain uninfected.

The whole problem with this traditional approach is that the emphasis is just on the «biological function». Besides, it is very negative and legalistic in its tendencies. As Poulin says, rather than saying what sexuality is, the emphasis is on what is forbidden hence, a great outline of sexual sins.[17]

---

[15] H. DAVIS, *Moral and Pastoral Theology*, II, 182.

[16] H. JONE – U. ADELMAN, *Moral Theology*, 1.

[17] C.H. POULIN, *Salvific Invitation and Loving Response*, 27.

2.1.2 Contemporary Approach and Understanding of Human Sexuality

As already seen in the manualist approach, the emphasis in understanding human sexuality hinges on the «biological function» as the exclusive meaning and purpose of sexuality. There emerged a growing dissatisfaction with this way of looking at human sexuality, hence the birth of the contemporary approach, which marks a great shift in emphasis and focus.

In the contemporary approach, the merely «genital and generative» is seen as common to animals, too, whereas human sexuality differs from that of the animals. Donald Goergen explains this fact thus:

> Human sexuality is distinct from other forms of sexuality. It cannot be reduced to animal sexuality. It has that and much more. Sexuality in men and women is human and not an expression of a lower nature. Human sexuality is filled with possibilities other than simply the potential for reproduction. There is more to human sexuality than this biological function. To explain sexuality in terms of its procreative function alone is to reduce it to prehuman sexuality.[18]

In this contemporary approach, the belief is that to really understand the meaning and purpose of human sexuality, it has to be within the context of the human person. That is to say, the whole person that consists of the physical and spiritual dimension. In other words, there should be no dichotomy. The human person in its totality must be the core for understanding human sexuality. William May expresses this view thus:

> Our bodies are not instruments attached to our selves, our persons. I am not one reality and my body another. I am a body, I am an animal. My body and my animality are, indeed, radically different in kind from the body and animality of other animals, precisely because the former are the body and the animality of that unique and special kind of animal that a human being is; but I am nonetheless an animal, and my body is an integral dimension of my self, my personhood. It is not subpersonal, subhuman, an element of physical nature that I can use apart from myself, now for one purpose, now for another.[19]

The whole idea is that there is no dichotomy between the body, which is physical, and the inner reality, which is spiritual. These two are the constitutive elements of the human person. Relating this to hu-

---

[18] D. GOERGEN, *The Sexual Celibate*, 51.
[19] W.E. MAY, *Human Existence, Medicine and Ethics*, 49.

man sexuality, it means then that the physical, the psychic, and the spiritual dimensions of the human person are involved and necessary for understanding the meaning of human sexuality. In this way, one sees the shift in emphasis in this contemporary approach. In this approach human sexuality is seen holistically, with the emphasis on the human person.[20]

In establishing the nature and meaning of human sexuality, the contemporary tendency turned to the revealed word, the Scriptures,[21] as its starting point. The scholars of this approach looked into what is revealed about the human person.

The book of Genesis unfolds for us a theological reflection about the creation of the world and everything in it, which includes the human person. Since the writers of this approach believed that human sexuality is to be understood in the context of the person, thus, they turned to the Scriptures to see what it reveals about our sexuality. The finding is that the first set of human persons, Adam and Eve, (and subsequent human beings), were created in the image and likeness of God. It is written, «God created man in his own image, in the image of God He created him: male and female He created them».[22] From this revelation, it is clear that there are two modes of being human and consequently, of being sexual persons, namely male and female.[23] Human sexuality, therefore, can be said to be a manifestation of how we are created in the image and likeness of God. Thus, human beings are sexual beings by God's design. Consequently, the first thing about human sexuality as revealed by God, and perceived and received in faith, is that we are sexual beings. The human person, however, is a male person or a female person. Thus we have two modes of being sexual, one of which is necessary in order to be a human person.

Being a female or a male is a constitutive aspect of personal identity; hence human sexuality is said to be «essentially personal».[24] As Poulin explains, this means:

---

20 K.T. KELLY, *New Directions in Sexual Ethics*, 35-36.

21 Since the two approaches are concerned with presenting and maintaining Christian Values with regard to sexuality they use the Scriptures in their presentation, but differ in the manner of bringing the scriptural message to bear on their presentations.

22 Gen 1:27. The word «man» is not to be understood here as referring to the masculine gender rather, it applies to the two human species: male and female.

23 It is to be noted, however, that this idea is being challenged in this contemporary time as we now have the «in between»: the transgender, transvestite, bisexual persons.

24 C.H. POULIN, «Human Sexuality», 3.

The sexual denomination of male or female is not a quality that pertains merely to one part or aspect of the individual person, but something that is said of the whole person. Nor does it have a meaning and purpose which is limited to any particular biological function or anatomical structure of the person. The whole person is male or the whole person is female.[25]

In this way, we see the personalistic tendency of the contemporary approach.

It is, however, important to note that the male and the female persons are complete in dignity themselves by virtue of being human persons. The dignity of the person is rooted in his or her nature as a being created in the image and likeness of God. Although the human persons, male and female are equal and complete in dignity, yet, the sexes are different.[26] The male person is not a female person and vice-versa. The differences are not only on the physical and biological levels, which are all too clear; the differences can also be perceived in the psychological and spiritual levels.

The book of Genesis also reveals another dimension of sexuality, which is seen in human nature, namely, that the human person is a procreative person, hence, sexuality is procreative.

The scholars of the contemporary approach opine that the word procreation means more than reproduction. It is pointed out that the statement of God and the blessing given to the human person in Gen. 1:28 to be fruitful and have many children, is different from the one given in Gen. 1:22 to the birds of the air and fish in the waters. «The birds and the fish were given the mandate to be reproductive but certainly not procreative».[27] The difference between the blessing and the command given to the human persons and to the birds, fish, etc., in Poulin's analysis is:

Procreative refers not merely to the fact that the woman and man can produce, or generate new life. It says much more not only about their total relationship to each other but it speaks of their relationship to the whole world as well. It is a revelation that God is sharing with them not only His creative power of bringing new life into being- that is, of persons who are conceived in love in the image of those who are their parents, — but that He also shares with them His dominion, or responsibility, as the Lord of creation. The procreativity of each person, man or woman says something

---

[25] C.H. POULIN, «Human Sexuality», 3.
[26] Cf. L.S. CAHILL, *Sex, Gender and Christian Ethics*, 1.
[27] C.H. POULIN, «Human Sexuality», 3.

about his or her total relationship to other persons, and to his or her responsibility in and for the world in which we live.[28]

According to this view, while procreation includes reproduction, it is much deeper than that. The reproductive dimension is also found among the lower creatures and they are not, and can never be procreative in the same way that human persons are. Thus, each and every human person is by nature procreative because of the way he or she relates to others, and to the community, which is not specifically genital or reproductive. This entails giving love, having intimacy, participating and maintaining human dominion over the world and things in the world. This also entails responsibility for participating with the Lord in His own «creative» power and continuing relationship with the community of His own people. In this regard, reproduction is part but not the totality of procreation.

From the account of Genesis chapter two, another dimension of human sexuality is deduced. Here human sexuality is perceived to be relational and complementary. This dimension is seen in the expression: «it is not good for man to be alone».[29] This shows that the «first» person needs a complementary being. In this account, even though God created the beasts, the birds, etc., along with the male human person, none of these other creatures proved suitable for him. He was still lonely until the female person, the «woman» was created, and who became his companion in such a way that they complemented each other. Applying this account to human sexuality, the contemporary approach thus sees sexuality also in the context of relationship: man and woman live in fellowship and complement each other. As Goergen says, «man finds companionship in nature, but a more perfect companion comes when a woman is created. Sexuality is not associated primarily here with propagation. It is a gift from God so that man might live in fellowship and not be lonely».[30] Hence, human person's male and female are relational beings; they live in fellowship and relate to each other. It is through this relationship that they will both understand themselves as individuals and then come to the perfect understanding of the other person. Therefore, human persons are not isolated beings they are relational beings. It is in this regard that they must love, and work together,

---

28 C.H. POULIN, «Human Sexuality», 4.

29 Cf. Gen 2:18-23. The particular verse quoted above specifically refers to the male person alone.

30 D. GOERGEN, *The Sexual Celibate*, 15.

and thereby, they will enrich one another and society, and achieve their good and fulfillment as male and female.

Furthermore, in this second account of Genesis, we see another dimension of human sexuality, namely, the unitive aspect. It is written, «that is why a man leaves his father and mother and clings to his wife, and two of them become one body».[31]   This aspect of sexuality taken literally refers primarily to what happens in marriage. Poulin, however, opines that:

> This unity which is achieved in the fullest form of sexual expression is not merely a physical union.... It transcends the physical, and establishes an intimate fellowship and companionship whereby one's identity as a man is discovered and expressed in his union with the woman and vice-versa.[32]

There is need for caution here as regards the unitive aspect of sexuality. Goergen calls for a proper use of the expression «sexual intercourse». According to him, «we speak of sexual intercourse when we actually mean genital intercourse. Hugging, kissing and personal conversations are also sexual intercourse».[33]   In other words, it is often misleading to use the term sexual intercourse limiting it to mean genital intercourse, since the genital conveys one aspect but not the only possible meaning of sexual intercourse. As sexual beings, there are parameters within which we may honestly share ourselves as male and female. These are not limited to just one level, that is, the physical or genital.[34] It is within this context, therefore, that the complementary and unitive dimensions of sexuality of the single, the celibate and the married couple can be grasped and appreciated better. From all that has been said then, the nature and meaning of human sexuality in the contemporary approach could be summed up in the following words of Goergen:

> Among other things, it means sexual differentiation being male and female. It also means being relational, — structured for the other- incomplete by oneself — inescapably social. Sexual existence is a social existence. In my social life I encounter other sexual beings of my own sex and other sexual beings of the other sex. Being sexual also means being bodily and physical. My body is a sexual reality and is involved in what I do and how I act.[35]

---

[31] Gen 2:24.
[32] C.H. POULIN, «Human Sexuality», 5.
[33] D. GOERGEN, *The Sexual Celibate*, 58.
[34] Cf. J. TIMMERMAN, «Sex, Sacred or Profane?», 47-54.
[35] D. GOERGEN, *The Sexual Celibate*, 26.

Thus, the meaning of sexuality as enunciated in this contemporary approach is seen within the holistic view of the person so that the emphasis in this approach is personalistic. The whole male is a complete human person and as such a sexual person, so also is the female person.

However, they differ, hence, we need to recognize and respect the differences. This then leads to the need for complementing one other and helping one another to achieve fulfillment and growth as a sexual person. The meaning of sexuality in this contemporary approach is such that it is not merely the genital and generative as we have it in the manualist approach, rather, it broadens the vision of the meaning of human person as a sexual being. The purpose of human sexuality could then be seen and understood in the light of its nature and meaning.

Reflecting on the human condition, we notice that a person's sexuality is a powerful and basic force. This force urges and pushes one to go out of himself or herself towards other people, to give himself or herself to them in relationships to seek union and communion with them, and in that union and communion, to find fulfillment and completion as a human person. Our sexuality, therefore, does not merely make it clear that we are not self-sufficient but also impels us, as men and women, to seek that sufficiency and completion where alone it can be found, namely, in relationships with other persons.

The quest for understanding the purpose of human sexuality is seen on the level of personalistic values. Thus the purpose of sexuality consists in personal relationships with others, which entails the promotion of love and loving relationships. Our sexuality thus impels us to open ourselves to others as persons and to seek to have others open themselves to us. It is essentially directed to others; by nature it is social, calling for the establishment of personal relationships leading to personal growth and maturity.

In this view, the purpose of human sexuality, therefore, is certainly not carnal pleasure, nor is it restricted to companionship in marriage, or children or the family, though it includes these and from the outset the majority of persons require all these. The ultimate purpose is to raise the person and through him or her, other persons to the most pure and exalted possible love of God. This entails that each person, as a sexual being, has to integrate his or her sexuality and bring it to bear in his or her relationships, depending on his or her state in life. Thus, sexuality is not just to be linked with marriage or merely genital.

2.3 *The Implications of the Contrasting Methodologies to HIV/AIDS Prevention*

I have tried to expose the Church's meaning of human sexuality as conceived and enunciated in the manualist and contemporary methodologies. These two approaches are concerned with the basis upon which evaluation of sexual moral acts should be made. It is in the light of this that we can see how these contrasting methodologies can help us to deal with the issue of HIV/AIDS prevention.

In the manualist approach to the understanding of human sexuality, the emphasis was on the «biological function», and this was then perceived and presented as the purpose of human sexuality. This approach is concerned primarily with the physiologic aspect of human sexuality. According to this approach, to maintain the physical integrity of sexual acts, the nature of persons as procreative must be respected. This procreative purpose is seen to be justified and legitimate only within marriage. This manualist methodology to understanding human sexuality is described by Lisa Sowle Cahill: «sex is approached with a narrow focus on the act of sexual intercourse with its natural procreative potential, and sees other dimensions of sexual experience as ancillary».[36] In this manualist approach, it is obvious that a great deal of emphasis is placed on the act, with the view of determining whether each and every sexual act fulfills the procreative meaning and purpose of sexuality.

The implication of this manualist approach to sexuality in this time of HIV/AIDS in my view should be very clear. It is one that depicts a picture of disaster. We have shown that this approach projects an act – centered morality. The act – centered approach of this methodology does not and cannot be of practical purpose in the prevention of HIV/AIDS. Some of the reasons for this assertion are the following:

In the first place, the act – centered sexual morality of the manualist tradition is legalistic and prohibitive. The legalistic attitude is seen in the fact that the dimension of sexuality and sexual morality is based on the sixth and ninth commandments. As a result, the emphasis is on what the precepts «explicitly» and «implicitly» forbids. In addition, this act – centered sexual morality in my view is very negative. It sees sexuality as evil, to be tolerated only when it has procreation in view. This approach makes it difficult for people to speak about their sexual needs and experiences.

---

[36] L.S. CAHILL, «Catholic Sexual Ethics», 22.

My objection to this methodology is that the «dos» and the «do nots» of the sexual ethics of this approach will not make people to change their sexual behavior and thereby reduce the spread of HIV. I do not believe that people will change their sexual behavior based on the fact of a law prohibiting them from acting the way they do. A concrete situation can be seen from the fact of the HIV/AIDS epidemic, now in its third decade since its manifestation, yet, we have cases of new infection, which means the behavioral change that is needed to curb the spread is still way off. This means then that we need a positive sexual ethic that will help us to embrace and appreciate our sexuality, as well as point out the task that our sexuality imposes on us.

The manualist approach will no doubt create difficulty for HIV couples in general, and the HIV-discordant couples in particular. For instance, HIV-discordant couples might find themselves in a difficult situation of resolving the tension between the need to be faithful to this manualist teaching and the need to remain committed to each other in their conjugal love despite the risk of infection that could occur.

Therefore, to accept the manualist understanding of human sexuality at this time of HIV/AIDS, seropositive couples must make a choice. They must choose either to bear children, with the possibility of having HIV-positive children or infecting their spouse, or, decide to abstain from genital intercourse for the rest of their lives. The reason is that the use of prophylactics means a deviation from the perceived meaning and purpose of sexuality that this approach considers as morally illicit. If we propose this teaching to people, we need to know how effective it will be in curbing the spread of HIV.

Shall we be helping people to live responsibly? Would it help couples in difficult situations of living with HIV/AIDS to maintain their life-long relationship or could that threaten their love life and lead to the collapse of their marriage? This is important, as the non-infected partner does not want to be infected and at the same time have the need to fulfill the unitive and the reproductive aspect of marriage.[37] A critical look at the manualist understanding of human sexuality reveals that this way of looking at sexuality contributes in no small way to the injustice suffered by women especially, as they are just seen as objects for procreation.

Relating the contemporary approach to HIV/AIDS prevention strategy, this understanding in the sex education program gives a more posi-

---

[37] Cf. S.C. BATE, «Differences in Confessional Advice», 213.

tive approach, that which could yield positive results, like how to deal with our sexuality as human persons depending on our life commitment.

The contemporary methodology as seen earlier on, offers a vision of equality and dignity of women and men. This vision can empower women to really be able to make choices about their sexual lives and sexual needs. In addition, it empowers those who are HIV infected that, despite their situation, their dignity is in no way compromised and they never cease to be sexual beings.

In addition, we see morality of persons rather than acts. That is to say, in making a moral evaluation of sexual acts, emphasis is on the person carrying out the sexual act. Thus to make a moral evaluation of a sexual act, it is necessary to probe beneath the surface of not only the act but of the person acting. The person's way of acting may be contrary to the values the person stands for, and which may be either because of lack of knowledge or some other problem.

The contemporary approach maintains that even in marriage, sexuality has to do with the needs of the person, that is, the total relationship of the spouse, their life-long relationship. The life- long relationship, in fact, appears to be far more important than just the reproductive dimension of their lives. This is a positive approach in this time of HIV/AIDS, especially with regard to a situation where one of the partners is infected and despite that they still try to express their loving relationship to the end.

Another aspect of the contemporary approach to sexuality that is important in HIV prevention strategy would be the need for each person to integrate his or her sexuality into his or her life commitment. In this way, sex education programs can be well received and appreciated. In this integration of one's sexuality to one's life commitment, abstinence and fidelity are very important. For instance, the married and the single are led to understand and appreciate their sexuality and know that they are called to responsible behavior. This is quite different from the approach that just puts emphasis on an aspect of sexuality, the genital, making it as if it were, the totality.

Based on the above, one is led by the contemporary theologians to the conviction that sex education programs for HIV/AIDS prevention will become practical and responsive to the needs of people, especially in this time of AIDS, if it is able to successfully present the positive message about human sexuality. As the contemporary approach has demonstrated, persons rather than acts should be the focal point. It is the person's clear understanding and perception of his or her sexuality that can lead to behavioral change, not just the act.[38]

3. The Prophylactics Debate

Before the advent of HIV/AIDS, the use of a prophylactic device, or condom as it is commonly called, had been seen and understood in relation to preventing pregnancy from taking place, that is, a condom was seen as a contraceptive device. While its effectiveness as a contraceptive device has been questioned,[39] nonetheless, the focus has now shifted from condom as a contraceptive to condom as a preventive device for HIV/AIDS infection.

It is in this context that one hears talks of «safe sex» or «safer sex». Thus, condom is now regarded as instrument for «safe sex» or «safer sex». Since HIV/AIDS became a global crisis, there has been debate whether the consistent use of condom is effective in the prevention of HIV/AIDS or not. My aim here, therefore, is to look at the arguments against and in favor of condom use, after which, I would attempt an evaluation by looking at some of the issues at stake.

3.1 *Arguments Against Prophylactics*

3.1.1 The Church and Condom Use

Jacques Suaudeau remarked that since the beginning of the HIV/AIDS epidemic, the Church has been in the forefront of the fight against HIV/AIDS.[40] Numerous conferences and seminars had been held both at the International and regional levels, all with the view of finding a solution to the numerous problems associated with the disease, as well as showing solidarity and support for those already infected with the disease.

Thus, the Church too, has shown concern for the need to curb the spread of the disease. The Church's recommendations for curbing the spread of the disease are, however, different from the recommendations of many governments of the world, scientists, and some medical personnel.

---

[38] It must be emphasized though that it is not enough to present a sound theology of sex and marriage without situating it in the understanding of human psychology and personal development. These are also necessary components of education for mature sexuality.

[39] See R. ALESSANDRI – Z. FRIEDMAN – L. TRIVELLI, «Condoms and Adolescent HIV», 62.

[40] See J. SUAUDEAU, «Prophylactics or Family Value?», *OR* 16-19 April 2000, 4.

The Church has always rejected condom use as it was seen as a contraceptive device, which is considered to be against the design of nature and hence, against the will of God. This position is well defined in *Humanae Vitae*,[41] paragraph 14 of which says: «every act that intends to impede procreation must be repudiated...Whether it is done in anticipation of marital intercourse, or during it, or while it is having its natural consequences».[42]

Following the tradition of *Humanae Vitae*, some Church leaders oppose the use of a condom for the prevention of HIV/AIDS, since its use is claimed to be an intrinsic evil.[43] The position of the Church regarding the use of condoms for the prevention of HIV/AIDS is emphasized in an unsigned article in the *L' Osservatore Romano* that says:

> To seek a solution to the problem of infection by promoting the use of prophylactics would be to embark on a way not only insufficiently reliable from a technical point of view, but also and above all, unacceptable from the moral aspect. Such a proposal for «safe» or at least «safer» sex — as they say — ignores the real cause of the problem, namely, the permissiveness which, in the area of sex as in that related to other abuses, corrodes the moral fiber of the people.[44]

Following the above quotation, the belief is that condom use corrodes the authentic meaning and purpose of human sexuality, and aids behavior that encourages indiscriminate sexual activity that is considered as serving egoistic interests.

John Paul II in a way emphasizes this point. While commenting on the problem of AIDS and its spread, he remarks, «certainly not far from the truth is the affirmation that, parallel to the spread of AIDS, there is a kind of immunodeficiency in existential values that cannot but be identified as a real pathology of the spirit».[45] And so, talking about prevention, he says:

> Prevention methods, which instead promote egoistic interests, deriving from considerations that are incompatible with the fundamental values of

---

[41] The main thesis of *Humanae Vitae* is that it is always illicit, to directly and willingly impede the natural biological finality of the sexual act. Prophylactics have been seen and understood to do that.

[42] PAUL VI, *Humanae Vitae*, no. 14.

[43] See J. HICKEY – al., «Reactions to AIDS Statement», 439-443. «It is never morally permissible to employ an intrinsically evil means to achieve a good purpose», p. 490.

[44] «Prevention of AIDS», *OR* March 10, 1988. Also cited in J. RATZINGER, «Letter on AIDS Document», 117-121.

[45] JOHN PAUL II, «Pope Addresses Vatican AIDS Conference», 664.

life and love, can only end up being contradictory as well as illicit, merely circling the problem without resolving it at its roots... It is extremely harmful to the dignity of the person, and therefore it is morally illicit, to support as AIDS prevention any method which violates the authentically human sense of sexuality and is a palliative for those deep needs which involve the responsibility of the individuals and of society: And right reason cannot admit that the fragility of the human condition — greater care — be used as a pretext for yielding to a way of moral degradation.[46]

In the above quotation, one notices that the Pope, though, never specifically mentioned condom use but it is implied in the whole trend of thought. Cardinal Ratzinger, the Prefect of the Congregation for the Doctrine of Faith, says «technical instructions in the use of prophylactic devices is an immoral practice».[47]

Carlo Caffarra,[48] one of the participants at the Vatican AIDS conference of 1989, writes that even in a situation involving HIV-discordant couple the use of condom for HIV prevention is morally illicit.[49] He argues from two levels. According to him, the use of the condom is a contraceptive act that is not morally licit for any reason or circumstance. He goes on to say, even if the use of condom is not as a contraceptive in itself or in the intention, yet, condom use is not morally licit in the case of HIV-discordant couple. This is because the genital act of the couple is not a conjugal sexual act; a barrier that prevents the couple from becoming one flesh destroys the conjugality.[50]

A high-ranking moral theologian, Dionigi Tettamanzi,[51] also emphasized the official position of the Church. According to him the use of prophylactics for the prevention of HIV/AIDS is not morally licit.[52] He goes on to say that even among the married HIV-discordant couples, prophylactics should not be encouraged because it falsifies the meaning of conjugal love and above all, even in relation to Humanae Vitae no. 15, it still cannot be justified since there exists an alternative, that is abstinence.[53]

---

[46] JOHN PAUL II, «Pope Addresses Vatican AIDS Conference», 664.

[47] J. RATZINGER, «Letter on AIDS Document», 118.

[48] Mons. Carlo Caffarra was then the President of the Institute of John Paul II for the study of Marriage and Family at the Pontifical Lateran University, Rome.

[49] C. CAFFARRA, «Aids: Aspetti Etici Generali», 70-74.

[50] C. CAFFARRA, «Aids: Aspetti Etici Generali», 71.

[51] Dionigi Tettamanzi is an Italian moral theologian and also the Cardinal Archbishop of Milano, Italy.

[52] D. TETTAMANZI, Bioetica, 359-360.

[53] D. TETTAMANZI, Bioetica, 360-361.

In an article that appeared in the *L'Osservatore Romano*, Jacques Suaudeau, of the Pontifical Council for the Family, emphasized again the official Church's position on prophylactics. According to him, «the most radical prevention of HIV/AIDS, the one which is absolutely effective and which no one can deny, is sexual abstinence for adolescents before marriage and conjugal chastity in marriage».[54] It is important to note, however, that Suaudeau also said that condoms were an effective means of containing the spread of HIV, were «actually a lesser evil», and «had a good result». According to him, «prophylactic is one of the ways to "contain" the sexual transmission of HIV/AIDS, that is, to limit its transmission». [55] This is an important issue that will be examined later.

Nonetheless, the teaching of the Church in the area of prevention is that sexual abstinence and fidelity are the only effective weapons for preventing the spread of HIV/AIDS. Hence, people must learn to have a faithful, permanent relationship with their partner, that is, for those who are married, while the unmarried must learn the virtue of chastity.[56]

3.1.2 Reasons for Objecting to the Use of Prophylactics

The Church objected to the use of prophylactics as a prevention device on various grounds. Condom use is seen to be inconsistent with the Church's sexual ethics and the values they promote. Firstly, it is believed that promoting the use of condoms does not attack the root cause of the problem or factors that enhance the spread of HIV/AIDS.[57] Also, prophylactics, it is argued, give a false sense of security and illusion, and this in turn could lead to promiscuity or indiscriminate sexual acts, since it did not offer any deeper value to the people, especially the young people.[58]

---

[54] J. SUAUDEAU, «Prophylactics or Family Value?», 9.

[55] J. SUAUDEAU, «Prophylactics or Family Value?», 9.

[56] See F.G. MELLIN, «The Places of Education in Values», 40. The Church affirms: «Chastity, self-control, education in real love, loyalty and individual and social responsibility».

[57] See JOHN PAUL II, «Pope Addresses Vatican AIDS Conference», 664. Also J. SUAUDEAU, «Prophylactics or Family Value?», 9.

[58] USCC ADMINISTRATIVE BOARD, «The Many Faces of AIDS», 486, suggests that this would be result of using condoms. See also, NCCB, «Called to Compassion and Responsibility», 424.

The Bishops of the Philippines in their pastoral letter express this fear:

> The moral dimension of the problem of HIV/AIDS urges us to take a sharply negative view of the condom-distribution to the problem. We believe that this approach is simplistic and evasive. It leads to a false sense of complacency on the part of the state, creating an impression that an adequate solution has been arrived at. On the contrary, it simply evades and neglects the heart of the solution, namely the formation of authentic sexual values.[59]

In addition, there is also the concern that the promotion of condoms for HIV/AIDS prevention could be a subtle manner of carrying out the population control agenda program. This feeling is strong among the African hierarchy in particular. A good example could be seen in the views of the Catholic Bishops of Zimbabwe, in conjunction with other Christian Church leaders. They criticized their government's HIV/AIDS prevention campaign program:

> The Churches question the manner in which the ministry of health appears to have surrendered to policies formulated by Western governments and agencies in the area of population control without any comprehension of the effect these policies will have on the cultural and moral attitudes of the people of Zimbabwe.[60]

In Nigeria, there has not been an official pronouncement against condom use by the Church's hierarchy, yet, on the individual level, some bishops maintain that the use of prophylactics are morally illicit and, as such, unacceptable for the prevention of HIV/AIDS transmission.

The Church's criticism of prophylactics as an effective means of HIV/AIDS prevention is corroborated with some data pointing to the unreliability of condoms as a guarantee against HIV/AIDS transmission.

Raul Alessandri, Zelig Friedman and Liliana Privelli, for instance, examined a good number of control studies that showed that condom use is not a sure guarantee against HIV/AIDS infection. These studies

---

[59] CATHOLIC BISHOPS' CONFERENCE OF THE PHILIPPINES, «In the compassion of Jesus», January 23, 1993.

[60] «Zimbabwe Church Leaders Chide State Anti-Aids Program», as reported in *Catholic News Service*, Washington, DC, March 18, 1996.

showed a high failure rate of condoms in preventing pregnancy,[61] hence, if high failure rates exist in that regard, that points out that it cannot be trusted to prevent HIV/AIDS infection. They therefore conclude that prophylactic use «is not only no solution at all, but it may be a multiplier of the problem».[62] An important element is brought out in the failure rate of the condom use. It is said that the failure rates of condoms do not depend on the kind of brand or quality of the condom.[63] The authors of these studies intended to say that whether or not good quality condoms are used, these condoms couldn't be expected to be hundred percent safe.

In a separate study, it was found that HIV/AIDS instruction is not associated with less risky sexual behavior.[64] This confirms the point made by Aristotle that knowing is not doing. In other words, knowledge and the practice of virtue do not always go hand in hand. The mere fact that one knows the good does not automatically mean one will do the good. Therefore those who oppose the use of condoms as effective means of prevention believe that «abstinence is the healthiest choice for adolescents, that sexual activity should be reserved for a committed, mature relationship and that character building is a desirable part of any educational system».[65]

Apart from the data, experts in different fields of human endeavor objected to the use of condoms for HIV/AIDS prevention. For instance, Mark Johnson objected to the reasoning given for condom use in a situation where one partner of a married couple is already HIV positive. He opines that the traditional Catholic teaching «provides direction, albeit unpopular direction for many, to most cases that would otherwise be subject to the practice of safe sex».[66] He criticized the idea of 'safe sex', which he said is not only misguided and is not a reality, but rather a «politically correct» presentation.[67] Despite this, he never really ar-

---

[61] See R. ALESSANDRI – Z. FRIEDMAN – L. TRIVELLI, «Condoms and Adolescent HIV», 62. Also W.R. GRADY – M.D. HAYWARD – J. YAGI, «Contraceptive Failure», 200-209; G.C. GRIFFIN, «Condoms and Contraceptives», 60-66.

[62] R. ALESSANDRI – Z. FRIEDMAN – L. TRIVELLI, «Condoms and Adolescent HIV», 62. Also Col. R.A. WATSON – L.S. WATSON, «Fidelity, Mutual Respect», 30-32.

[63] J. TRUSSELL – D.L. WARNER – R.A. HATCHER, «Condom Slippage», 20-23.

[64] J.E. ANDERSON – al., «HIV/AIDS Knowledge», 6-16.

[65] R. ALESSANDRI – Z. FRIEDMAN – L. TRIVELLI, «Condoms and Adolescent HIV», 70.

[66] M. JOHNSON, «The Principle of Double Effect», 83.

[67] M. JOHNSON, «The Principle of Double Effect», 83.

gued that the use of prophylactics was itself wrong, especially in the case of his point of departure; rather, he questioned the principle used to argue for that position.[68]

Glen Griffin also assented to that which some Church leaders affirm by saying «the only really safe sex is between two faithful marriage partners who are free of sexually transmitted diseases. This is not only «no-risk sex», it is also worth waiting for».[69] Richard Watson and Leonie Watson on their part said that providing condoms and making it a slogan of «safe sex» is not the key, rather «saved sex» is the key. «Saved sex», they explain means «abstinence, self-respect and self control, not sort - of - safe self-indulgence».[70]

From all that has been said, one notices that the main reasons for opposing the use and distribution of condoms are that such action could promote and encourage promiscuity and negative values.[71] Condoms, it is argued, give a false sense of security, yet, it is unreliable to protect against the virus. Thus, the best method of prevention, and the only safe and secure one is abstinence, and fidelity in marriage.

3.2 *Arguments in Support of Prophylactics as Preventive Measure*

I would like to emphasize from the outset that there are two categories of arguments that I wish to examine here. The first category deals with scientific studies and data in support of condom use for the prevention of HIV/AIDS. The second category is that which involves Catholic theologians, especially moralists. These are people who are genuinely concerned with the enormity of the problem the epidemic poses to humanity, thus, using the moral tradition of the Church and with the data available, are arguing in favor of prophylactics for the prevention of HIV transmission. My own reaction to the debate will be offered later on as a way of conclusion to this whole chapter.

3.2.1 Scientific Studies Showing the Effectiveness of Condoms

One of the arguments against condom use is that since the failure rate has been recorded in its use for preventing pregnancy, hence, it

---

[68] See J.F. KEENAN, ed., *Catholic Ethicists,* 20.

[69] G.C. GRIFFIN, «Condoms and Contraceptives», 65.

[70] R.A. WATSON – L.S. WATSON, «Fidelity, Mutual Respect», 31.

[71] It is important to point out that there are data in the public health literature to refute these claims. These data will be presented under the examination of those who argue in favor of prophylactics.

cannot be relied on to prevent transmission of HIV/AIDS virus. However, several studies have shown the effectiveness of condoms to reduce HIV transmission, especially as no vaccine or cure has been found for the virus. Jon Fuller[72] gives a lengthy description of three studies that show that condom use had helped to reduce the spread of HIV/AIDS.[73] In one of these studies, among 121 HIV-discordant couples that reported inconsistent condom use, 12 infections occurred, whereas among the 124 who reported consistent use there were no infections despite an estimated 15,000 acts of intercourse.[74] In another study in which condom promotion was carried out among female sex workers, it is said that condom promotion did help to reduce and bring about a major decline of HIV incidence among this group of people.[75] Anne M. Johnson also makes the affirmation that condoms really can save lives.[76]

The same trend is found in a report of the Surgeon General, US Public Health Service. Although it is accepted that only sexual abstinence or mutual monogamy between uninfected partners completely eliminates the risk of sexual transmission of HIV, this report, based on numerous studies, concludes that latex condoms that are consistently used are highly effective in reducing the risk of sexual exposure to HIV.[77]

According to the center for AIDS Prevention Studies of University of California, San Francisco, the affirmation is made that condoms can absolutely save life. «Condoms that are readily available, effectively promoted, and used correctly and consistently, play an important public health role in HIV prevention».[78] While the possibility of the failure rate is recognized and accepted, it has also been proven in the laboratory that latex condoms are very effective at blocking transmission of HIV because the pores in latex condoms are too small to allow the passage of the virus.[79]

---

[72] Jon Fuller, S.J., M.D., is associate Professor of Medicine and also assistant director of the Clinical AIDS Program at the Boston Medical Center, Boston University School of Medicine.

[73] J. FULLER, «AIDS Prevention», 13-20.

[74] J. FULLER, «AIDS Prevention», 17.

[75] M. LAGA – al., «Condom Promotion», 246-248.

[76] A.M. JOHNSON, «Condoms and HIV Transmission», 391-392.

[77] A.C. NOVELLO – al., «From the Surgeon General», 2840.

[78] P. DE CARLO, «Do Condoms Work?». http://www.ama-assn.org/special/hiv/prevention/prevent2.htm.

[79] P. DE CARLO, «Do Condoms Work?». http://www.ama-assn.org/special/hiv/prevention/prevent2.htm.

In addition, another reason for objecting to the use of condoms is that it promotes or encourages promiscuity. But recent studies have shown that this is not necessarily the case. In a study carried out in ten Seattle high schools, condoms were made available through vending machines, baskets in school clinics, or both. This study examined the number of condoms that the students obtained and subsequent changes in sexual behavior and condom use. The finding is that the availability of condoms in these schools enabled students to obtain large number of condoms but amazingly did not lead to increases in either sexual activity or condom use.[80] This means that making condoms available for these students does not mean that they will become sexually promiscuous. In a separate study on Latino Youth, the same conclusion is arrived at, namely, that HIV prevention program that included the promotion and distribution of condoms did not increase sexual activity among the adolescents in the study.[81]

What these scientific data point to is that if condoms are consistently and correctly used, there will be a drop in the rate of infection with the virus of HIV/AIDS. This is particularly important if people cannot be discouraged from having sex in the first place, hence the effectiveness of condoms for HIV/AIDS prevention.

3.2.2 The Use of Condoms in an Acceptable Theological Framework

Here we find Catholic theologians and Ethicists who maintain the Church's teaching on sexuality by emphasizing the importance of abstinence and fidelity, yet, still believe that there is room for prophylactics as a means of preventing HIV transmission, which is in accordance with the Church's long standing tradition. These moralists believe that the Catholic moral tradition can help to mediate in a constructive manner in the face of apparent clash of values, without undermining the long-standing tradition.[82]

One of the earliest Catholic contributions to the debate about prophylactic use for preventing HIV transmission began after the United States Catholic Conference (USCC) Administrative Board issued a document titled, «The Many Faces of AIDS: A Gospel Response».[83] This document seeks to address the situation of those suffering from this

---

80 D. KIRBY – al., «The Impact of Condom Distribution», 182-187.
81 D.E. SELLERS – S.A. MCGRAW – J.B. MCKINLAY, «Does the Promotion», 1952-1959.
82 See J.F. KEENAN, ed., Catholic Ethicists, 13.
83 USCC ADMINISTRATIVE BOARD, «The Many Faces of AIDS», 482-489.

this human tragedy, as well as present the teaching of the Church on sexual ethics. The document explicitly rejects the «Safe sex» approach to prevention. The landmark contribution and the controversy this document generates come from the educational aspect. The document, after stressing the need for abstinence and fidelity, goes on to say:

> Because we live in a pluralistic society, we acknowledge that some will not agree with our understanding of human sexuality. We recognize that the public educational programs addressed to a wide audience will reflect the fact that some people will not act as they can and should; that they will not refrain from the type of sexual or drug abuse behavior, which can transmit AIDS. In such situations educational efforts, if grounded in the broader moral vision outlined above, could include accurate information about prophylactic devices or other practices proposed by some medical experts as potential means of preventing AIDS...

> We are not promoting the use of prophylactics, but merely providing information that is part of the factual picture.[84]

In the appendix of this same document, another significant line of reasoning was made. This will also become contentious. Again, while rejecting the «safe sex» slogan, the document advised that those who have the virus or who are at risk should be invited «to live a chaste life». It adds, «if it is obvious that the person will not act without bringing harm to others, then the traditional Catholic wisdom with regard to one's responsibility to avoid inflicting greater harm may be appropriately applied».[85] Here it is intended that the health care professional could on a personal level advise on the use of prophylactics.[86] Some people, including members of the United States Episcopal Conference, disagreed with this document, which they thought sent a wrong message to the faithful and the public at large about the teaching of the Church.[87] There are still others, including moralists, who believe that the document is a fine piece of work and its position is justified and is in line with the Church's tradition.[88]

---

[84] USCC ADMINISTRATIVE BOARD, «The Many Faces of AIDS», 486.

[85] USCC ADMINISTRATIVE BOARD, «The Many Faces of AIDS», 489.

[86] See J.F. KEENAN, «Prophylactics, Toleration, and Cooperation», 205.

[87] «Reaction to AIDS Statement», *Origins* 17.28 (1987) 489-493; F. STAFFORD, «Continued Reaction to AIDS Statement», *Origins* 17.30 (1988) 516-522; J. RATZINGER, «Letter on AIDS Document», 117-121.

[88] See R. MCCORMICK, *The Critical Calling,* 319-323; J.F. KEENAN, «Prophylactics, Toleration, and Cooperation», 205-207; ID., «Applying the Seventh-Century Casuistry», 492-512.

Apart from the United States Bishops, there have been some other Catholic Bishops' Conferences and individual bishops who do not rule out the possibility of accepting condom use in the fight against HIV/AIDS spread. For instance, the French bishops, too, had shown their willingness to examine the issue of condoms for the prevention of HIV/AIDS. In 1996, the Social Commission of the French Bishops Conference issued a document entitled: *SIDA La Société en Question*, which allows for the inclusion of information about condoms as an integral, but not the solitary, element of HIV/AIDS prevention education.[89] In this document the French bishops are of the opinion that condoms may be necessary but insufficient means for battling AIDS. The statement of the French bishops is significant because it calls for honesty and sincerity both on the part of those who advocate the use of condoms for HIV prevention and also from those who oppose its use.

In his reaction to the statement of the French bishops as regards condoms for HIV prevention, the Archbishop of Vienna, now Cardinal Schonborn said that condoms' use could be morally acceptable for the prevention of HIV in some given situations. According to him, «love can never bring death... In given situations, the condom can be seen as the lesser evil».[90]

Since the beginning of the debate, there have been a good number of Catholic theologians, especially moralists, who have explored the richness of the Catholic tradition and come to the conclusion that condom use in the prevention of HIV/AIDS transmission can be, and is morally licit.

In the first instance, the theologians who support the use of condoms for the prevention of HIV/AIDS made it abundantly clear that they do not approve the sexual acts which facilitate the transmission of the virus, especially those acts engaged in by teenagers and unmarried couples.[91] The object of their support is to safeguard life and protect the common good.

Enda McDonagh, the Irish theologian, using the biblical theme of *kairos* time states:

---

[89] COMMISSION SOCIALE DE L'EPISCOPAT, *SIDA: La Société en Question*. Also cited by R.J. VITILLO, «HIV/AIDS Prevention Education», 5.

[90] EDITORIAL, «Vienna Archbishop». Quoted also by R.J. VITILLO, «HIV/AIDS Prevention Education», 6; J. NORTON, «Theologians».

[91] See E.P. FLYNN, «Teaching about HIV Prevention», 149, 154; E. MCDONAGH, «Theology in a Time of AIDS», 84ff.

With all the risks of misunderstanding both in regard to the «safety» of so
– called safe sex and to the apparent endorsement of promiscuity, it may
be socially necessary and morally legitimate to accept the use of condoms.
However, it must be made clear that this is in no way regarded as good in
itself. It is tolerated as an interim measure to protect life and allow time for
the personal and social conversion, which the coming of the kingdom calls
for....[92]

Meanwhile, he strongly emphasized what has been said earlier that
«if condoms are introduced as a cover for endorsing promiscuity or
exploiting the sex trade, that should be exposed and opposed».[93] Thus
the motive for endorsement of condom is important in the final analysis.

Eileen Flynn on her part, although favoring the use of condoms for
preventing HIV transmission, nonetheless believes in the strong need to
reverse the sexual permissiveness of the present time. She says that the
«reality» that people, especially young people, cannot do without genital sexuality is something that has been culturally created, and as such
could be reversed.[94] This culture, in her view, has led to a significant
loss in the understanding of the seriousness and significance of sexual
intimacy. While she holds this view, she however concedes that in the
face of the reality of a deadly disease like HIV/AIDS, the use of condoms can then be permitted, especially for those who are sexually active and unmarried.[95]

David Kelly on his part examines the situation of married couples
whereby one partner is infected and the other not. In a situation such as
this, the risk of transmission of the virus is high if the couple continues
to engage in genital intercourse. The ethical questions then is, is it legitimate to advise this couple to use a condom? In answering this question and concern, Kelly stresses that in a situation such as this, it is not
only morally permitted to use condoms, but more importantly, such
couples are morally «required» to use them.[96] The use of a condom in
this case, according to Kelly, is not contraception, that is, preventing
pregnancy; rather, it is a question of prevention of a life – threatening
disease. For him, it is more appropriate to see the warning as a right
action intended to minimize the negative consequence of a wrong ac-

---

[92] E. McDonagh, «Theology in a Time of AIDS», 84-85.
[93] E. McDonagh, «Theology in a Time of AIDS», 86.
[94] E.P. Flynn, «Teaching about HIV Prevention», 153.
[95] E.P. Flynn, «Teaching about HIV Prevention», 155-156.
[96] D.F. Kelly, Critical Care Ethics, 206.

tion than seeing it as cooperation in the evil act.[97] He goes on to say that by asking people to use a condom (even though the object of their act may be immoral), can even be seen as at most, a «remote» or «indirect» cooperation, a principle that finds a place in the Catholic tradition.[98]

John Tuohey is another person that looks at the issue of couples with HIV and condoms use. According to him, the use of a condom in a situation where one of the couples is already infected and the other not, does not in any way contradict the teaching and tradition of the Church. He specifically looked at the teaching of *Humanae Vitae*. The understanding of *Humanae Vitae*, he says, is that the moral character of a contraceptive act is found in its direct intention to impede the coming to be of a possible life.[99] Hence, it is the contraceptive intention, which morally defines the use of condom as contraceptive. Given this fact, Touhey argues that the use of condoms by couples that stand the risk of infection has a different view or perspective. The use of condoms in this case is not contraceptive, but a protective means.[100] He said even though the act is the same, yet, there is a significant difference in purpose and intention. Thus the use of condoms in time of HIV/AIDS serves only as a means of prevention. The contraceptive consequence of a condom, though foreseen, is not a means to a good end; it is not directly intended, either as a means or as an end.[101] The intention of condom use in the case at hand is to save life.

Nader Michel, too, thinks in the situation of couples faced with the risk of HIV, condom use could be justified. According to him, the reasons for allowing the use of condoms are «to preserve life, a supreme good, and to protect the dimensions of love and unity in this stable married couple».[102] The contraception that results from the action is nothing but a secondary effect of that which is pursued-namely, the protection of life. To advocate abstinence for this couple may not be a prudent thing to do since that entails not fulfilling one of their marriage commitments and that in turn could «hurt their love in its greatest and most intimate expression, and condemn them to neuroses and their mar-

---

[97] D.F. KELLY, *Critical Care Ethics*, 207.
[98] D.F. KELLY, *Critical Care Ethics*, 207.
[99] J. TUOHEY, «Methodology and Ideology», 53-69.
[100] J. TUOHEY, «Methodology and Ideology», 59.
[101] J. TUOHEY, «Methodology and Ideology», 61.
[102] N. MICHEL, «Fighting AIDS», 157.

riage to dissolution».[103] He reiterated the value that the Church offers on love and sexuality, but at the same time challenged the Church to be alive to her mission of saving and protecting life. While condom use provides no education of love or adult sexuality, yet he maintains, «in the face of death, the Church can't act for death».[104] The use of a condom is just a means of protection.

Richard McCormick, too, supports the use of prophylactics as a strategy for HIV prevention. According to him, when prophylactics are used to prevent HIV infection during heterosexual intimacy, «such usage does not merit the name contraception».[105]

Jon Fuller combines his medical knowledge and theological insight to call our attention to the need to see condom use as a means of preventing HIV infection, thereby saving lives.[106] He calls on the Church to recognize the «signs of the times», by discerning well the tradition, as well as her responsibility to protect life, which has been the hallmark of the Church's mission.

James Keenan, who remains one of the known leading Catholic moral theologians in the field of HIV/AIDS, favors the recommendation of condom use in a time of HIV/AIDS. This recommendation, he points out, is not an endorsement of contraception, but of prophylaxis.[107] He points out that the use of prophylactics does not in any way contradict the tradition of the Church, instead, using the same tradition, one can see why such action is morally licit.[108]

3.2.3 Principles Invoked in Support of Prophylactics

The moralists and all those who are genuinely moved at the enormous impact of HIV/AIDS and thus support prophylactics to curb the further infection, believe that there is higher value at stake, namely life. These people are also convinced that their position is also in keeping with the tradition of the Church to which many of them belong. So what are the Church's traditional principles they invoked, to support their claims?

---

[103] N. MICHEL, «Fighting AIDS», 157.
[104] N. MICHEL, «Fighting AIDS», 158.
[105] R. McCORMICK, *The Critical Calling*, 323.
[106] J. FULLER, «AIDS Prevention», 13-20.
[107] J.F. KEENAN, «Living with HIV/AIDS», 701; J.F. KEENAN, ed., *Catholic Ethicists*, 24.
[108] J.F. KEENAN, «Prophylactics, Toleration, and Cooperation», 205-220; ID., «Applying the Seventh-Century Casuistry», 492-512.

a) *The Principle of Toleration*

Although the USCC Administrative Board insists on chastity and the avoidance of drug use, they however, accepted the idea of public educational programs that include factual information about prophylactics.[109] In addition, they also recommended that in the case that someone would not act responsibly as he or she ought to, then, it is important to do everything not to bring harm to others,[110] meaning that he or she could be advised to use prophylactics.

In accepting these facts, the writers of the document made recourse to the principle of toleration of the lesser evil.[111] Invoking this principle, and as they consistently maintained, they are not tolerating immoral or illicit sexual activity but rather given the factual situation of AIDS, they «tolerate» information about prophylactics. The object of their toleration is not the action that led to the need for the program, but given the activity, they believe it is necessary to limit the actual physical effects of the illicit activity.[112]

Expectedly, there are those who disagreed with the document's position and the principle invoked to justify the position, for instance, here, we find Cardinal Ratzinger who says:

> It hardly seems pertinent to appeal to the classical principle of tolerance of the lesser evil on the part of those who exercise responsibility for the temporal common good of society. In fact, even when the issue has to do with educational programs promoted by the civil government, one would not be dealing simply with a form of Passive toleration but rather with a kind of behavior which would result in at least the facilitation of evil.[113]

There are many bishops of the United States, who criticized and rejected the Administrative Board document,[114] among which we find Archbishop Francis Stafford of Denver, who gave a detailed critique of the structure of the document. According to him, the traditional principle of toleration of the lesser evil, especially as put forward by Aquinas, applies only to civil government thus, cannot be invoked in the same way in the affairs of the Church.[115] Besides, the way Pius XII

---

[109] USCC ADMINISTRATIVE BOARD, «The Many Faces of AIDS», 486.

[110] USCC ADMINISTRATIVE BOARD, «The Many Faces of AIDS», 489.

[111] USCC ADMINISTRATIVE BOARD, «The Many Faces of AIDS», 489, footnote 7.

[112] See J.F. KEENAN, «Prophylactics, Toleration, and Cooperation», 206.

[113] J. RATZINGER, «Letter on AIDS Document», 117.

[114] «Reaction to AIDS Statement», *Origins* 17.28 (1987) 489-493; F. STAFFORD – *al.*, «Continued Reaction to AIDS Statement», 516-522.

[115] F. STAFFORD – *al.*, «Continued Reaction to AIDS Statement», 519.

invoked the principle, Stafford says, is «radically different» from the way it was assumed in the document «Many Faces», which, is not a question of passive toleration.[116]

There are those who agreed with and supported the document. For instance, Richard McCormick not only sees the document as pastorally sound, an excellent piece, but also agreed with the principle invoked to justify their positions.[117]

On his part, James Keenan calls the document a «pastorally sensitive and fundamentally ethically and theologically correct»,[118] hence, he supports it. But he thinks the principle of toleration invoked is not adequate, hence, he proposes that an adequate principle needed in this regard is the principle of cooperation.[119]

b) *The Principle of Cooperation*

The principle of cooperation is seen as guaranteeing the support for the use of prophylactics as a preventive device.

According to Keenan, who strongly proposes this alternative principle, he argues that the second position in the document of the «Many Faces» is not a detached attention, hence does not merit to be seen as toleration.

«Cooperation understood in the moral sense is concurrence with another person in a sinful act».[120] This is to say the participation of more than one person in the same immoral or criminal action. This concurrence can occur in two ways either by acting with another in the same sin or by supplying the other with what is helpful in performing the sinful action.[121] It is important to note, however, that circumstances may arise in which a person is associated, to a greater or lesser degree, with someone else in a situation that is contrary to right order. Such an associate may be equally guilty with the wrongdoer or less guilty, or perhaps not guilty at all.

---

[116] F. STAFFORD – *al.*, «Continued Reaction to AIDS Statement», 519.

[117] R. McCORMICK, *The Critical Calling*, 321.

[118] J.F. KEENAN, «Prophylactics, Toleration, and Cooperation», 205.

[119] J.F. KEENAN, «Prophylactics, Toleration, and Cooperation», 205-220.

[120] E. HEALY, *Moral Guidance*, 43; H. DAVIS, *Moral and Pastoral Theology*, II, 341. T.J. O'DONNELL, *Medicine and Christian Morality*, 34-39. See also J.F. KEENAN, «Prophylactics, Toleration, Cooperation», 207-220.

[121] E. HEALY, *Moral Guidance*, 43; H. DAVIS, *Moral and Pastoral Theology*, II, 341. T.J. O'DONNELL, *Medicine and Christian Morality*, 34-39. See also J.F. KEENAN, «Prophylactics, Toleration, Cooperation», 207-220.

However, the key to understanding this principle rests on a number of issues. One of such issue for instance, is in the distinction between formal or material cooperation, proximate or remote, necessary or contingent.[122]

Formal cooperation occurs when the assisting agent participates in the evil intention or in an essential aspect of the action of the main agent. It is a kind of approval of the evil action of the main agent. As a result the assisting agent is equally guilty of wrongdoing.[123]

As regards material cooperation, the cooperation may or may not be sinful depending on the circumstances of each case. Material cooperation with another person's evil act is allowed when one has a proportionate reason for acting or cooperating,[124] and when scandal can be avoided.[125] It is, however, important to note that material cooperation is not justifiable in all cases.[126] Nonetheless, it is said that for such material cooperation to be licit, the action performed by the cooperator must in itself be good or indifferent, even though the main agent to act immorally can use it.

Applying this principle to the issue of distribution, and advising the use of condoms for the prevention of HIV/AIDS infection, the belief is that this falls under material cooperation and that there is sufficient reason for doing that. The disease is life – threatening whereas, condoms can reduce or eliminate the chances of infection thereby protecting and saving lives. At the same time, it protects the common good.

Given the above, one sees clearly that the principle of cooperation is about action, not about mere tolerance or passivity. Toleration implies detachment. This is what Keenan rightly points out: that cooperation seeks to know or ask, «what should I do?» rather than «what should I allow to happen?»[127] The fact remains however that knowing the right course of action is not always easy to determine.

---

[122] E. HEALY, *Moral Guidance*, 43-47; J.J. FERRER, «Needle Exchange», 177-189.

[123] E. HEALY, *Moral Guidance*, 43-44; H. DAVIS, *Moral and Pastoral Theology*, II, 341.

[124] E. HEALY, *Moral Guidance*, 45-46.

[125] Cf. CONGREGATION FOR DOCTRINE OF FAITH, «Questions on Sterilization», March 13, 1975, *AAS* 68 (1976) 738-740, especially at p. 739, «In applicatione principii de materiali cooperatione, ubi casus ferat, omnino scandalum et periculum cuiusvis confusionis mentium caveatur per opportunam explicationem realitatis».

[126] J.J. FERRER, «Needle Exchange», 187.

[127] J.F. KEENAN, «Prophylactics, Toleration, and Cooperation», 207. He gives a detailed analysis of all that is involved in invoking this principle. I rely on the analysis too.

c) *Other Traditional Principles:*
   Double Effect, Lesser of Two Evils

Some authors have even gone further to justify the use of condoms for HIV prevention by using the principle of double effect.[128]

According to this principle, «actions and omissions are permissible only when their gravely bad effects are allowed for good reason («proportional reason») and are unintended».[129]

The premise of this principle dates back to Thomas Aquinas' discussion on self-defense. In his analysis Aquinas writes:

> I reply that it must be said that nothing prevents there being two effects of one act, of which one effect alone would be in the intention and the other would be beyond the intention. But moral acts receive their species according to what is intended, not from what is beyond intention, since the latter is accidental as appears from what has been said above.
>
> Therefore, from the act of someone defending himself a double effect can follow: one is the preservation of his own life, the other is the killing of the attacker. An act of this kind in which the preservation of one's own life is intended does not have the character of the unlawful, since it is natural for everyone to preserve himself in his being as far as he can.
>
> But some act, arising from a good intention can be made unlawful if it is not proportionate to the end. And so, if someone is defending his own life uses greater violence than is necessary, it will be unlawful. But if he moderately repels violence, it will be a lawful defense.[130]

---

[128] D.F. KELLY, *Critical Care Ethics,* 208; see Maurizio Faggioni, as reported in the Catholic News Service. For an excellent treatment of this principle, see, L. UGORJI, *The Principle of Double Effect.* Significant literature about this principle can be found in C.E. CURRAN – R. McCORMICK, ed., *Readings in Moral Theology.* See also C.E. CURRAN, *Ongoing Revision,* 173-209; J.L. GARCIA, «Double Effect», 636-641.

[129] J.L. GARCIA, «Double Effect», 636.

[130] Thomas Aquinas, *Summa Theologiae,* II-II, q. 64, a. 7. «Respondeo dicendum quod nihil prohibet unius actus esse duos effectus, quorum alter solum sit in intentione, alius vero sit praeter intentionem. Morales autem actus recipiunt speciem secundum id quod intenditur, non autem ab eo quod est praeter intentionem, cum sit per accidens, ut ex supra dictis patet. Ex actu igitur alicuius seipsum defendentis duplex effectus sequi potest: unus quidem conservatio propriae vitae; alius autem occisio invadentis. Actus iqitur huiusmodi ex hoc quod intenditur conservatio propriae vitae, non habet rationem illiciti: cum hoc sit cuilibet naturale quod se conservet in esse quantum potest. Potest tamen aliquis actus ex bona intentione proveniens illicitus reddi si non sit proportionatus fini. Et ideo si aliquis ad defendendum propriam vitam

Although there have been various interpretations and usages of this principle,[131] nonetheless, there are four basic conditions that almost have become the standard for the use of this principle. These four conditions are:

1. The action itself is good or indifferent.
2. The good effect is not produced by means of evil effect.
3. The evil effect is not directly intended.
4. A proportionate reason supports causing or tolerating the evil effect.[132]

These four conditions, as Gula notes, are not free from some problems.[133] However, traditionally, the principle of double effect uses the distinction of the direct and indirect intention, since certain actions are regarded as intrinsically evil.

Applying this principle to justify the use of prophylactics for the prevention of HIV/AIDS, David Kelly argues that the distribution of condoms is not itself intrinsically evil; the good effect, that of saving lives, is not caused by the bad effect, the immoral sex. Again, those who distribute or advise condom use do not will, or support, the immoral sexual acts.

Maurizio Faggioni on his part says that condom use might be justified among Catholic couples especially when one of the spouses has AIDS, but the justification holds as long as the «exclusive and primary intent» is to defend the healthy partner from infection and not to prevent pregnancy. In this case, the principle of double effect comes to play as the person's good action has an unintended bad effect.[134]

Salvino Leone also argued in favor of the use of condoms to prevent the transmission of HIV/AIDS within the context of marriage where one partner is infected and the other not yet infected. Using a rigorous phenomenological analysis, he argued that the use of prophylactics for contraceptive purpose is quite different from the use of prophylactics as preventive measure for HIV/AIDS. The mechanism of prophylactics as contraceptive is explicitly meant to block the sperm from reaching the ovules. The mechanism of prophylactics as a preventive measure

---

utatur maiori violentia quam oporteat, erit illicitum. Si vero moderate violentiam repellat, erit licita defensio».

[131] Cf. R. GULA, *Reason Informed by Faith,* 270.

[132] R. GULA, *Reason Informed by Faith,* 270. See also, A. SPAGNOLO, *Bioetica,* 46.

[133] R. GULA, *Reason Informed by Faith,* 271.

[134] Maurizio Faggioni, as reported by J. NORTON, «Theologians», 2000.

against HIV/AIDS infection is that of blocking the virus from entering the organism of the uninfected partner.[135]

The principle of lesser of two evils has also been invoked to justify the moral liceity of condoms when it comes to the prevention of HIV/AIDS.[136] This principle is just saying that given a situation where one is determined to act immorally or pursue an evil action, since it is certain that such a person is not willing to change, it is permissible to counsel for the lesser of two evils. Two conditions are necessary for one to validly make recourse to the principle of lesser evil. First, the person counseled is determined to and prepared for the commission of the greater evil; secondly, there is no other way of preventing the greater evil.

In relation to condoms and HIV prevention, the advice to use condoms could be justified and ethically permissible using the principle of lesser evil if the person is going to be sexually active, especially among HIV-discordant couples.[137] In this case, the principle of lesser evil is counseled *sub specie boni*. That is to say it is recognized that to engage in sexual intercourse when one is HIV-positive is an evil act. Given a situation where this individual does not want to abstain from sex, instead of exposing the uninfected partner to infection, which is a greater evil, it is advisable to use condoms that minimize the risk of exposure to the virus (the lesser evil) by the uninfected partner. The intention here is to protect the healthy partner from being infected with the deadly virus. The greater evil is death by AIDS, while the lesser evil is the use of condoms for HIV prevention.

As a matter of fact, even within the Church that consistently rejects condom use, one sees divergent views. For instance, in the article of Suaudeau, it is accepted implicitly that «prophylactics is one of the ways to "contain" the sexual transmission of HIV/AIDS, that is, to limit its transmission».[138] James Keenan and Jon Fuller see this position as a

---

[135] S. LEONE, «L'approccio etico ai problemi dell'AIDS»,14-19.

[136] See EDITORIAL, «Vienna Archbishop». Also, J.J. FERRER, «Needle Exchange», 190. Though he invoked this principle with regard to Needle Exchange Program yet his arguments fit into prophylactics discussion.

[137] Cf. M. VIDAL, *Diccionario de Etica Teologica*, 555. He says: «Cuando la conducta sexual sea correcta, por ejemplo entre casados uno de los cuales es seropositivo, no parece incorrecto el uso del preservativo come un <mal menor> para evitar males mayores».

[138] J. SUAUDEAU, «Prophylactics or Family Value?», 9.

positive sign coming from the Church's high officials.[139] However, in a reaction to the article of Fuller and Keenan, Suaudeau said these two Jesuits had unjustly amplified one point of his article, which referred to condoms as a lesser evil in the case of Thai prostitutes. According to him, the overall thrust of his article is that condom use «could not be proposed as a model of humanization and development».[140] In addition, he said his use of the term of «lesser evil» was not so unusual and that the phrase did not signify an official Vatican endorsement, a phrase that some moral theologians criticized.

The issue is that many Church officials believe that condom use could be accepted for HIV prevention but there are divergent opinions on the principles invoked to justify such position. For instance, one of the theologians who criticized the principle of lesser evil is Maurizio Faggioni. He said he do not see the «lesser evil» principle as helpful. He recognizes the fact that some moralists accept it and that it is part of the Church's tradition, but he thinks «it doesn't seem a (moral principle) which helps. A Christian can never do evil, even the lesser evil».[141] He nonetheless said that condom use to protect against AIDS could be tolerated on other grounds. For example, prostitutes who show no immediate intention of leaving their profession could use condoms, in this situation, the use of condoms according to him, is a step «in a progression of human liberation».[142] Gonzalo Miranda on his part said that using a condom in a situation involving prostitutes with AIDS could be described as a «lesser evil» if one meant it as a social or health evil and not a moral evil.

Given the above, one notices that there is a tension between those who oppose condom use and those who argue in its favor. The future will tell how this tension will be resolved. Although Georges Cottier, who is John Paul II's in-house theologian, said that there is «an ongoing debate among Catholic theologians».[143] Before this tension is resolved, however, given the fact that HIV infection occurs on daily basis, I believe that what is needed is to propose a comprehensive approach. By this I mean, first is the need to emphasize and encourage

---

[139] J.D. FULLER – J.F. KEENAN, «Tolerant Signals», 6-7. After the publication of this article, Suaudeau claimed that his article is not an endorsement by the Vatican for condom use and that Fuller and Keenan do not adequately reflect his position.

[140] J. NORTON, «Theologians». Also, EDITORIAL, «Signs of the Times», 4.

[141] J. NORTON, «Theologians». Also, EDITORIAL, «Signs of the Times», 4.

[142] J. NORTON, «Theologians». Also, EDITORIAL, «Signs of the Times», 4.

[143] J. NORTON, «Theologians». Also, EDITORIAL, «Signs of the Times», 4.

abstinence, mutual monogamy and fidelity in existing relationships. In this way, young people especially, should be encouraged to have a delayed experience of genital intercourse until they are married. This then will effectively cater for the expressed fear of promiscuity. For the HIV-discordant couples, one can encourage them to abstain from sex as much as they can, but when and where such advice is not followed or accepted, then condom use may be recommended. Secondly, moral values are needed in our public health campaign programs.

At the same time, we must not fail to take into cognizance the fact that the majority of cases and the spread of the HIV infection worldwide occur during sexual intercourse. Thus, in a situation where people will not refrain from those activities which potentially expose them to infections, as with the exposure to the highly concentrated fluids as in genital intercourse, then condom use could be recommended since it can reduce the risk. It must, however, be emphasized that condoms cannot be taken as an absolute guarantee against infection during intercourse. Therefore, the recommendation for condom use has to be done on a case-by-case situation.

Meanwhile, the teaching of *Humanae Vitae* must not be forgotten since that is the basis upon which some Church's leaders based their rejection of condom use. In number 15 of *Humanae Vitae*, the Church accepts as licit whatever therapeutic means is necessary to cure diseases of the human organism, even if that results in contraception, provided the contraceptive result is not directly intended or willed.[144] In other words, *Humanae Vitae* gives room for exceptions so that contraceptive devices can sometimes be legitimate. I think this vision should hold equally now as regards the use of condoms for preventing the spread of HIV infection. Although, HIV/AIDS was not known at the time *Humanae Vitae* was written, yet, I believe the vision of Paul VI in making the exception in no. 15 is very important and must be commended. It is this vision that should be a guiding principle in the efforts to confront the problem of the HIV/AIDS of this present time.

Unfortunately, a lot of people tend to ignore this aspect of the Church's teaching as if it does not exist. It is even surprising to note that the present pope, who praised the encyclical of his predecessor, and referred to it in some of his writings, was nonetheless silent on

---

[144] PAUL VI, «Humanae Vitae», no.15. «Ecclesia autem illas medendi rationes haud illicitas existimat, quae ad morbos corporis curandos necessariae sunt, etiamsi exinde oriatur procreationis impedimentum, licet praevisum, dummodo ne hoc impedimentum ob quamlibet rationem directo intendatur».

Humanae Vitae no.15.

As mentioned earlier, John Paul II has not made a categorical or explicit statement on the use of condoms for the prevention of HIV/AIDS. At the same time, one notices in his writings that he only reaffirms and emphasizes the teaching that the use of a contraceptive device is not open to procreation. For instance, in his Apostolic Exhortation, *Familiaris Consortio*,[145] he reaffirms and supports the teaching of *Humanae Vitae*. In no. 32,[146] for example, John Paul II made references to nos. 7, 12, 13 and 14 of *Humanae Vitae*, but then, was silent on no.15. This same pattern is seen in his other writings, like *Gratissimam Sane*,[147] where he spoke of the grave difficulties families sometimes face, and also in *Evangelium Vitae*.[148] In fact, no distinction is made between the «contraceptive mentality» and the use of contraceptive for the prevention of a deadly disease such as HIV/AIDS.

Therefore, condom use in the time of HIV/AIDS is for prevention of a deadly disease. One may argue that those infected can practice abstinence;[149] this is perfectly right. But in case they choose not to abstain from sex, especially HIV-discordant couples, then, it is also legitimate to see the use of prophylactics in this situation as preventive measure, not as contraceptive since they want to preserve the unitive aspect of their marriage as well. In this regard I find Bernard Haring's insight very stimulating. In his analysis of *Humanae Vitae* 15, he rightly pointed out the phrase was constructed with the biological understanding of medicine as restoration of organism. Medicine is no longer based on the mere restoration of the organism but the wholeness of a person in community.[150] It is in this context, too, that the use of prophylactics for the prevention of HIV/AIDS among HIV-discordant couples can be situated and hence, permitted as morally licit.

Finally, in the field of medicine, preventive medicine is an important aspect of therapeutic medicine. Therefore, giving room for condom use to prevent the transmission of HIV does not in my view compromise the teaching of the Church.

---

[145] JOHN PAUL II, *Familiaris Consortio* (November 22, 1981).

[146] JOHN PAUL II, *Familiaris Consortio, no.* 32.

[147] JOHN PAUL II, *Gratissimam Sane*, (February 2, 1994). See nos. 5, 12 and 37 in particular.

[148] JOHN PAUL II, *Evangelium Vitae*, (March 25, 1995). See no. 100. 2.

[149] Cf. D. TETTAMANZI, *Bioetica*, 360-361.

[150] B. HARING, «The Inseparability of the Unitive», 153-167, especially, pp.159-160.

4. The Needle Exchange Programs

Although it has been pointed out that there are no known cases of HIV transmission as a result of drug injection in Nigeria, yet it is important to examine the effectiveness of the needle exchange program.

There are people who strongly argue that like the issue of prophylactics, given the fact that infections occur as a result of the use of contaminated needles and syringes for injecting drugs, it is necessary to engage in the distribution of new needles and syringes for the drug users. The concern is that a program such as this will help to reduce or eliminate the cases of infection that occur through the practice of drug injection.

As with the prophylactic debate, there have been arguments in support, as well as against this idea.[151] For those who argue against a program like this, the claim is that embarking on it may seem to be giving tacit approval for drug use. Those who argue in favor of the needle exchange program claim that embarking on such a program does not in any way promote or encourage the illicit use of drugs. Rather, the object of concern is to protect and save lives given the fact that these addicts are not willing or able to give up their illicit drug use.

Again, Jon Fuller cited some findings that show that needle exchange programs do not increase the frequency of injection among those who participate in the program; neither did it increase the number of new injection drug users.[152]

Jorge Ferrer also argues along this line and goes on to support such programs by invoking the principles of cooperation and the lesser of two evils.[153] He concludes by saying that such action is not only justifiable but probably obligatory as well.

5. Concluding Remarks

The problem that the preventive effort faces lies only with the above specific areas of prevention namely, the use of prophylactics and the needle exchange programs. The main criticism against distribution or advice on the use of condoms is that it promotes or encourages promiscuity, while neglecting the basic human values, especially in the area of sexuality. There is no doubt that those who argue in support of condoms and needle exchange programs also consider this criticism. It is

[151] See J.F. KEENAN, ed., *Catholic Ethicists*, 26-28.
[152] J. FULLER, «A Needle Exchange», 18.
[153] J.J. FERRER, «Needle Exchange», 177-191.

accepted that the criticism has «an explicit factual claim and an implicit moral claim».[154] Yet, those who support the use of condoms and needle exchange believe that these approaches are important and necessary to save lives[155] given the fact that no effective cure has been found.

I would conclude this chapter by noting that in Nigeria, as in most of the developing nations, the majority of the cases of HIV infection are spread through heterosexual intercourse, and so, any intervention that reduces the risk of transmission must be viewed as potentially life-saving. The use of condoms here cannot and should not be equated to contraception. The people in this part of the world love to have children and a large family, hence the contraceptive spirit is not as high as in the developed countries.

---

[154] J.J. FERRER, «Needle Exchange», 181.
[155] J. FULLER, «A Needle Exchange», 18.

SUMMARY AND CONCLUSION

In the foregoing pages, I demonstrated that the HIV/AIDS situation in the world at large, and Nigeria in particular, should be a cause of concern for everyone in order to avoid the disaster that comes with the explosion of the epidemic. As the HIV/AIDS epidemic continues, it has dawned on many people that this disease is everyone's tragedy. If this consciousness is accepted, then the prevention of its further spreading would be everyone's concern. It is in the light of this consciousness that I undertook to do a doctoral research on this crucial issue.

In chapter one, a general overview was given of HIV/AIDS. There, it pointed out the inconclusive or rather, the divergent views about the origin of the disease. It also highlighted and explained its modes of transmissions. One crucial point is that it pointed out with data that the disease is not contracted casually, hence, that should help to alleviate fear and unwarranted discriminations towards the people already infected with the virus.

In chapter two I examined the situation of HIV/AIDS in Nigeria, according to the different states and zones. Here, I discussed the factors that enhanced the rapid spread of the disease in the country, which are basically economic, socio-moral, political and cultural. However, it was argued that economic rather than cultural reasons are the main factors for the rapid spread of the disease. The effects of the epidemic, both immediate and long-term were also said to have both economic and social dimensions. It should be emphasized again that the epidemic has affected all social groups, although at different levels. However, the conclusion that could be drawn from the analysis made is that HIV/AIDS in one aspect is a revelation of inequality and injustice.

The third chapter deals with the preventive approach that Nigeria needs to undertake. The idea in this chapter is that for any preventive strategy to make a meaningful difference, the social and economic to political factors that were examined in chapter two must be tackled and addressed decisively. The contention, therefore, is that the war against HIV/AIDS would not be won if based solely on isolated vertical programs. For instance, a program on general awareness about HIV/AIDS is not enough unless it includes other factors contributing to the spread of the disease. Thus, the need to focus on the issue of economic and social justice, especially as it affects women, who bear the burden of the disease much more. Consequently, the chapter examined the principles of responsibility, non-discrimination, confidentiality and justice, which are considered to be important components of a meaningful preventive strategy. It also argued that everyone must be involved from the government to religious institutions, non-governmental and individual citizens in this preventive strategy. The chapter concludes by examining the ways to realize the preventive goals which include: information and enlightenment campaign, testing and screening for HIV, counseling those already infected and the renewal of traditional values and customs that frown against immoral sexual behaviors. The last point is very essential as it calls for a dialogue to make a constructive Christian engagement with traditional customs and values.

The final chapter examined some specific moral issues in the prevention of HIV/AIDS, like the use of prophylactics (condoms) and needle exchange programs. By examining the debates over the use of condoms for HIV/AIDS prevention, I portrayed the sense and values of the Catholic teaching on abstinence and marital fidelity along with others who share similar views. However, given the fact that many people do not follow the teachings on abstinence and marital fidelity, and so many individuals are at risk of becoming HIV-infected, it is equally important for the Church to listen and to be faithful to her teachings, like the principles of double effect, lesser of two evils, etc. to argue for the use of prophylactics as a necessary component of HIV/AIDS prevention.

Having noted the above, the starting point for the prevention of HIV/AIDS in Nigeria would be the need to eliminate poverty, injustice and inequality that exist, especially that to which women are subjected. There is also the need for behavioral changes that put people at the risk of infection. However, it is also necessary to admit the fact that not all people will be positively disposed to behavioral change, hence, the need to move toward common interests based on prudence, compassion and reciprocal advantage of protecting and saving lives.

Table 1: **Summary Results of HIV Prevalence in Zone A (South East)**

STATE	SITE	SITE STATUS	TOTAL SAMPLE	NUMBER POSITIVE	%HIV	95% C.I
ABIA	UMUAHIA	MC	300	7	2,3	1.0-4.6
	ABA	OMC	207	8	3,9	1.8-7.2
	TOTAL		507	15	3	
ANAMBRA	AWKA	MC	298	25	8,4	5.6-12.0
	EKWULOBIA	OMC	300	11	3,7	1.9-6.3
	TOTAL		598	36	6	
EBONYI	ABAKALIKI	MC	153	17	11,1	6.8-16.8
	ONUEKE	OMC	160	12	7,5	4.1-12.4
	TOTAL		313	29	9,3	
ENUGU	ENUGU	MC	300	15	5	2.8-8.1
	ONUEKE	OMC	164	7	4,2	1.7-8.5
	TOTAL		464	22	4,7	
IMO	OWERRI	MC	300	16	5,3	3.1-8.5
	ORLU	OMC	264	28	10,6	7.2-15.0
	TOTAL		564	44	7,8	
ZONAL TOTAL			**2446**	**146**	**6**	

Minimum Value:	2,3
Maximum Value:	11,1
Median Value:	**5,2**

MC = Major City.
OMC = Outside Major City.
Source: National AIDS/STD Control Programme/Federal Ministry of Health, 2000.

Table II: Summary Results of HIV Prevalence in Zone B (South West)

STATE	SITE	SITE STATUS	TOTAL SAMPLE	NUMBER POSITIVE	%HIV	95% C.I
EKITI	ADO EKITI	MC	300	5	1,7	0.5 3.8
	IKOLE EKITI	OMC	284	8	2,8	1.2-5.5
	TOTAL		584	13	2,2	
LAGOS	IKEJA	MC	300	21	7	4.4-10.5
	EPE	OMC	220	14	6,4	3.5-10.4
	TOTAL		520	35	6,7	
OGUN	ABEOKUTA	MC	300	3	1	0.2-2.9
	IJEBU-ODE	OMC	298	12	4	0.2-2.9
	TOTAL		598	15	2,5	
ONDO	AKURE	MC	293	8	2,9	1.2-5.3
	ONDO	OMC	301	9	3	1.4-5.6
	TOTAL		594	17	2,9	
OSUN	OSOGBO	MC	300	8	2,7	1.2-5.2
	ILESHA	OMC	300	14	4,7	2.6-7.7
	TOTAL		600	22	3,7	2.1-5.5
OYO	IBADAN	MC	300	8	2,7	1.2-5.2
	SAKI	OMC	300	13	4,3	2.3-7.3
	TOTAL		600	21	3,5	
ZONAL TOTAL			3496	123	3,5	

Minimum Value:	1,7
Maximum Value:	4,3
Median Value:	3,5

MC = Major City.
OMC = Outside Major City.
Source: National AIDS/STD Control Programme/Federal Ministry of Health, 2000.

Table III: **Summary Results of HIV Prevalence in Zone C (North West)**

STATE	SITE	SITE STATUS	TOTAL SAMPLE	NUMBER POSITIVE	%HIV	95% C.I
JIGAWA	DUTSE	MC	299	6	2	0.7-4.3
	HADEJIA	OMC	301	4	1,3	0.4-3.4
	TOTAL		600	10	1,7	
KADUNA	KADUNA	MC	298	24	8,1	5.2-11.7
	KAFANCHAN	OMC	299	45	15,1	11.2-19.6
	TOTAL		597	69	11,6	
KANO	KANO	MC	300	11	3,6	1.8-6.5
	RANO	OMC	300	15	5	2.8-8.1
	TOTAL		600	26	4,3	
KATSINA	KATSINA	MC	299	9	3	1.3-5.6
	FUNTUA	OMC	299	5	1,7	0.5-3.9
	TOTAL		598	14	2,3	
KEBBI	BIRININ KEBBI	MC	300	12	7,3	2.1-6.9
	ORGUNGU	OMC	300	10	3,3	1.6-6.0
	TOTAL		600	22	3,7	
SOKOTO	SOKOTO	MC	300	8	2,7	1.2-5.2
	ARGUNGU	OMC				
	TOTAL		300	8	2,7	
ZAMFARA	GUSAU	MC	299	5	1,7	0.6-3.9
	TALATA-MARAFA	OMC	298	11	3,7	1.9-6.5
	TOTAL		597	16	2,7	
ZONAL TOTAL			3892	165	4,2	

Minimum Value:	1,3
Maximum Value:	15,1
Median Value:	**3,2**

MC = Major City.   /   OMC = Outside Major City.

Source: National AIDS/STD Control Programme/Federal Ministry of Health, 2000.

Table IV: **Summary Results of HIV Prevalence in Zone D (North East)**

STATE	SITE	SITE STATUS	TOTAL SAMPLE	NUMBER POSITIVE	%HIV	95% C.I
ADAMAWA	YOLA	MC	310	17	5,5	3.2-8.6
	MUBI	OMC	290	13	4,5	2.4-7.5
	TOTAL		600	30	5	
BAUCHI	BAUCHI	MC	300	16	5,3	3.1-8.5
	AZARE	OMC	299	2	0,6	0.1-2.4
	TOTAL		599	18	3	
BORNO	MAIDUGURI	MC	300	13	4,3	2.3-7.3
	BIU	OMC	300	14	4,7	2.6-7.7
	TOTAL		600	27	4,5	
GOMBE	GOMBE	MC	299	10	3,3	1.6-6.1
	KALTUNGO	OMC	300	18	6	3.6-9.3
	TOTAL		599	28	4,7	
TARABA	JALINGO	MC	300	12	4	2.1-6.9
	ZING	OMC	300	21	7	4.4-10.5
	TOTAL		600	33	5,5	
YOBE	DAMATURU	MC	353	9	2,5	1.2-4.8
	GEIDAM	OMC	184	1	0,5	0.0-2.0
	TOTAL		537	10	1,9	
ZONAL TOTAL			**3535**	**146**	**4,1**	

Minimum Value:	0,5
Maximum Value:	7
Median Value:	**4,5**

MC = Major City.
OMC = Outside Major City.
Source: National AIDS/STD Control Programme/Federal Ministry of Health, 2000.

Table V: **Summary Results of HIV Prevalence in Zone E (North Central)**

STATE	SITE	SITE STATUS	TOTAL SAMPLE	NUMBER POSITIVE	%HIV	95% C.I
BENUE	MAKURDI	MC	300	38	12,7	9.1-17
	OTUKPO	OMC	300	63	21	16.5-26.1
	TOTAL		600	101	16,8	
FCT	GARKI	MC	300	24	8	5.2-11.6
	GWAGWALADA	OMC	300	19	6,3	3.9-9.7
	TOTAL		600	43	7,2	
KOGI	LOKOJA	MC	300	11	3,7	1.8-6.5
	ANKPA	OMC	300	20	6,7	4.1-10.1
	TOTAL		600	31	5,2	
KWARA	ILORIN	MC	358	11	3,1	1.5-5.4
	OFFA	OMC	240	8	3,3	1.4-6.5
	TOTAL		598	19	3,2	
NASARAWA	LAFIA	MC	300	41	13,7	10.0-18.1
	N/EGGON	OMC	240	18	7,3	4.5-11.6
	TOTAL		540	59	10,8	
NIGER	MINNA	MC	300	27	9	6.0-12.8
	WUSHISHI	OMC	300	13	4,3	2.3-7.3
	TOTAL		600	40	6,7	
PLATEAU	JOS	MC	321	25	7,8	5.1-11.3
	SHENDAM	OMC	299	14	4,3	2.3-7.3
	TOTAL		620	38	6,1	
ZONAL TOTAL			**4158**	**331**	**7,9**	

Minimum Value:	3,1
Maximum Value:	21
Median Value:	**7**

MC = Major City.
OMC = Outside Major City.
Source: National AIDS/STD Control Programme/Federal Ministry of Health, 2000.

Table VI: **Summary Results of HIV Prevalence in Zone F (South-South)**

STATE	SITE	SITE STATUS	TOTAL SAMPLE	NUMBER POSITIVE	%HIV	95% C.I
AKWA IBOM	UYO	MC	300	35	11,7	8.3-15.9
	ESSEIN-UDIM	OMC	300	40	13,3	9.7-7.7
	TOTAL		600	75	12,5	
BAYELSA	YENOGOA	MC	267	9	3,4	1.6-6.3
	BRASS	OMC	262	14	5,3	3.0-8.8
	TOTAL		529	23	4,3	
CROSS RIVER	CALABAR	MC	300	19	6,3	3.9-9.7
	IKOM	OMC	300	16	5,3	3.1-8.5
	TOTAL		600	35	5,8	
DELTA	WARRI	MC	299	10	3,3	1.6-6.1
	AGBOR	OMC	300	15	5	2.8-8.1
	TOTAL		599	25	4,2	
EDO	BENIN CITY	MC	300	12	4	2.1-6.9
	AUCHI	OMC	244	20	8,2	5.1-12.4
	TOTAL		544	32	5,9	
RIVERS	PORTHACOURT	MC	300	14	4,7	2.6-7.7
	BORI	OMC	290	3	1	0.2-0.3
	TOTAL		590	17	3,3	
ZONAL TOTAL			**3462**	**207**	**6**	

Minimum Value: 1
Maximum Value: 13,3
Median Value: 5,2

MC = Major City
OMC = Outside Major City.
Source: National AIDS/STD Control Programme/Federal Ministry of Health, 2000.

TABLE I – Federal Government Budget Estimates (Capital Expenditure) [Million Naira]

	1986	1987	1988	1989	1990	1991	1992	1993	1994	1995	1996
Administration	574,1	275,5	1306,5	993,9	1969,7	2942,9	3404,6	6788	10832,7	16858,5	13328,4
General Administration	200,4	163,9	595,2	559,5	955,1	1950,8	1740,1	4156,1	6719,4	11139,2	6731,3
Defence	164,7	92,1	400	310	818,2	581	981,3	1546,3	2826,5	3688,1	3927
Internal Security	209	18,5	271,3	124,1	196,4	411,1	683,2	1085,6	1286,8	2031,2	2670
Economic Services	2836,7	1957,9	2604,4	2325,4	3751,6	1673,7	2355,1	5475,6	9902,5	22527,9	21036,7
Agric.& Natural Resources	892,5	365,1	595,7	981,5	1758,5	551,2	763	1820	2800,1	4691,7	3892,8
Manufacturing,Craft, Mining and Quarrying	1094	452	994,4	529,8	729,5	561,9	751,4	1659,3	4313,6	7103,3	1741,2
Transport and Communication	516,1	375,1	703,7	683,8	877,4	353,4	625,3	1436,7	1293,5	3800,3	8819,7
Special Projects											-
Others	334,1	775,7	310,6	130,3	386,2	207,2	215,4	559,6	1495,3	6932,6	6583
Special and Community Services	789,6	715	1407,4	1043,9	1359,7	1329,5	1777,8	4826,9	6064,8	5032,6	5832,4
Education	442	139,1	281,8	221,9	331,7	289,1	384,1	1563	2405,7	3307,4	3215,8
Health	81,2	69,5	183,2	126	257	137,6	188	352,9	961	1725,2	1659,5
Housing	-	-	239,4	273,1	523,4	840,5	1079,9	2468,2	2683,6	-	465
Others	266,4	506,4	703	422,9	247,6	62,3	125,8	442,8	14,5	-	492,1
Transfers	1245,5	1812	1263,9	1946,2	1974,6	3645	8438,4	1509,5	4200	140	7802,5
Other Financial Obligations	79	174	241	166,2	-	-	-	-	4200	-	609,1
Capital Repayment	1166,5	938	522,9	1200	1631	150	n.a	n.a	-	-	-
Outstanding Liabilities	n.a.	700	500	100	260	3395	4000	n.a	-	-	-
Public Debt Charges								n.a			
Minor Adjustments					83,6	100	4438,4	1509,5	-	140	211,5
Capital Supplimentations						3494,3	n.a	1024,5	-	-	5425
Phased Commitments Due				480							
Add (i) External Loans (External Drawdowns)			1506,4	2500	3500			n.a	n.a	-	-
(ii) Special Projects			2500	488,1	-	-	-	485	-	-	1556,9
Loans On-Lent to State Governments	n.a.	n.a	n.a	n.a.	n.a	n.a	n.a.	n.a	n.a	-	-
Loans to Parastatals of Govt. Owned Companies	n.a.	n.a	n.a	n.a.	n.a	n.a	n.a.	n.a	n.a	-	-
Federal Government Own											
Capital expenditure	5445,9	4759,4	10588,6	9297,1	12555,6	13085,4	15975,9	18600	31000	44559	48000

Source: *Central Bank of Nigeria Statistical Bulletin*, Vol.7, No.2, Dec. 1996.

TABLE II – Federal Government Budget Estimates (Capital Expenditure) [Million Naira]

	1986	1987	1988	1989	1990	1991	1992	1993	1994	1995	1996
Administration	2008,4	2214,3	3856	3646	5404,5	7413,7	8842,6	18769,1	20851,7	32824,8	49138
General Administration	869,2	1106,2	2481	2017	2864,1	4061,2	5076,1	12851,2	11924,4	25449,3	25931,8
Defence	742,4	717,7	830	957,3	1410,5	1834,2	2023,4	3085,4	4205,1	5344,4	11425,7
Internal Security	396,8	390,4	545	617,7	1129,9	1518,3	1743,1	2832,5	4722,2	2031,1	11780,5
Economic Services	598,2	494,4	874,9	991,4	1135,9	1325,4	2379,3	3603,4	4210,9	5802,1	5017,5
Agriculture	32,9	29,2	54,3	81,1	208,1	121,1	161,5	1015,3	919	2236	1681,2
Construction	329,8	259,1	43,3	449,6	342,1	412,6	1066,3	1272,5	1438,8	494,7	984,4
Transport and Communication	125,8	114,2	142,8	170,4	232,4	245,4	356,3	350,1	381,4	890	2183,6
Others	109,7	91,9	244,8	283,3	353,3	546,3	795,2	965,5	1471,7	2181,1	168,3
Social and Community Services	1144,6	778	1298,3	2337,4	2945,9	2693,4	3081,5	8767,7	11114,3	12757	16879,1
Education	652,8	514,4	802,3	1719,9	1962,6	1265,1	1676,3	6436,1	7878,1	9421,3	12136
Health	279,2	166,9	260	326,6	401,1	619,4	837,4	2331,6	2066,8	3335,7	3192
Others	212,6	96,7	236	290,9	582,2	808,9	567,6	-	1169,4	0,0	1551,1
Transfers	1884,7	7262,5	7679,4	13835,2	17722,1	14148	21756,6	62360,3	43023,1	57552,7	60385,6
Public Dept Charges	1509	6578,5	6915,6	13030	16872	13247	20442	58400	41000	55000	56000
Internal	-	2666,2	3000	(4210)	(5105)	-	n.a	(17900)	(1400)	11000	12000
External	-	3912,3	3915	(8820)	(11767)	-	n.a	(40500)	(39600)	44000	44000
Pension and Gratuities	367,7										
Contingencies/Subventions	-	80	100	100	100	100	250	250	250	250	250
Other/Other CFR Charges	8	604	663,8	705,2	750,1	801	1064,6	3708,3	1773,1	2302,7	4135,6
Federal Government Own Recurrent Expenditure	5635,9	10749,2	13708,6	20810	27208,4	25580,5	36060	93500,5	79200	108936,6	131420,2
Add: Statutory Appropriation;											
(i) To State Governments								n.a	n.a	n.a	n.a
(ii) Local Governments								n.a	n.a	n.a	n.a
(i), (ii)											
(iii) For development of Producing Areas								n.a	n.a	n.a	n.a
(iv) Ecological								n.a	n.a	n.a	n.a
(v) Derivation								n.a	n.a	n.a	n.a
(iii), (iv), (v)								n.a	n.a	n.a	n.a
(vi) Transfer to Development Fund								n.a	n.a	n.a	n.a
Extra Budgetary Expenditure								n.a	n.a	n.a	n.a
Others								n.a	n.a	n.a	n.a
Total	5635,9	10749,2	13708,6	9297,1	27208,4	25580,5	36060	93500,5	79200	108936,6	131420,2

Source: *Central Bank of Nigeria Statistical Bulletin*, Vol.7, No.2, Dec. 1996, p.118

ABBREVIATIONS

AAS	*Acta Apostolicae Sedis*
AIDS	Acquired Immunodeficiency Syndrome
AIDS	*Acquired Immunodeficiency Syndrome* (review)
AIM	*Annals of Internal Medicine*
AJOG	*American Journal of Obstetrics and Gynecology*
AJPH	*American Journal of Public Health*
BJVD	*British Journal of Venerology Diseases*
BSP	*Bullentin of Social Pathology*
Cf.	Confer.
CIA	Central Intelligence Agency
Conc	*Concilium*
DH	*Dolentium Hominum*
Dt	Deuteronomy
ed.	Editor (s)
Ex	Exodus
Gen	Genesis
FMOH	Federal Ministry of Health
FMOH/NACA	FEDERAL MINISTRY OF HEALTH/NATIONAL ACTION COMMITTEE ON AIDS, *Situation Analysis Report on STD/HIV/ AIDS in Nigeria*, Abuja 2000.
FPP	*Family Planning Perspective*
HIV	Human Immunodeficiency Virus
Ibid.	*Ibidem* (Same work)
ID.	Same Author
IPhR	*International Philosophical Quarterly*
IThQ	*International Theological Quarterly*
JAMA	*Journal of the American Medical Association*
JID	*Journal of Infectious Diseases*
JRSM	*Journal of Royal Social Medicine*
LS	*Louvain Studies*
NACA	National Action Committee on AIDS
NASCP	National AIDS/STD Control Programme

NASCP/FMOH	NATIONAL AIDS/STD CONTROL PROGRAMME, FEDERAL MINISTRY OF HEALTH, *1999 HIV/Syphilis Sentinel Sero-Prevalence Survey in Nigeria: Technical Report,* Abuja 1999.
NCCB	National Conference of Catholic Bishops
NEJM	*New England Journal of Medicine*
No.	Number
op.cit.	*opus citatum* (work already cited)
OR	*L'Osservatore Romano*
p./pp.	page/pages
PID	*Pediatric Infectious Deseases*
RID	*Review of Infectious Deseases*
SSM	*Social Science and Medicine*
TS	*Theological Studies*
UNAIDS	United Nations Programme on HIV/AIDS
USCC	United States Catholic Conference
WHO	World Health Organization

BIBLIOGRAPHY

1. Sources

1.1 *Dictionaries*

CINA, F. – LOCCI, E. – ROCCHETTA, C. – SANDRIN, L., ed., *Dizionario di Teologia Pastorale Sanitaria*, Torino 1997.

COMPAGNONI, F. – PIANA, G. – PRIVITERA, S., ed., *Nuovo Dizionario di Teologia Morale*, Cinisello Balsamo, MI 1990.

LEONE, S. – PRIVITERA, S., ed., *Dizionario di Bioetica*, Acireale – Bologna 1994.

MACQUARRIE, J. – CHILDRESS, J., ed., *A New Dictionary of Christian Ethics*, London 1986.

ROSSI, L. – VALSECCHI, A., ed., *Dizionario Enciclopedico di Teologia Morale*, Roma 1981.

VIDAL, M., *Diccionario de Etica Teologica*, Estella, Navarra 1991.

WALTON, J. – BEESON, P. – SCOTT, R., ed., *The Oxford Companion to Medicine*, I, New York 1986.

1.2 *Nigerian Government Documents*

CENTRAL BANK OF NIGERIA, *Statistical Bulletin*, VII/2, Lagos 1996.

FEDERAL MINISTRY OF HEALTH AND NATIONAL AIDS/STD CONTROL PROGRAMME, *1999 HIV/Syphilis Sentinel Sero-Prevalence Survey in Nigeria: Technical Report*, Abuja 1999.

FEDERAL MINISTRY OF HEALTH AND NATIONAL ACTION COMMITTEE ON AIDS, *Situation Analysis Report on STD/HIV/AIDS in Nigeria*. Abuja 2000.

1.3 *American Government Documents*

CENTERS FOR DISEASE CONTROL, «Pneumocystis Pneumonia: Los Angeles», *Morbidity and Mortality Weekly Report*, June 5 (1981) 250-252.

CENTERS FOR DISEASE CONTROL, «Kaposi's Sarcoma and Pneumocystis Pneumonia Among Homosexual Males – New York City and California», *Morbidity and Mortality Weekly Report* 30 (1981) 305-308.

————, «Follow-up on Kaposi's Sarcoma and Pneumocystis Pneumonia», *Morbidity and Mortality Weekly Report* 30 (1981) 409-410.

————, «Diffuse, Undifferentiated Non-Hodgkins Lymphoma Among Homosexual Males – United States», *Morbidity and Mortality Weekly Report* 31 (1982) 277-279.

————, «Recommendations for Assisting in the Prevention of Perinatal Transmission of Human T-Lymphotropic Virus Type III/Lymphadenopathy-Associated Virus and Acquired Immunodeficiency Syndrome», *Morbidity and Mortality Weekly Report* December 6 (1985) 721-726, 731-732.

————, «Interpretive Criteria used to Report Western Blot Results for HIV-I Antibody Testing- United States», *Morbidity and Mortality Weekly Report* 40 (1991) 694-695.

CIA, *The World Factbook-Nigeria*, 2001. Cf. http://www.odci.gov/cia/publications/factbook.

INSTITUTE OF MEDICINE – NATIONAL ACADEMY OF SCIENCES, *Confronting AIDS: Directions for Public Health, Health Care and Research*, Washington, DC 1986.

NATIONAL SECURITY COUNCIL, *NSSM 200 – Implications of Worldwide Population Growth for US Security and Overseas Interests*, Washington, DC 1974.

1.4 *International Organization*

WHO – UNAIDS, *The AIDS Epidemic Update*, Geneva, December 1, 1998.

————, *Report on the Global HIV/AIDS epidemic*, Geneva 1998.

————, *Statistical Report: Adults and Children Estimated to Be Living with HIV/AIDS as of End 1999*, Geneva, December 1, 1999.

————, *Statistical Report: Adults and Children Estimated to Be Living with HIV/AIDS as of End 2000*, Geneva, December 1, 2000.

1.5 *Church Documents*

1.5.1 Papal Teaching

PIUS XI, *Divini Redemptoris* (March 19,1937), *AAS* 29 (1937) 65-106.

JOHN XXIII, *Mater et Magistra* (May 15, 1961), *AAS* 53 (1961) 401-464.

PAUL VI, *Humanae Vitae* (July 25, 1968), *AAS* 60 (1968) 481-503.

PAUL VI, *Octogesima Adveniens* (May 14, 1971), *AAS* 63 (1971) 401-441.

JOHN PAUL II, «Pope Addresses Vatican AIDS Conference», November 15,1989, *Origins*, 19.6 (1989) 434-436; *AAS* 82 (1990) 662-669.

——— , «The Church in the Face of Twofold Challenge of AIDS: Prevention in Keeping with the Dignity of the Human Person and True Solidary Care», November 15, 1989, *DH* 13 (1990) 6-9; *AAS* 82 (1990) 662-669.

——— , *Familiaris Consortio* (November 22, 1981), *AAS* 74 (1982) 81-191.

——— , *Gratissimam Sane* (February 2, 1994), *AAS* 86 (1994) 868-925.

——— , *Evangelium Vitae* (March 25, 1995), *AAS* 87 (1995) 401-522.

1.5.2 Episcopal Teaching

CATHOLIC BISHOPS' CONFERENCE OF THE PHILIPPINES, «In the Compassion of Jesus: A Pastoral Letter on AIDS», January 23, 1993.

COMMISSION SOCIALE DE L'EPISCOPAT, *SIDA. La Société en Question,* Paris 1996.

NCCB, «Economic Justice for All: Catholic Social Teaching and the US Economy», *Origins* 16.3 (1986) 33-76.

——— , «Called to Compassion and Responsibility: A Response to HIV/AIDS Crisis», *Origins* 19.26 (1989) 421-434.

RATZINGER, J., « Letter on AIDS Document», *Origins* 18.8 (1988) 117-121.

«Reaction to AIDS Statement», *Origins* 17.28 (1987) 489-493 [Bishops of the United States].

STAFFORD, F. – *al.*, «Continued Reaction to AIDS Statement», *Origins* 17.30 (1988) 516-522

USCC ADMINISTRATIVE BOARD, «The Many Faces of AIDS: A Gospel Response», *Origins* 17.28 (1987) 482-489.

2. **Books and Articles**

ACHEBE, C., *The Trouble with Nigeria,* London 1984.

ADEKEYE, F., «Before They Die», *Newswatch*, Lagos, March 8, 1999, 42 [newspaper's article].

ALAUSA, K.O. – OSABA, A.O., «Epidemiology of Gonococal Valvo Vaginith's among Children in the Tropics», *BJVD* 50 (1980) 239-242.

ALESSANDRI, R. – FREIDMAN, Z. – TRIVELLI, L., «Condoms and Adolescent HIV: A Medical Evaluation», *Linacre Quarterly* 61 (1994) 62-74.

ALISON, J., *Catholics and AIDS: Questions and Answers*, London 1987.

ALLEN, S.A. – KARITA, E. – N'GANDU, N. – TICHACEK, A., «The Evolution of Voluntary Testing and Counseling as an HIV Prevention Strategy», in L. GIBNEY – R.J. DICLEMENTE – S.H. VERMUND, ed., *Preventing HIV in Developing Countries,* New York 1999, 87-108.

ALMOND, B., ed., *AIDS: A Moral Issue. The Ethical, Legal and Social Aspects,* New York 1996.

ALTMAN, D., *Power and Community: Organizational and Cultural Responses to AIDS,* London 1994.

——— , «HIV, Homosexuality, and Vulnerability in the Developing World», in J.M. MANN – D.J. M. TARANTOLA, ed., *AIDS in the World II: Global Dimensions, Social Roots, and Responses,* New York, 1996, 254-258.

ALTMAN, L.K., «Rare Cancer Seen in 41 Homosexuals», *New York Times,* July 3, 1981 [newspaper's article].

ALUBO, S.O., «Debt Crisis, Health and Health Services in Africa», *SSM* (1990) 639-648.

AMADORI, A. – ZANOVELLO, P., *Immunologia Cellulare e Molecolare,* Padova 1998.

AMAT-ROSE, J.M. – al., «La géographie de l'infection par les virus de l'immunodeficience humaine (VIH) en Afrique noire: mise en évidence de facteurs d'épidemisation et de regionalisation», *BSP* 83 (1990) 137-140.

ANDERSON, J. – al., «HIV/AIDS Knowledge and Sexual Behavior Among High School Students», *FPP* 23 (1991) 6-16.

ANGELL, M., «A Dual Approach to the AIDS Epidemic», in K.R. OVERBERG, ed., *AIDS, Ethics and Religion,* Maryknoll, NY 1994, 178-182.

ANTONIO, G., *The AIDS Cover - Up?: The Real and Alarming Facts about AIDS,* San Francisco 1986.

AOKI, B. – NGIN, C.P. – MO, B. – JA, D.T., «AIDS Prevention Models in Asian-American Communities», in V.M. MAYS – G.W. ALBEE – S.F. SCHNEIDER, ed., *Primary Prevention of AIDS: Psychological Approaches,* Newbury Park, CA 1989, 290-308.

ARNO, P.S. – FEIDEN, K.L., *Against the Odds: The Story of AIDS, Drug Development, Politics & Profits,* New York 1992.

ASHLEY, B. – O'ROURKE, K.D., *Healthcare Ethics: A Theological Analysis,* Washington, DC 1997.

BABAGINDA, I., «AIDS Patients Need Care and Love», *The Road Journal,* 2 (4) 1992, 10.

BACKE, J., «AIDS: A Serious and Special Opportunity for Ministry», in K.R. OVERBERG, ed., *AIDS, Ethics and Religion*, Maryknoll, NY 1994, 249-261.

BALLARD, J., «Australia: Participation and Innovation in a Federal System», in KIRP, D.L. – BAYER, R., *AIDS in the Industrialized Democracies*, New Brunswick, NJ 1992, 134-167.

BASTERRA, F.J.E., *Bioethics,* Middlegreen, UK 1994.

BATE, S.C., «Differences in Confessional Advice in South Africa», in J.F. KEENAN, ed., *Catholic Ethicists on HIV/AIDS Prevention*, New York 2000, 212-221.

BAYER, R. – LEVINE, C. – WOLFE, S., «HIV Antibody Screening», *JAMA* 256 (1986) 1768-1774.

BAYER, R. – STRYKER, J., «Ethical Challenges Posed by Clinical Progress in AIDS», in T.L. BEAUCHAMP – L. WALTERS, ed., *Contemporary Issues in Bioethics*, Belmont, CA 1999, 723-727.

BAYER, R., *Private Acts, Social Consequences: AIDS and the Politics of Public Health,* New Brunswick 1991.

———— , «Public Health Policy and the AIDS Epidemic: An End to HIV Exceptionalism?», *NEJM* 324 (1991) 1500-1504.

BAYLEY, A., *One New Humanity: The Challenge of AIDS,* London 1996.

BEAUCHAMP, D.E., *The Health of the Republic: Epidemics, Medicine, and Moralism as Challenges to Democracy,* Philadelphia 1998.

BEAUCHAMP, T.L. – CHILDRESS, J.F., *Principles of Biomedical Ethics*, New York 1994[4].

BEAUCHAMP, T. – WALTERS, L., ed., *Contemporary Issues in Bioethics*, Belmont, CA 1999[5].

BELLO, C.S. – DADA, J.D., «Sexually Transmitted Disease in Northern Nigeria», *BJVD* 59 (1983) 202-205.

BENNET, R. – ERIN, C. A., ed., *HIV and AIDS: Testing, Screening, and Confidentiality*, New York 1999.

BERMEJO HIGUERA, J.C., «A Spaniard Resists Disclosing His HIV Status to His Girlfriend», in J.F. KEENAN, ed., *Catholic Ethicists on HIV/AIDS Prevention*, New York 2000, 239-246.

BLACK, D., «Absolute Confidentiality?», in T.L. BEAUCHAMP – L. WALTERS, ed., *Contemporary Issues in Bioethics,* Belmont CA 1999, 172-176.

BLATTNER, W. – GALLO, R. – TEMIN, H., «HIV Causes AIDS», *Science* 241 (1988) 514-517.

BRENNAN, R. – D. DURACK, «Gay Compromise Syndrome», *Lancet* 2 (1981) 1338-1339.

BRUSCUGLIA, L., ed., *Aids Pediatrico: Problematiche Giuridiche e Medico-Sociali,* Milano 1997.

BUJO, B., *The Ethical Dimension of Community: The African Model and The Dialogue Between North and South,* Nairobi 1998.

BURGGRAEVE, R., «From Responsible to Meaningful Sexuality: An Ethics of Growth as an Ethics of Mercy for Young People in this Era of AIDS», in J.F. KEENAN, ed., *Catholic Ethicists on HIV/AIDS Prevention,* New York 2000, 303-316.

BURKE, D.S. – *al.,* «Measurement of False Positive Rate in a Screening Program for Human Immunodeficiency Virus Infections», *NEJM* 319 (1988) 961-964.

CAFFARA, C., «AIDS: Aspetti Etici Generali», *DH* 13 (1990) 70-74.

CAHILL, L.S., «Catholic Sexual Ethics and the Dignity of the Person: A Double Message», *TS* 50 (1989) 49-64.

———— , *Sex, Gender and Christian Ethics,* Cambridge, UK 1996.

———— , «AIDS, Justice, and the Common Good», in J.F. KEENAN, ed., *Catholic Ethicists on HIV/AIDS Prevention,* New York 2000, 282-293.

CALLAHAN, D., «The WHO Definition of Health», in S.E. LAMMERS – A. VERHEY, ed., *On Moral Medicine: Theological Perspectives in Medical Ethics,* Grand Rapids, Michigan 1998[2], 253-261.

CAMERON, C. – *al.,* «Female to Male Transmission of Immunodeficiency Virus Type I. Risk Factors for Sero-Conversion in Men», *Lancet* 2 (1983) 403-407.

CAMPOS, C., «A Catholic Hospital in India is Asked to Cooperate With An HIV Prevention Program», in J.F. KEENAN, ed., *Catholic Ethicists on HIV/AIDS Prevention,* New York 2000, 199-211.

CANTWELL, A., *Queer Blood: The Secret AIDS Genocide Plot,* Los Angeles 1988.

———— , *AIDS and the Doctor of Death: An Inquiry into the Origin of the AIDS Epidemic,* Los Angeles 1988.

CARMODY, D.L., *Christian Ethics: An Introduction through History and Current Issues,* Englewood Cliffs, NJ 1993.

CATTORINI, P., ed., *AIDS: Etica, giustizia e politica sanitaria,* Cinisello Balsamo, MI 1993.

CATTORINI, P. – MINNUCCI, P. – MORELLI, D., ed., *AIDS. AIDS e Bioetica: Materiali e linee. Guida per formazione del personale di assistenza sanitaria,* Milano 1992.

CHILDRESS, J.F., «Mandatory HIV Screening and Testing», in F. REAMER, ed., *AIDS and Ethics,* New York 1991, 50-76

CHILDRESS, J.F., «Mandatory HIV Screening and Testing», in T.L. BEAU-
     CHAMP – L. WALTERS, ed., *Contemporary Issues in Bioethics*,
     Belmont, CA 1999[5], 741-758.

CHRISTENSEN, J., «AIDS in Africa: Dying by the Numbers», CNN
     INTERACTIVE, March 28, 2000. Cf. http://cnn.com/SPECIALS/2000/
     aids/ stories/overview.

CLELAND, J. – FERRY, N., ed. *Sexual Behaviour and AIDS in the Developing
     World,* London 1995.

COHEN, R.L., ed., *Justice: Views from the Social Sciences*, New York 1986.

COLEMAN, G.D., *Human Sexuality: An All-Embracing Gift,* New York 1992.

CONNOR, E. – al., «Reduction of Maternal Infant Transmission of HIV Type
     with Zidovudine Treatment», *NEJM* 331 (1994) 1173-1180.

COSSTICK, V., ed., *AIDS: Meeting the Community Challenge,* London 1987.

CRIBB, J., *The White Death,* Sydney 1996.

CUNNINGHAM, F., ed., *The Christian Life,* Dubuque, Iowa 1959.

CURRAN, C.E., *Ongoing Revision: Studies in Moral Theology,* Notre Dame
     1975.

CURRAN, C.E. – MCCORMICK, R., ed., *Readings in Moral Theology*, No.1:
     Moral Norms and Catholic Tradition, New York 1979).

CURTIS, T., «The Origin of AIDS: A Startling New Theory Attempts to
     Answer the Question "Was it an Act of God or an Act of Man?"»,
     Rolling Stone, 626, 19 March 1992, 54-59, 61, 106, 108
     [newspaper's article].

DALGLEISH, A. – WEISS, R., ed., *HIV and the New Viruses,* San Diego, CA
     1999.

DAVID WEST, T., «Obasanjo's Problem is Obasanjo», *Newswatch*, Lagos,
     May 22, 2000 [newspaper's article].

DAVIS, H., *Moral and Pastoral Theology. II. Precepts.* London 1936.

DE CARLO, P., «Do Condoms Work?», *Center for AIDS Prevention Studies*,
     University of California San Francisco, cf. http://www.ama-assn.
     org/special/hiv/prevention/prevent2.htm.

DEL CORONA, M., «L'AIDS divora l'Africa. Crociata dell'Onu», *Corriere
     della Sera*, Roma, 11 Gennaio, 2000, 14 [newspaper's article].

DOMINIAN, J., *Sexual Integrity: The Answer to AIDS*, London 1987.

DUESBERG, P., «HIV is not the Cause of AIDS», *Science* 241 (1988) 514-517.

————— , *Infectious AIDS. Have We Been Mislead?* Berkeley, CA 1995.

————— , *Inventing the AIDS Virus*, Washington, DC 1996.

EDITORIAL, «10% have HIV in South Africa», *International Herald Tribune*, April 19, 2000 [newspaper's article].

EDITORIAL, «Beaming Light on Recovered Loot», *This Day*, Lagos, May 21, 2000 [newspaper's article].

EDITORIAL, «Cover Story/Computer Whizz Kid: This Man is Hot», *New African*, July/August 1996 [newspaper's article].

EDITORIAL, «Lawmakers Loot Nigeria», *Tell,* Lagos, April 24, 2000 [newspaper's article].

EDITORIAL, «Nigeria to Make Pre-Marriage HIV Check Compulsory», *The Guardian*, Lagos, March 30, 2000 [newspaper's article].

EDITORIAL, «Nigerian Authorities Worry over Prostitution Rings», *All Africa News Agency*, Nairobi, June 5, 2000 [newspaper's article].

EDITORIAL, «Nigerian Woman Bags International Science Award», *The Guardian*, Lagos, April 12, 2001 [newspaper's article].

EDITORIAL, «No tears from AIDS workers as FG scraps PTF» *AIDS News Service*, a monthly News Bulletin of Journalists Against AIDS (JAAIDS) Nigeria, vol. 2, Issue 1, July 1999, pp. 1-2 [newspaper's article].

EDITORIAL, «Signs of the Times: Roman Theologians Say Condom Use OK in Certain Cases», *America*, 2000.

EDITORIAL, «Vienna Archbishop Says Condoms Morally Acceptable to Fight AIDS», *Catholic News Service*, Washington, DC, April 3, 1996 [newspaper's article].

EGBOH, M., «A Pathfinder to AIDS Cure», *The Guardian*, Lagos, March 25, 2000.

EGUNJOBI, G., «Save the Mothers», *The Guardian*, Lagos, April 1, 2000 [newspaper's article].

EHRHARDT, A.A., «Sexual Behavior Among Homosexuals», in J. MANN – D. TARANTOLA, ed., *AIDS in the World II: Global Dimensions, Social Roots, and Responses*, New York 1996, 259-261.

EIDSON, T., ed., *The AIDS Caregiver's Handbook,* Revised Edition, New York 1993.

ELIZARI, J., «Segreto professionale e Aids», *DH* 13 (1990) 240-242.

ELOIKE, T., «AIDS Control in Nigeria: Problems and Prospects», Paper presented at National Conference on AIDS in Enugu, 1992

ELSWOOD, B.F. – STRICKER, R.B., «Polio Vaccines and the Origin of AIDS», *Medical Hypotheses* 42 (1994) 347-354.

ENAHORO, P., «The Ugly Nigerian», *The Vanguard Daily*, Lagos, May 31, 2000 [newspaper's article].

ENGELHARDT, T.H., *The Foundations of Bioethics,* New York 1986.

ESSEX, M. – KANKI, P. – *al.,* «Antigens of Human T Lymphotropic Virus Type III/Lymphadenopathy-Associated Virus», *AIM* 103 (1985) 700-703.

FAGGIONI, M.P., «An HIV – Infected Italian Woman Seeking to Have Children», in J.F. KEENAN, ed., *Catholic Ethicists on HIV/AIDS Prevention,* New York 2000, 246-254.

FARMER, P., *Infections and Inequalities: The Modern Plagues,* Berkeley – Los Angeles 1999.

FERRER, J.J., *Sida y Bioetica: de la Autonomia a la Justicia,* Madrid 1997.

———— , «Needle Exchange in San Juan, Puerto Rico: A Traditional Roman Catholic Caustic Approach», in J.F. KEENAN, ed., *Catholic Ethicists on HIV/AIDS Prevention,* New York 2000, 177-189.

FILOCHOWSKI, J., «A Measure of Our Humanity», in K.R. OVERBERG, ed., *AIDS, Ethics and Religion,* Maryknoll, NY 1994, 262-272.

FINNIS, J., *Natural Law and Natural Rights,* New York 1993.

FLECK, L. – ANGELL, M., «Please Don't Tell: A Case about HIV and Confidentiality», in T.A. MAPPES – D. DEGRAZIA, ed., *Biomedical Ethics,* New York 2001[5], 216-219

FLYNN, E.P., *Issues in Medical Ethics,* Kansas City, MO 1996.

———— , *Issues in Health Care Ethics,* Upper Saddle River, NJ 2000.

———— , «Teaching about HIV Prevention in an American Catholic College Classroom», in J.F. KEENAN, ed., *Catholic Ethicists on HIV/AIDS Prevention,* New York 2000, 148-155

FOREMAN, J., «Suicides Raise Questions on AIDS Testing», *The Boston Globe,* February 2, 1987, 17 [newspaper's article].

FRIEDLAN, G.H., «Risk of HTLV-II/LAV Transmission to Household Contacts», *NEJM* 315 (1986) 258.

FRIEDLAN, G.H. – *al.,* «Lack of Transmission of HTLV-III/LAV Infection to Household Contacts of Patients with AIDS or AIDS-Related Complex with Oral Candidiasis», *NEJM* 314 (1986) 344-349.

FRIEDLAN, G.H. – KLEIN, R.S., «Transmission of the Human Immuno-deficiency Virus», *NEJM* 317 (1987) 1125-1135.

FULLER, J.D., «AIDS Prevention: A Challenge to the Catholic Moral Tradition», *America* 175, no. 20, 1996, 13-20.

———— , «A Needle Exchange: Saving Lives», *America,* 1998, 8-11.

———— , «HIV/AIDS: An Overview», Boston, 1999. Mimeographed Article.

FULLER, J. – KEENAN, J., «Tolerant Signals: The Vatican's New Insights on Condom for HIV Prevention», *America,* 2000, 6-7.

FUMENTO, M., *The Myth of Heterosexual AIDS,* Washington, DC 1993.

GAFO, J. – BRAS, L.A., *Sida y Tercer Mundo: Una Llamada a la Etica y a la Solidaridad,* Madrid 1998.

GALLIN, R. S. – FERGUSON, A. – HARPER, J., ed., *Women in Development Annual,* III, Boulder, CO 1993.

GALLO, R., *Virus Hunting. AIDS, Cancer and the Human Retrovirus: A Story of Scientific Discovery,* New York 1991.

GAO, F. – *al.* «Origin of HIV-I in the Chimpanzee Pan Troglodytes Troglodytes», *Nature,* 397 (1999) 436-441.

GARCIA, J.L., «Double effect», in REICH, W.T., ed., *Encyclopedia of Bioethics,* II, New York 1995, 636- 641.

GARDNER, E.C., *Justice and Christian Ethics,* Cambridge, UK 1995.

GIBNEY, L. – DICLEMENTE, R.J. – VERMUND, S.H., ed., *Preventing HIV in Developing Countries: Biomedical and Behavioral Approaches,* New York 1999.

GLEESON, G. – LEARY, D., «When Fidelity and Justice Clash: Testing the limits of Confidentiality in Australia», in J.F. KEENAN, ed., *Catholic Ethicists on HIV/AIDS Prevention,* New York 2000, 221-230.

GOERGEN, D., *The Sexual Celibate,* New York 1974.

GOLDSMITH, M.F., «HIV and Intravenous Drug Users», in K.R. OVERBERG, ed., *AIDS, Ethics and Religion,* Maryknoll, NY 1994, 101-104.

GOSTIN, L., ed., *AIDS and the Health Care System,* New Haven 1990.

GOTTLIEB, M.S. – *al.,* «Pneumocystis Carinii Pneumonia and Mucosal Candidiasis in Previously Healthy Homosexual Men: Evidence of a New Acquired Cellular Immunodeficiency», *NEJM* 305 (1981) 1425-1438.

GOUDSMIT, J., *Viral Sex: The Nature of AIDS,* New York 1997.

GOULD, J.M. – GOLDMAN, B.A., *Deadly Deceit: Low-Level Radiation High-Level Cover-Up,* New York 1990.

GRADY, W.R. – HAYWARD, M.D. – YAGI, J., «Contraceptive Failure in the United States: Estimates from the 1982 National Survey of Family Growth», *FPP* 18/5 (1986) 200-209.

GRAY, J.N. – LYONS, P.M. – MELTON, G.B., *Ethical and Legal Issues in AIDS Research,* Baltimore 1995.

GRIFFIN, G.C., «Condoms and Contraceptives in Junior High and High School Clinics», *Linacre Quarterly* 60 (1993) 60-66.

GRMEK, M., *History of AIDS,* Princeton, NJ 1990.

GULA, R., *Reason Informed by Faith: Foundations of Catholic Morality,* Mahwah, NJ 1989.

GULTMACHER, S., *Testing for AIDS: The Dilemmas of Controlling Disease*, Newbury Park, CA 1992.

GUPTA, G.R. – WEISS, E., «Women's Lives and Sex: Implications for AIDS Prevention», in R.G. PARKER – J.H. GAGNON, ed., *Conceiving Sexuality; Approaches to Sex Research in PostModern World*, New York 1995, 259-270.

HAG, C., «Data on AIDS in Africa: An Assessment», in N. MILLER – R. C. ROCKWELL, ed., *AIDS in Africa: The Social and Policy Impact*, 9-29.

HARDY, B.D., «Cultural Practices Contributing to Transmission of Human Immunodeficiency in Africa», *RID* 9 (1987) 1109-1119.

HARING, B., «The Inseparability of the Unitive – Procreative Functions of the Marital Act», in C.E. CURRAN – R.A. MCCORMICK, ed., *Readings in Moral Theology* No. 8: *Dialogue About Catholic Sexual Teaching*, New York – Mahwah 1993, 153-167.

HAUGHEY, J.C., ed., *The Faith That Does Justice*, New York 1977.

HAYGOOD, W., «Prostitution Plays Key Role in Fuelling Africa's AIDS Crisis», *The Boston Globe*, October 11, 1999, A 25 [newspaper's article].

HEALY, E., *Moral Guidance*, Chicago 1942.

HICKEY, J. – *al.*, «Reactions to AIDS Statement», *Origins* 17-30 (1988) 439-443.

HOOPER, E., *The River: A Journey back to the Source of HIV and AIDS*, London 1999.

HOROWITZ, L.G., *Deadly Innocence*, Rockport, MA 1994.

————, *Emerging Viruses: AIDS and Ebola, Nature, Accident or Intentional?* Rockport, MA 1996.

HUNTER, N.D. – RUBENSTEIN, W.B., ed., *AIDS Agenda: Emerging Issues in Civil Rights*, New York 1992.

IGHODARO, J., «3 Nigerians Bag NEST awards», *Vanguard*, Lagos, April 12, 2001 [newspaper's article].

JACKSON, R., «Hiltler's Lab Created AIDS Virus», *Sun*, January 3,1989 [newspaper's article].

JETER, J., «AIDS Cripples Economics of Sub-Saharan Africa», *International Herald Tribune*, December 13, 1999 [newspaper's article].

JOHNSON, A.M., «Condoms and HIV Transmission», *NEJM* 331 (1994) 391-392.

JOHNSON, M., «The Principle of Double Effect and Safe Sex in Marriage: Reflections on a Suggestion», *Linacre Quarterly* 60 (1993) 82-89.

JONE, H. – ADELMAN, U., *Moral Theology*, Westminster, MD 1961[16].

KALEEBA, N., *We Miss You All*, Harare 1991.

KAPLAN, J.E. – *al.*, «Evidence Against the Transmission of Human T - Lymphotropic Virus Type III/Lymphadenopathy-Associated Virus (HTLV-III/LAV) in Families of Children with the Acquired Immunodeficiency Syndrome», *PID* 4 (1985) 468-471.

KASUN, J.., *The War Against Population,* San Francisco 1988.

KAWAMUR, M. – *al.*, «HIV-2 in West Africa in 1966», *Lancet* 1 (1989) 385.

KEANE, P.S., *Sexual Morality: A Catholic Perspective,* New York 1977.

KEENAN, J.F., «Prophylactics, Toleration and Cooperation: Contemporary Problems and Traditional Principles», *IPhQ* 29, no. 2 (1989) 205-220.

———, «Notes on Moral Theology: Confidentiality, Disclosure and Fiduciary Responsibility», *TS* 54 (1993) 142-146.

———, «Living with HIV/AIDS», *The Tablet* (1995).

———, «Making a Case for Casuistry: AIDS and its Ethical Challenges», in J. WETLESEN, ed., *HVA er Kasuistikk?,* Oslo 1998, 163-185.

———, «Applying the Seventh Century Casuistry of Accommodation to HIV Prevention», *TS* 60 (1999) 492-512.

———, ed., *Catholic Ethicists on HIV/AIDS Prevention*, New York 2000.

KELLY, D.F., *Critical Care Ethics,* Kansas City 1991.

KELLY, K.T., *New Directions in Sexual Ethics: Moral Theology and the Challenge of AIDS*, London 1998.

KIRBY, D. – *al.*, «The Impact of Condom Distribution in Seattle Schools on Sexual Behavior and Condom Use», *AJPH* 89 (1999) 182-187.

KIRP, D.L. – BAYER, R., *AIDS in the Industrialized Democracies*, New Brunswick, NJ 1992.

KISEMBO, B. – MASEGA, L. – SHORTER, A., *African Christian Marriage*, Nairobi 1998.

KOLATA, G., «Origins of AIDS Remain Murky», *International Herald Tribune*, January 31, 2002, 8 [newspaper's article].

KUHSE, H. – SINGER, P., ed., *Bioethics: An Anthology,* Oxford 1999.

KYLE, W., «Simian Retroviruses, Polio Vaccine, and Origins of AIDS», *Lancet* 339 (1992) 600-601.

LAGA, M. – *al.*, «Condom Promotion, Sexually Transmitted Disease Treatment, and Declining Incidence of HIV-1 Infection in Female Zairian Sex Workers», *Lancet* 344 (1994) 246-248.

LAMMERS, S.E. – VERHEY, A., ed., *On Moral Medicine: Theological Perspectives in Medical Ethics,* Grand Rapids, Michigan 1998[2].

LAURENCE, J., «Zidovudine in Pregnancy – More Questions Than Answers», *AIDS Reader* 4 (1994) 74-76.

LEIBOWITCH, J., *A Strange Virus of Unknown Origin,* New York 1985.

LEONE, S., «L'approcio etico ai problemi dell'AIDS», *Bioetica e Cultura* III/5 (1994) 9-31.

———, ed., *AIDS: Problemi Sanitari, Sociali e Morali,* Roma 1995.

LEVINE, C. – BAYER, R., «The Ethics of Screening for Early Intervention in HIV Disease», *AJPH* 79 (1989) 1661-1667.

LIAGIN, E., *Excessive Force: Power, Politics and Population Control,* Washington, DC 1996.

LUPTON, D., *Moral Threats and Dangerous Desires: AIDS in the News Media,* London 1994.

LYNCH, C., «AIDS is Security Threat», *International Herald Tribune,* January 11, 2000 [newspaper's article].

MANN, J. – TARANTOLA, D., *AIDS in the World II: Global Dimensions, Social Roots, and Responses,* New York 1996.

MAPPES, T.A. – DEGRAZIA, D., *Biomedical Ethics,* New York 2001[5].

MARZUK, P. – al., «Increased Risk of Suicide in Persons with AIDS», *JAMA* 259 (1988) 1333-1337.

MASEGA, L., «Recognizing the Reality of African Religion in Tanzania», in J.F. KEENAN, ed., *Catholic Ethicists on HIV/AIDS Prevention,* New York 2000, 76-84.

MASUR, H.M. – al., «An Outbreak of Community-Acquired Pneumocystis Carinii Pneumonia: Initial Manifestation of Cellular Immune Dysfunction», *NEJM* 305 (1985) 1431-1438.

MAY, W.E., *Human Existence, Medicine and Ethics,* Chicago 1977.

MAYER, K.H. – al., «Human T-lymphotropic Virus Type-III in High Risk, Antibody Negative Homosexual Men», *AIM* 104 (1986) 194-196.

MAYS, V.M. – ALBEE, G.W. – SCHNEIDER, S.F., ed., *Primary Prevention of AIDS: Psychological Approaches,* Newbury Park, CA 1989.

MCCORMICK, R.A., *The Critical Calling: Reflections on Moral Dilemmas Since Vatican II,* Washington, DC 1989.

MCDANIEL, J.S. –ISENBERG, D.J. – MORRIS, D.G. – SWIFT, R.Y., «Delivering Culturally Sensitive AIDS Education in Rural Communities», in D.C. UMEH, ed., *Confronting the AIDS Epidemic: Cross-Cultural Perspectives on HIV/AIDS Education,* Trenton, NJ 1997, 169-179.

MCDONAGH, E. «Theology in a Time of AIDS», *IThQ* 60 (1994) 81-89.

MELLIN, F.G., «The Places of Education in Values», *DH* 44 (2000) 37-40.

MESSERLI, F.H., «Transmission of AIDS: The Case against Casual Contagion», *NEJM* 314 (1986) 379-380.

MICHEL, N., «Fighting AIDS in a Society Where We Egyptians Don't Talk About It», in J.F. KEENAN, ed., *Catholic Ethicists on HIV/AIDS Prevention*, New York 2000, 155-161.

MILLER, N. – ROCKWELL, R.C., ed., *AIDS in Africa: The Social and Policy Impact*, Lewiston/Queenston 1988.

MINKOFF, H. – AUGENBRAUM, M., «Antiretoviral Therapy for Pregnant Women», *AJOG* 176 (1997) 478-489.

MODIBBO, I., «Vice-President Wife Sets up Body to Tackle Prostitution, Child Labour», *Newswatch*, Lagos, May 16, 2000 [newspaper's article].

MOLONEY, M., *On Life and Love: Teenagers Sex and Love*, Nairobi 2000.

MORRISON, L. – GURUGE, S., «We Are A Part of All That We Have Met: Women and AIDS», in D.C. UMEH, ed., *Confronting the AIDS Epidemic: Cross-Cultural Perspectives on HIV/AIDS Education*, Trenton, NJ 1997, 197-214.

MUMFORD, S.D., *The Life and Death of NSSM 200,* Research Triangle Park, North Carolina 1996.

MURPHY, T., *Ethics in an Epidemic: AIDS, Morality, and Culture,* Berkeley, CA 1994.

NATIONAL ACADEMY OF SCIENCES, «Symposium on Chemical and Biologial Warfare», *Proceedings NAS* 65 (1970) 250-259.

———, *The Social Impact of AIDS in the United States,* Washington, DC 1993.

NICOLSON, R., *God in AIDS? A Theological Enquiry*, London 1996.

NORTON, J., «Theologians Say Condom Use OK in Certain Cases, Not as Policy», *Catholic News Service*, Washington, DC. September 22, 2000 [newspaper's article].

NOVELLO, A.C. – al., «From the Surgeon General, US Public Health Service», *JAMA* 269 (1993) 2840ff.

NWOSU, P., «Nigeria Leaders Stole N400b... Reveals US Congressman», *Post Express*, Lagos, May 31, 2000 [newspaper's article].

O'DONNELL, T.J., *Medicine and Christian Morality*, Third Revised and Updated Edition, New York 1996.

O'MALLEY, P., ed., *The AIDS Epidemic: Private Rights and the Public Interest,* Boston 1989.

OGBU, CH. – OZOR, CH., «Utomi, Gana, Akingbola Set Economic Agenda», *Post Express*, October 4, 2000 [newspaper's article].

OGUNJIMI, T., «Out to Recover IBB's Loot», *The News*, Lagos, May 17, 2000 [newspaper's article].

OKAFOR, J.O., «AIDS Campaign in Nigeria: The Efforts of the Federal Government», in D.C. UMEH, ed., *Confronting the AIDS Epidemic: Cross-Cultural Perspectives on HIV/AIDS Education,* Trenton, NJ 1997, 105-115.

OKWE, J., «Research Reveals Rate of Birth Among Young Girls», *Post Express*, Lagos, May 30, 2000 [Article found on web at Africa News Online].

OLADEPO, W., «AIDS Body Indicts Nigeria», *Newswatch*, Lagos, March, 1991 [newspaper's article].

ONISHI, N., «Against Tough Odds, Nigeria Bets on Reform», *New York Times*, August 20, 2000 [newspaper's article].

ORUBULOYE, I.O., «Patterns of Sexual Behavior of High Risk Population and the implication for STDS and HIV/AIDS Transmission in Nigeria», in R.G. PARKER – J. H. GRAGNON, ed., *Conceiving Sexuality: Approaches to Sex Research in PostModern World,* New York 1995, 235-246.

OSUNTOKUN, B.O., «Biomedical Ethics in the Developing World: Conflicts and Resolutions», in E. PELLEGRINO – P. MAZZARELLA – P. CORSI, ed., *Transcultural Dimensions in Medical Ethics,* Frederick, Maryland 1992, 105-143.

OVERBERG, K.R., ed., *AIDS Ethics and Religion*, Maryknoll, NY 1994.

PADOVESE, L., «Segreto», in F. COMPAGNONI – G. PIANA – S. PRIVITERA, ed., *Nuovo Dizionario di Teologia Morale,* Cinisello Balsamo, MI 1990, 1205-1212.

PARKER, R. – GAGNON, J.H., ed., *Conceiving Sexuality: Approaches to Sexual Research in a Post-Modern World,* New York 1995.

PASCAL, L., «What Happens When Science Goes Bad: The Corruption of Science and Technology», *Analysis Research Program of the University of Wollongong,* Working paper no. 9, 1992.

PATERSON, G., *Women in the Time of AIDS,* New York 1996.

PELÀEZ, J.H., «Educating for HIV Prevention in a Medical School in Colombia», in J.F. KEENAN, ed., *Catholic Ethicists on HIV/AIDS Prevention,* New York, 2000, 142-148.

PELLEGRINO, E. – MAZZARELLA, P. – CORSI, P., ed., *Transcultural Dimensions in Medical Ethics,* Frederick, Maryland 1992.

PESCHKE, H.C., *Christian Ethics. II. A Presentation of special Moral Theology in the light of Vatican II,* Dublin 1978.

PHAIR, J.P. – WOLINSKY, S., «Diagnosis of Infection with the Human Immunodeficiency Virus», *Clinical Infectious Disease* 15 (1992) 13-16.

PIOT, P. – *al.*, «AIDS in a Heterosexual Population in Zaire», *Lancet* (1984).

POULIN, C.H., *Salvific Invitation and Loving Response: The Fundamental Christian Dialogue,* Quezon City 1989.

———, «The Theology of Human Sexuality: General Introduction and a Contemporary Perspective on Theological Method», Ibadan: SS. Peter and Paul Seminary, 1992. Mimeographed Lecture Notes.

———, «Human Sexuality: A Historico-Theological Over-view», Ibadan: SS. Peter and Paul Seminary, 1992. Mimeographed Lecture Notes.

«Prevention of AIDS: Christian Ethical Aspect», *OR,* March 10, 1988 [newspaper's article].

PREWITT, K., «AIDS in Africa: The triple Disaster», Foreword in N. Miller & R. C. Rockwell, ed., *AIDS in Africa: The Social and Policy Impact,* Lewiston/Queenston 1988, IX-XII.

RANSOME-KUTI, O., «The HIV/AIDS Epidemic in Nigeria», *National Health Digest,* June 1999, 20-21.

REAMER, F.G., *AIDS and Ethics,* New York 1991.

RENSE, J., *AIDS Exposed: Secrets, Lies and Myths,* Goleta, CA 1996.

ROTTER, H., «AIDS: Some Theological and Pastoral Considerations», *Theology Digest* 39 (1992) 235-240.

ROWE, P., «US Expert Panel Reaffirms Benefit of Perinatal Zidovudine», *Lancet* 349 (1997) 258.

RUSHING, W.A., *The AIDS Epidemic: Social Dimensions of an Infectious Disease,* Boulder, CO 1995.

SANDE, M.A. «Transmission of AIDS: The Case against Casual Contagion», *NEJM* 314 (1986) 380-382.

SARAT, A. – KEARNS, T.R., ed., *Justice and Injustice in Law and Legal Theory*, Ann Arbor, MI 1996.

SASHA, A., ed., *You Can Do Something About AIDS,* Boston 1988.

SCHOEPF, B.G., «Gender, Development, and AIDS: A Political Economy and Culture Framework», in R.S. GALLIN – A. FERGUSON – J. HARPER, ed., *Women in Development Annual,* III, Boulder, CO 1993, 53-85.

SCHOUB, B.D., *AIDS and HIV in Perspective*, Cambridge, UK 1999[2].

SEALE, J., «AIDS Virus Infection: Prognosis and Transmission», *JRSM* 78 (1985) 613-615.

SELLERS, D. – MCGRAW, S.A. – MCKINLAY, J.B., «Does the Promotion and Distribution of Condoms Increase Teen Sexual Activity? Evidence

From an HIV Prevention Program for Latino Youths», *AJPH* 84 (1994) 1952-1959.

SETEL, P.W. – LEWIS, M. – LYONS, M., ed., *Histories of Sexually Transmitted Diseases and HIV/AIDS in Sub-Saharan Africa*, Westport 1999.

SHANNON, T., *An Introduction to Bioethics,* Mahwah, NJ 1987.

SHARP, R.R. – GAO, D.F. – HAHN, B., «Origins and Diversity of Human Immunodeficiency Viruses», *AIDS* 8 (1994) 527-543.

SHELP, E.E., ed., *Justice and Health Care,* Boston 1981.

SHERR, L., «Counseling and HIV Testing: Ethical Dilemmas», in R. BENNETT – C.A. ERIN, ed., *HIV and AIDS: Testing, Screening, and Confidentiality,* New York 1999), 39-60.

SHILTS, R., *And the Band Played On: Politics, People, and the AIDS Epidemic*, New York 1987.

SHOKUNBI, L., «AIDS, harbinger of Poverty in Nigeria», *The Guardian*, Lagos, March 5, 1999, 15.

SHORTER, A. – ONYANCHA, E., *The Church and AIDS in Africa, A Case Study: Nairobi City,* Nairobi 1998.

SIEGLER, M., «Confidentiality in Medicine. A Decrepit Concept», in T.L. BEAUCHAMP – L. WALTERS, ed., *Contemporary Issues in Bioethics*, Belmont, CA 1999[5], 169-171

SLAFF, J. – BRUBAKER, J.K., *The AIDS Epidemic,* New York 1985.

SONSTAG, S., *Illness as Metaphor and AIDS and its Metaphors,* London 1991.

SPAGNOLO, A., *Bioetica nella ricerca e nella prassi medica,* Torino 1997.

SPOHN, W.C., «The Moral Dimensions of AIDS», *TS* 49 (1988) 89-109.

SUAUDEAU, J., «Prophylactics or Family Value? Stopping The Spread of HIV/AIDS», *OR*, 16-19 April 2000 [newspaper's article].

TALIERCIO, G., «Segreto», in L. ROSSI – A. VALSECCHI, ed., *Dizionario Enciclopedico di Teologia Morale,* Roma 1981, 987-993.

TETTAMANZI, D., *Bioetica: Difendere le frontiere della vita,* Casale Monferrato (AL) 1996[3].

TIMMERMAN, I., «Sex, Sacred or Profane?», in C.E. CURRAN – R. MC CORMICK, ed., *Readings in Moral Theology, No. 8: Dialogue About Catholic Sexual Teaching,* New York 1993, 47-54.

TOLTZIS, P. – al., «Zidovudine – Associated Embryonic Toxicity in Mice», *JID* 163/6 (1991) 1212-1218.

TRUSSELL, J. – WARNER, D.L. – HATCHER, R.A., «Condom Slippage and Breaking Rates», *FPP* 24/1 (1992) 20-23.

TUOHEY, J., «Methodology and Ideology: The Condom and a Consistent Sexual Ethic», *LS* 15 (1990) 53-69.

UGORJI, L., *The Principle of Double Effect,* Frankfurt au Main 1985.

UMEH, D.C., ed., *Confronting the AIDS Epidemic: Cross-Cultural Perspectives on HIV/AIDS Education,* Trenton, NJ 1997.

UWAKWE, C., «Socio-Cultural Factors that Predispose Women to HIV/AIDS in the Middle-Belt of Nigeria," in D.C. UMEH, *Confronting the AIDS Epidemic: Cross-Cultural Perspectives on HIV/AIDS Education,* Trenton, NJ 1997, 39-45.

VIDAL, M., «The Christian Ethic: Help or Hindrance? The Ethical Aspects of AIDS», *Conc* 75 (1997) 89-98.

VITILLO, R.J., «HIV/AIDS Prevention Education: A Special Concern for the Church», Presentation for discussion at the Caritas Internationalis/ CAFOD Theological Consultation on HIV/AIDS, April 14-17, 1998, Pretoria, 5.

WAITE, G., «The Politics of Disease: The AIDS Virus and Africa», in N. MILLER – R. C. ROCKWELL, ed., *AIDS in Africa: The Social and Policy Impact*, Lewiston/Queenston 1988, 145-164.

WALTERS, L., «Ethical Issues in the Prevention and Treatment of HIV Infection and AIDS», in T.L. BEAUCHAMP – L. WALTERS, *Contemporary Issues in Bioethics*, Belmont, CA 1999[5], 708-718.

WALTON, J. – BEESON, P.B. – SCOTT, R.B., ed., *The Oxford Companion to Medicine,* I, New York 1986.

WATSON, R.A. – WATSON, L.S., «Fidelity, Mutual Respect Best Shield Against AIDS», *Linacre Quarterly* 61 (1994) 30-32.

WAY, P.O. – STANECKI, K.A. *The Impact of HIV/AIDS on World Population,* Washington, DC 1994.

WENIGER, B.G. – BERKLEY, S., «The Evolving HIV/AIDS Pandemic», in J. MANN – D. TARANTOLA, D., ed., *AIDS in the World II: Global Dimensions, Social Roots, and Responses*, New York 1996, 57-70.

WERT, N.J., «The Biblical and Theological Basis for Risking Compassion and Care for AIDS Patients», in K.R. OVERBERG, ed., *AIDS, Ethics and Religion*, Maryknoll, NY 1994, 231-242.

WILLIAM, E. – al., «Implementation of an AIDS Prevention Program among Prostitutes in the Cross River State of Nigeria», *AIDS* 6 (1992) 629-630.

WINSLADE, W.J., «Confidentiality», in W.T. REICH, ed., *Encyclopedia of Bioethics*, I, New York 1995, 451-459.

WISTON, M., «AIDS and a Duty to Protect», *Hasting Center Report* (1987) 22ff.

ZION, B., «The Orthodox Church and the AIDS Crisis», in K.R. OVERBERG, ed., *AIDS, Ethics and Religion*, Maryknoll, NY 1994, 243-248.

AUTHORS' INDEX

TABLE OF CONTENTS

TESI GREGORIANA

Since 1995, the series «Tesi Gregoriana» has made available to the general public some of the best doctoral theses done at the Pontifical Gregorian University. The typesetting is done by the authors themselves following norms established and controlled by the University.

Published Volumes [Series: Theology]

1. NELLO FIGA, Antonio, *Teorema de la opción fundamental. Bases para su adecuada utilización en teología moral*, 1995, pp. 380.

2. BENTOGLIO, Gabriele, *Apertura e disponibilità. L'accoglienza nell'epistolario paolino*, 1995, pp. 376.

3. PISO, Alfeu, *Igreja e sacramentos. Renovação da Teologia Sacramentária na América Latina*, 1995, pp. 260.

4. PALAKEEL, Joseph, *The Use of Analogy in Theological Discourse. An Investigation in Ecumenical Perspective*, 1995, pp. 392.

5. KIZHAKKEPARAMPIL, Isaac, *The Invocation of the Holy Spirit as Constitutive of the Sacraments according to Cardinal Yves Congar*, 1995, pp. 200.

6. MROSO, Agapit J., *The Church in Africa and the New Evangelisation. A Theologico-Pastoral Study of the Orientations of John Paul II*, 1995, pp. 456.

7. NANGELIMALIL, Jacob, *The Relationship between the Eucharistic Liturgy, the Interior Life and the Social Witness of the Church according to Joseph Cardinal Parecattil*, 1996, pp. 224.

8. GIBBS, Philip, *The Word in the Third World. Divine Revelation in the Theology of Jen-Marc Éla, Aloysius Pieris and Gustavo Gutiérrez*, 1996, pp. 448.

9. DELL'ORO, Roberto, *Esperienza morale e persona. Per una reinterpretazione dell'etica fenomenologica di Dietrich von Hildebrand*, 1996, pp. 240.

10. BELLANDI, Andrea, *Fede cristiana come «stare e comprendere». La giustificazione dei fondamenti della fede in Joseph Ratzinger*, 1996, pp. 416.

11. BEDRIÑAN, Claudio, *La dimensión socio-política del mensaje teológico del Apocalipsis*, 1996, pp. 364.

12. GWYNNE, Paul, *Special Divine Action. Key Issues in the Contemporary Debate (1965-1995)*, 1996, pp. 376.

13. NIÑO, Francisco, *La Iglesia en la ciudad. El fenómeno de las grandes ciudades en América Latina, como problema teológico y como desafío pastoral*, 1996, pp. 492.

14. BRODEUR, Scott, *The Holy Spirit's Agency in the Resurrection of the Dead. An Exegetico-Theological Study of 1 Corinthians 15,44b-49 and Romans 8,9-13*, 1996, pp. 300.

15. ZAMBON, Gaudenzio, *Laicato e tipologie ecclesiali. Ricerca storica sulla «Teologia del laicato» in Italia alla luce del Concilio Vaticano II (1950-1980)*, 1996, pp. 548.

16. ALVES DE MELO, Antonio, *A Evangelização no Brasil. Dimensões teológicas e desafios pastorais. O debate teológico e eclesial (1952-1995)*, 1996, pp. 428.

17. APARICIO VALLS, María del Carmen, *La plenitud del ser humano en Cristo. La Revelación en la «Gaudium et Spes»*, 1997, pp. 308.

18. MARTIN, Seán Charles, *«Pauli Testamentum». 2 Timothy and the Last Words of Moses*, 1997, pp. 312.

19. RUSH, Ormond, *The Reception of Doctrine. An Appropriation of Hans Robert Jauss' Reception Aesthetics and Literary Hermeneutics*, 1997, pp. 424.

20. MIMEAULT, Jules, *La sotériologie de François-Xavier Durrwell. Exposé et réflexions critiques*, 1997, pp. 476.

21. CAPIZZI, Nunzio, *L'uso di Fil 2,6-11 nella cristologia contemporanea (1965-1993)*, 1997, pp. 528.

22. NANDKISORE, Robert, *Hoffnung auf Erlösung. Die Eschatologie im Werk Hans Urs von Balthasars*, 1997, pp. 304.

23. PERKOVIĆ, Marinko, *«Il cammino a Dio» e «La direzione alla vita»: L'ordine morale nelle opere di Jordan Kuničić, O.P. (1908-1974)*, 1997, pp. 336.

24. DOMERGUE, Benoît, *La réincarnation et la divinisation de l'homme dans les religions. Approche phénoménologique et théologique*, 1997, pp. 300.

25. FARKAŠ, Pavol, *La «donna» di Apocalisse 12. Storia, bilancio, nuove prospettive*, 1997, pp. 276.

26. OLIVER, Robert W., *The Vocation of the Laity to Evangelization. An Ecclesiological Inquiry into the Synod on the Laity (1987), Christifideles laici (1989) and Documents of the NCCB (1987-1996)*, 1997, pp. 364.

27. SPATAFORA, Andrea, *From the «Temple of God» to God as the Temple. A Biblical Theological Study of the Temple in the Book of Revelation*, 1997, pp. 340.

28. IACOBONE, Pasquale, *Mysterium Trinitatis. Dogma e Iconografia nell'Italia medievale*, 1997, pp. 512.

29. CASTAÑO FONSECA, Adolfo M., *Δικαιοσύνη en Mateo. Una interpretación teológica a partir de 3,15 y 21,32*, 1997, pp. 344.

30. CABRIA ORTEGA, José Luis, *Relación teología-filosofía en el pensamiento de Xavier Zubiri*, 1997, pp. 580.

31. SCHERRER, Thierry, *La gloire de Dieu dans l'oeuvre de saint Irénée*, 1997, pp. 328.

32. PASCUZZI, Maria, *Ethics, Ecclesiology and Church Discipline. A Rhetorical Analysis of 1 Cor 5,1-13*, 1997, pp. 240.

33. LOPES GONÇALVES, Paulo Sérgio, *Liberationis mysterium. O projeto sistemático da teologia da libertação. Um estudo teológico na perspectiva da regula fidei*, 1997, pp. 464.

34. KOLACINSKI, Mariusz, *Dio fonte del diritto naturale*, 1997, pp. 296.

35. LIMA CORRÊA, Maria de Lourdes, *Salvação entre juízo, conversão e graça. A perspectiva escatológica de Os 14,2-9*, 1998, pp. 360.

36. MEIATTINI, Giulio, *«Sentire cum Christo». La teologia dell'esperienza cristiana nell'opera di H.U. von Balthasar*, 1998, pp. 432.

37. KESSLER, Thomas W., *Peter as the First Witness of the Risen Lord. An Historical and Theological Investigation*, 1998, pp. 240.

38. BIORD CASTILLO Raúl, *La Resurrección de Cristo como Revelación. Análisis del tema en la teología fundamental a partir de la Dei Verbum*, 1998, pp. 308.

39. LÓPEZ, Javier, *La figura de la bestia entre historia y profecía. Investigación teológico-bíblica de Apocalipsis 13,1-8*, 1998, pp. 308.

40. SCARAFONI, Paolo, *Amore salvifico. Una lettura del mistero della salvezza. Uno studio comparativo di alcune soteriologie cattoliche postconciliari*, 1998, pp. 240.

41. BARRIOS PRIETO, Manuel Enrique, *Antropologia teologica. Temi principali di antropologia teologica usando un metodo di «correlazione» a partire dalle opere di John Macquarrie*, 1998, pp. 416.

42. LEWIS, Scott M., *«So That God May Be All in All». The Apocalyptic Message of 1 Corinthians 15,12-34*, 1998, pp. 252.

43. ROSSETTI, Carlo Lorenzo, *«Sei diventato Tempio di Dio». Il mistero del Tempio e dell'abitazione divina negli scritti di Origene*, 1998, pp. 232.

44. CERVERA BARRANCO, Pablo, *La incorporación en la Iglesia mediante el bautismo y la profesión de la fe según el Concilio Vaticano II*, 1998, pp. 372.

45. NETO, Laudelino, *Fé cristã e cultura latino-americana. Uma análise a partir das Conferências de Puebla e Santo Domingo*, 1998, pp. 340.

46. BRITO GUIMARÃES, Pedro, *Os sacramentos como atos eclesiais e proféticos. Um contributo ao conceito dogmático de sacramento à luz da exegese contemporânea*, 1998, pp. 448.

47. CALABRETTA, Rose B., *Baptism and Confirmation. The Vocation and Mission of the Laity in the Writings of Virgil Michel, O.S.B.*, 1998, pp. 320.

48. OTERO LÁZARO, Tomás, *Col 1,15-20 en el contexto de la carta*, 1999, pp.312.

49. KOWALCZYK, Dariusz, *La personalità in Dio. Dal metodo trascendentale di Karl Rahner verso un orientamento dialogico in Heinrich Ott*, 1999, pp. 484.

50. PRIOR, Joseph G., *The Historical-Critical Method in Catholic Exegesis*, 1999, pp. 352.

51. CAHILL, Brendan J, *The Renewal of Revelation Theology (1960-1962). The Development and Responses to the Fourth Chapter of the Preparatory Schema* De deposito Fidei, 1999, pp. 348.

52. TIEZZI, Ida, *Il rapporto tra la pneumatologia e l'ecclesiologia nella teologia italiana postconciliare*, 1999, pp. 364.

53. HOLC, Paweł, *Un ampio consenso sulla dottrina della giustificazione. Studio sul dialogo teologico cattolico luterano*, 1999, pp. 452.

54. GAINO, Andrea, *Esistenza cristiana. Il pensiero teologico di J. Alfaro e la sua rilevanza morale*, 1999, pp. 344.

55. NERI, Francesco, *«Cur Verbum capax hominis». Le ragioni dell'incarnazione della seconda Persona della Trinità fra teologia scolastica e teologia contemporanea*, 1999, pp. 404.

56. MUÑOZ CÁRDABA, Luis-Miguel, *Principios eclesiológicos de la «Pastor Bonus»*, 1999, pp. 344.

57. IWE, John Chijioke, *Jesus in the Synagogue of Capernaum: the Pericope and Its Programmatic Character for the Gospel of Mark. An Exegetico-Theological Study of Mk 1:21-28*, 1999, pp. 364.

58. BARRIOCANAL GÓMEZ, José Luis, *La relectura de la tradición del éxodo en l libro de Amós*, 2000, pp. 332.

59. DE LOS SANTOS GARCÍA, Edmundo, *La novedad de la metáfora κεφαλή – σῶμα en la carta a los Efesios*, 2000, pp. 432.

60. RESTREPO SIERRA, Argiro, *La revelación según R. Latourelle*, 2000, pp. 442.

61. DI GIOVAMBATTISTA, Fulvio, *Il giorno dell'espiazione nella Lettera agli Ebrei*, 2000, pp. 232.

62. GIUSTOZZO, Massimo, *Il nesso tra il culto e la grazia eucaristica nella recente lettura teologica del pensiero agostiniano*, 2000, pp. 456.

63. PESARCHICK, Robert A., *The Trinitarian Foundation of Human Sexuality as Revealed by Christ according to Hans Urs von Balthasar. The Revelatory Significance of the Male Christ and the Male Ministerial Priesthood*, 2000, pp. 328.

64. SIMON, László T., *Identity and Identification. An Exegetical Study of 2Sam 21–24*, 2000, pp. 386.

65. TAKAYAMA, Sadami, *Shinran's Conversion in the Light of Paul's Conversion*, 2000, pp. 256.

66. JUAN MORADO, Guillermo, *«También nosotros creemos porque amamos». Tres concepciones del acto de fe: Newman, Blondel, Garrigou-Lagrange. Estudio comparativo desde la perspectiva teológico-fundamental*, 2000, pp. 444.

67. MAREČEK, Petr, *La preghiera di Gesù nel vangelo di Matteo. Uno studio esegetico-teologico*, 2000, pp. 246.

68. WODKA, Andrzej, *Una teologia biblica del dare nel contesto della colletta paolina (2Cor 8–9)*, 2000, pp. 356.

69. LANGELLA, Maria Rigel, *Salvezza come illuminazione. Uno studio comparato di S. Bulgakov, V. Lossky, P. Evdokimov*, 2000, pp. 292.

70. RUDELLI, Paolo, *Matrimonio come scelta di vita: opzione – vocazione – sacramento*, 2000, pp. 424.

71. GAŠPAR, Veronika, *Cristologia pneumatologica in alcuni autori cattolici postconciliari. Status quaestionis e prospettive*, 2000, pp. 440.

72. GJORGJEVSKI, Gjoko, *Enigma degli enigmi. Un contributo allo studio della composizione della raccolta salomonica (Pr 10,1–22,16)*, 2001, pp. 304.

73. LINGAD, Celestino G., Jr., *The Problems of Jewish Christians in the Johannine Community*, 2001, pp. 492.

74. MASALLES, Victor, *La profecía en la asamblea cristiana. Análisis retórico-literario de 1Cor 14,1-25*, 2001, pp. 416.

75. FIGUEIREDO, Anthony J., *The Magisterium-Theology Relationship. Contemporary Theological Conceptions in the Light of Universal Church Teaching since 1835 and the Pronouncements of the Bishops of the United States*, 2001, pp. 536.

76. PARDO IZAL, José Javier, *Pasión por un futuro imposible. Estudio literario-teológico de Jeremías 32*, 2001, pp. 412.

77. HANNA, Kamal Fahim Awad, *La passione di Cristo nell'Apocalisse*, 2001, pp. 480.

78. ALBANESI, Nicola, *«Cur Deus Homo»: la logica della redenzione. Studio sulla teoria della soddisfazione di S. Anselmo arcivescovo di Canterbury*, 2001, pp. 244.

79. ADE, Edouard, *Le temps de l'Eglise. Esquisse d'une théologie de l'histoire selon Hans Urs von Balthasar*, 2002, pp. 368.

80. MENÉNDEZ MARTÍNEZ, Valentín, *La misión de la Iglesia. Un estudio sobre el debate teológico y eclesial en América Latina (1955-1992), con atención al aporte de algunos teólogos de la Compañía de Jesús*, 2002, pp. 346.

81. COSTA, Paulo Cezar, *«Salvatoris Disciplina». Dionísio de Roma e a Regula* fidei *no debate teológico do terceiro século*, 2002, pp. 272.

82. PUTHUSSERY, Johnson, *Days of Man and God's Day. An Exegetico-Theological Study of ἡμέρα in the Book of Revelation*, 2002, pp. 302.

83. BARROS, Paulo César, *«Commendatur vobis in isto pane quomodo unitatem amare debeatis». A eclesiologia eucarística nos Sermones ad populum de Agostinho de Hipona e o movimento ecumênico*, 2002, pp. 344.

84. PALACHUVATTIL, Joy, *«He Saw». The Significance of Jesus' Seeing Denoted by the Verb εἶδεν in the Gospel of Mark*, 2002, pp. 312.

85. PISANO, Ombretta, *La radice e la stirpe di David. Salmi davidici nel libro dell'Apocalisse*, 2002, pp. 496.

86. KARIUKI, Njiru Paul, *Charisms and the Holy Spirit's Activity in the Body of Christ. An Exegetical-Theological Study of 1Cor 12,4-11 and Rom 12,6-8*, 2002, pp. 372.

87. CORRY, Donal, *«Ministerium Rationis Reddendae». An Approximation to Hilary of Poitiers' Understanding of Theology*, 2002, pp. 328.

88. PIKOR, Wojciech, *La comunicazione profetica alla luce di Ez 2–3*, 2002, pp. 322.

89. NWACHUKWU, Mary Sylvia Chinyere, *Creation–Covenant Scheme and Justification by Faith. A Canonical Study of the God-Human Drama in the Pentateuch and the Letter to the Romans*, 2002, 378 pp.

90. GAGLIARDI, Mauro, *La cristologia adamitica. Tentativo di recupero del suo significato originario*, 2002, pp. 624.

91. CHARAMSA, Krzysztof Olaf, *L'immutabilità di Dio. L'insegnamento di San Tommaso d'Aquino nei suoi sviluppi presso i commentatori scolastici*, 2002, pp. 520.

92. GLOBOKAR, Roman, *Verantwortung für alles, was lebt. Von Albert Schweitzer und Hans Jonas zu einer theologischen Ethik des Lebens*, 2002, pp. 608.

93. AJAYI, James Olaitan, *The HIV/AIDS Epidemic in Nigeria. Some Ethical Considerations*, 2003, pp. 212.